STEEL GATE TO FREEDOM

STEEL GATE TO FREEDOM

The Life of Liu Xiaobo

Yu Jie

Translated by HC Hsu

ROWMAN & LITTLEFIELD
Lanham • Boulder • New York • London

Published by Rowman & Littlefield
A wholly owned subsidiary of
The Rowman & Littlefield Publishing Group, Inc.
4501 Forbes Boulevard, Suite 200, Lanham, Maryland 20706
www.rowman.com

Unit A, Whitacre Mews, 26-34 Stannary Street, London SE11 4AB,
United Kingdom

British Library Cataloguing in Publication Information Available

Library of Congress Cataloging-in-Publication Data
Yu, Jie, 1973–
[Liu Xiaobo zhuan. English]
Steel gate to freedom : the life of Liu Xiaobo / Yu Jie ; translated by HC Hsu.
pages cm
Includes bibliographical references and index.
ISBN 978-1-4422-3713-1 (cloth : alk. paper) — ISBN 978-1-4422-3714-8
(electronic)
1. Liu, Xiaobo, 1955– 2. Political prisoners—China—Biography. 3. Dissenters—China—Biography. 4. Nobel Prize winners—Biography. I. Hsu, H. C.,
1982– II. Title. III. Title: Life of Liu Xiaobo.
CT1828.L595Y82513 2015
365'.45092—dc23
[B]
2015008574

♾ ™ The paper used in this publication meets the minimum requirements of
American National Standard for Information Sciences Permanence of Paper
for Printed Library Materials, ANSI/NISO Z39.48-1992.

Printed in the United States of America

CONTENTS

FOREWORD

Jean-Philippe Béja

When Liu Xiaobo was awarded the Nobel Peace Prize in October 2010, journalists and scholars of China were very much aware of his numerous writings on politics. Some remembered the "black horse" who shook up the literary scene in 1986 with his iconoclastic piece denouncing China's contemporary literature at a time permeated by a self-congratulatory air. But no one knew who the real Liu Xiaobo was or understood how the 1980s maverick had become the astute political analyst who drew up a thorough diagnosis of the ills of the current Chinese regime.

This book by fellow dissident and long-time friend Yu Jie fills that gap. Yu has known Liu for over ten years. In the years before his arrest, almost every time I had lunch or dinner with Liu, Yu was there, taking part in the discussion, poring over the fine points. A political dissident and fine writer himself, Yu had attracted Liu's attention with the publication of his first book.

It's important to note that since his release from reeducation through labor in 1999, Liu has assumed a central role in the Chinese dissident movement. So it was only natural newly christened dissidents should gravitate toward him. That is what happened to Yu. A long and deep friendship developed, but one would be wrong to think Yu's critical spirit is dampened here.

As someone deeply respected by and who deeply respects Liu, Yu is in the best position to write his biography. He knows most of Liu's friends, his wife Liu Xia, and his family. A literary critic like Liu, Yu has a profound empathy with Liu's work. In this book, partly based on interviews with numerous acquaintances in China as well as the United States, Yu takes the reader on a journey through the "roaring eighties," a decade that, for its ups and downs, was marked by a renewed curiosity for the outside world and experimentation in all manners of Chinese daily life. Liu enthusiastically took part in this renaissance. He founded a poetry journal at his alma mater, Jilin University, and, on arriving at the epicenter of Beijing, published scathing articles, most notably in *China*, a new review started by Ding Ling, criticizing the inability of intellectuals to have distinct personalities. His book *Critique of Choice: Conversations with Li Zehou*, a criticism of the influential intellectual at the time, sounded a loud ring through the public. Furthermore, the confident young man didn't hesitate taking contemporary Chinese writers' penchant for self-pity to task: in "Reflection without Escape: The Picture of the Intellectual in Recent Fiction," Liu "panned influential writers and filmmakers for airbrushing intellectuals—themselves—and making them up like Christ figures" at a time when "scar literature" presented them as heroic victims of the Cultural Revolution. When authorities shut down *China*, Liu became furious and launched a petition. It was his first time as a protest organizer, and the experience would help him in his later endeavors.

Yu rightly describes Liu Xiaobo as a prime example of Northeastern Chinese, who "have a tough exterior and unyielding interior, . . . [are] loud and never get cold feet, . . . [are] bright and open and value camaraderie over the law, and . . . love making friends. There is a 'gangster' attitude to their way of life, and this was already apparent in Liu in his early years." The young child raised by a stern father and a doting mother (a situation quite common in Chinese families, as Yu notes) cultivated a strong fighting spirit that found an expression during the Cultural Revolution. "I am grateful for the Cultural Revolution. I was a kid then. I could do whatever I wanted. My parents were off 'revolutionizing,' schools stopped, and I was for a time able to be rid of the constraints of an 'education,' to do whatever I wanted to do, to play, to fight. I lived a happy life." This period of his life no doubt reinforced Liu's individualism and deepened his hunger for self-achievement.

This personality further manifested itself when, during the eighties, Liu—who had been married early to Tao Li, the daughter of an intellectual family—refused to be bound by the trappings of marriage. As Yu observes, he was always surrounded by pretty girls and was a womanizer. This attitude was also typical of the eighties when, after years of Cultural Revolution puritanism, the sexual revolution was regarded as a healthy reaction against Mao's reign.

During this decade, Liu, fascinated by Nietzsche, was an ultra-individualist. His writings were meant to be shocking, and they did what they set out to do. It is in this context his declaration that "Chinese writers . . . can't write creatively themselves—they simply don't have the ability—because their very lives don't belong to them," which so stunned progressive audiences, should be interpreted: Liu didn't shy from agitating mainstream opinion. His heretical views on literature made him a celebrity in the literary scene, and young people used to fight for a seat to attend the slightly stuttering star's talks on the most prestigious Chinese campuses. Though thought provoking, his individualism kept him from getting directly involved in politics.

Like most successful Chinese intellectuals in the 1980s, Liu was invited to lecture abroad, and he spent three months in Norway, where he was quite disappointed by the country's quiet serenity, and in the United States. But in contrast to his colleagues, as the 1989 pro-democracy movement fermented in Beijing, he became restless and, after careful consideration, decided to go home to take part in this historical event. He spent all his time at Tiananmen Square, living with the students but also not holding back on criticizing them. Despite, or because of, his forthrightness, he earned their esteem and admiration. His hunger strike and the role he played in persuading the students to leave the square helped change the intellectual provocateur into a reasoned political actor.

However, it was undeniably the June 4 massacre that transformed him. He was arrested in June 1989 and sent to Qincheng Prison. As the papers were filled with long articles painting him as the black hand behind the movement, he was convinced he would be dealt a heavy sentence. In August 1990, his then wife, Tao, asked for a divorce. He agreed, knowing it was the only way for their son to lead a normal life. China had not changed much since the 1950s, when relatives and loved ones were pressured into "tracing a line of demarcation" (*huaqing jiexian*) with the "rightists." Yu shows that Liu was deeply affected by the divorce but does not say whether this was what led him to write the confession that would allow him to get a light sentence. In any case, Liu has said, "My confession was a true lie. I didn't believe it; I had to say it to save my life. I caved in to the lies of others, to violence. . . . I signed it out of weakness. I didn't hold out until the end." This capitulation has weighed on him ever since:

> When I sold out my own dignity, I also sold out the souls of the dead. I had notoriety; many cared about me. What about the many who died? Who lost the ability to live? Who are still sitting in a dark cell to this day? Who knows them? Who remembers them? Who cares about them? . . . The only way to redeem myself is to resist, to go back to prison. It's the only way for me to realize my beliefs, my ideals, my integrity.

After his 1991 release, Liu changed: no longer the Nietzschean superman, Liu devoted all his time to the promotion of democracy and to keeping the memory of the Tiananmen Square massacre. In the many writings he published through the Hong Kong press—he has been banned from publishing in China—he formulated extremely thoughtful analyses of the CPC regime. Hailing the expansion of an unofficial public space (*minjian kongjian*), he showed that most reforms carried out by the CPC leadership were the result of pressure by society. He himself contributed to the development of what some call "civil society" by organizing a great number of petitions to protest human rights violations and documenting the evolution of this increasingly autonomous space through writing. Refusing to submit to pressures, though he had been under close surveillance since 1991, Liu, very much bolstered by his love for Liu Xia, decided to "live in truth," as Havel and Solzhenitsyn had done before him. And, just like them, he accepted that he would pay the price: he was arrested in December 2008 and sentenced to eleven years in jail in December 2009. To this day, he is serving his sentence at Jinzhou Prison, in Liaoning. His wife, Liu Xia, is under house arrest, deprived of the Internet, and allowed to visit Liu only half an hour every month.

Yu Jie's book offers much insight into Liu Xiaobo's personal life and depicts the multifaceted personality of one of the most prolific and original Chinese intellectuals of this century. Reading Yu Jie's biography is an indispensable introduction to the reading of Liu Xiaobo's works and, in this sense, is a must for anyone who wishes to understand the challenges confronting the future great power of the twenty-first century.

I

THE YOUNG BOY ON THE BLACK SOIL

SON OF A COMMUNIST MAN

Under a dictatorship, if you want to be a dissident and uphold the truth, the first thing you have to do is give up a normal home life.

To fight for democracy with her fellow Burmese, Aung San Suu Kyi stayed in Burma and gave up being a comfortable housewife in Oxford, England. The Burmese government denied her family entry and tried to force her to leave. When her husband, Aris, was diagnosed with terminal cancer, she couldn't go to him. She couldn't even see him one last time before he died. However, according to her, it's a decision they made together, out of loyalty to their vows of love and honor.

While Liu Xiaobo was fighting a tyrannical regime, he also had to give up being a good husband, son, and father. After the 1989 Tiananmen Square massacre, what pained him most was the divorce from his wife, Tao Li. When the divorce papers were delivered to him in prison, it was the single most difficult signature he had to sign in his life.

In the settlement, both parties agreed to place custody of their son, Liu Tao, with Tao Li. Liu was still in prison and couldn't raise a child. Even after his release he had no livelihood, being under constant police surveillance. He had no choice but to leave Liu Tao with the child's mother and grandparents.

This period was the lowest point in Liu Xiaobo's life. He writes: "I refused all media interviews and minimized my social circle as much as I could. I especially didn't want to see anyone associated with Tiananmen. I read, studied English, spent time with my girlfriend, chatted with friends, and often went to see my sick ex-wife and eight-year-old son."

Shortly after, Tao Li moved to the United States, leaving Liu Tao with his grandparents, where he stayed until he graduated from high school and went to college in the States. In those few years, Liu was able to see his son on occasion. This was the only limited contact they'd had. During the three years he was at a labor reeducation camp, Liu sent his new wife, Liu Xia, to see the boy. After Liu Xia visited Liu Xiaobo in prison, she would go to see Liu Tao, becoming a channel of communication between father and son. Yet when Liu Xiaobo was released for the third time, his son had already gone to study stateside.

For more than ten years, Tao Li's parents, the elderly couple Tao Dezhen and Pu Manting, put tremendous effort into raising their grandson. They took turns day and night feeding and clothing him, helping with his homework, attending parent-teacher conferences, and taking him out to play, including to gatherings with their friends. Little snot-nosed Tao-tao next to his grandfather in his sixties seemed less like a grandson than simply a fourth member of the family, Grandma and Grandpa's little hanger-on.

In a memoir about her father, Liu Tao's aunt Tao Ning writes:

> Not only does your dearest grandson Tao-tao look more like you than we do, broad-shouldered and thick-waisted, but—my God—in manners and speech he is practically cut from the same cloth as you. Looking at this kid Mom and I would often suddenly be dumbfounded: before our eyes is clearly a younger version of you. His unusually good academics, his compassion and integrity, brain and heart, his kindness and respect for his elders astonish everyone around him. Often people would ask Sister what her secret was, how she raised such a good kid, and she would always tell them, this kid was raised by his grandfather!

A son should resemble his father. Liu Tao's father was absent from his life, so his grandfather took on the role. After Tao Dezhen passed, Liu Tao writes in a memoir: "I grew up in my grandfather's house. Throughout my childhood and youth I was lucky enough to experience a grandfather's love beyond anyone's imagination." His grandfather took him to the market every day, and every time they walked into the store, Liu Tao would run straight to the dessert counter. Liu Tao had a particular fondness for the store's French pastries, and each time he would ask his grandfather to buy a couple of different kinds. A pastry cost four yuan, which, unknown to a child, was a lot of money. His grandfather never balked at the price in front of him and simply let him pick whatever he wanted. Maybe his grandfather thought, poor kid, his father was in and out of prison and his mother was abroad, the least he could do was provide for him materially.

Only years later, after Liu Tao had grown, did he realize how extravagant spending twenty yuan a month on pastries was for this family. At the time, his grandfather was a university professor and made only two hundred yuan a month, so a tenth of their household income went to pastries for their grandson alone. To save money to buy the pastries for his grandson, Grandfather himself ate only porridge and pickles for breakfast.

Under these circumstances, the bond between Liu Tao and his grandfather was deep, while the bond between his father and he was shallow. When Liu Xiaobo received the Nobel Peace Prize in 2010, Liu Tao had just turned twenty-seven and had been living in the States for more than ten years, perhaps already a naturalized US citizen. This child, who had at six lost his father, long graduated college, and probably even started a career and family of his own, never once spoke publicly about his father. Maybe one day, Liu Tao will understand the great sacrifice his father has made to lay a path for democracy for his country and be proud to have such a father.

Liu Xiaobo has confided in friends that in the past few years he's had very little contact with his son. In a way, in the Tiananmen massacre he lost his only child—maybe not forever, but the pain is real all the same.

With his child gone, Liu Xiaobo is certainly not an adequate father. But a thousand times more tragic were the many children who died that night and that dawn, the many mothers and fathers who overnight were no longer mothers and fathers. In this cold world, those children whose smiles blossomed can no longer be found, but they are not gone, because Liu Xiaobo is convinced: "Each night / The souls of the dead touch their mother's sky / Like being inside the womb / And listening to their mother's heartbeat." From that night on, Liu Xiaobo has lived for the children who died.

But does he still remember the child growing up running on the black soil of the Black Dragon River?

It would be a distant memory of himself.

* * *

On December 28, 1955, Liu Xiaobo was born in the city of Changchun, the capital of the province of Jilin in northeast China.

Liu spent most of his childhood and youth in Changchun. Jilin University, where he studied, was also in Changchun. The seventeen years he spent there was second only to the time he would spend in Beijing. He speaks with a heavy Changchun accent. The Changchun dialect tends to add r's to the end of words; it is full of life and humor, exaggerated but self-deprecating—all things you hear when Liu speaks. He spits out vulgarities and expletives like watermelon seeds, another characteristic of northeastern Chinese dialects. Even after he received his doctorate and became a professor he couldn't kick the northeastern accent and common way of speaking, with expletives never far from his mouth.

Scholars of Chinese regional cultures point out that among the Chinese, northeasterners' personalities are the most singularly unmistakable: they have a tough exterior and unyielding interior, they're loud, they never get cold feet, they're bright and open and value camaraderie over the law, and they love making friends. There is a "gangster" attitude to their way of life, and this was already apparent in Liu in his early years. At middle age, Liu has gradually gotten rid of some of the aspects of this gangster attitude such as narcissism, egotism, and unbridled brazenness and distilled it down more and more to its essence—truthfulness, directness, and the courage to blaze new trails. His temperament is like the Three Gorges Dam rising out of the Yangtze River, emerging from tempestuous winds and raging waves to become simply a lofty expansiveness.

Liu had a stern father and a doting mother and therefore, in a way, a somewhat classic Chinese family. His father, Liu Ling, was born in 1931 in Huaide County in Jilin Province, graduated from the prestigious Northeast Normal University with a degree in Chinese language, and stayed on to teach. He was promoted to associate professor in the Chinese Language and Literature Department in 1979 and transferred to the Dalian Army Academy to the south. Liu Ling studied, worked, and lived at the Northeast Normal University for more than thirty years, and it became an ineradicable part of Liu Xiaobo's childhood.

Liu Xiaobo never shies from speaking frankly about his family. In his view, among the generations of intellectuals in modern China, his father's generation was the most tragic. They spent their best years amid political movements. In terms of treatment, they were regarded far less favorably than those who finished university before 1949, when the People's Republic was founded; in terms of thought, they were more rigid than both the previous generation (before 1949) and the subsequent generation (after 1976). They were blind, conservative, craven, and even as they railed against Communist Party culture, their heads were still filled with Communist Party culture. This was the cruel irony of fate: even if they had the opportunity, they would still be reluctant to cut themselves loose from the binds of partisan culture. Their worldview, their manners and dispositions, how they thought, and how they lived had already been thoroughly shaped and molded by the party.

When Liu was little, Father was master of the house. His words were the law. He never had a chitchat or heart-to-heart talk with the children. Discipline meant yelling or hitting. It all appeared very macho to Liu, who recalls: "In my young mind Father was a hateful monster. I hated him so much I often wondered how nice it'd be if I didn't have a dad." He laments: "Father expressed his love through an ideological, loveless language, and this love became part of the Communist Party culture."

Liu's mother, Zhang Suqin, worked at the university's day-care center and, after 1973, in reception in the administrative unit. Of the brothers, Liu was his mother's favorite. His mother would always shield him from the lashes of his father's tongue and the strikes of his fists. Liu's arrest after Tiananmen and subsequent incarceration were more of a blow to her than anyone else. She cried every day and never got a good night's sleep, often waking from nightmares, startled, and then sobbing until dawn. She would talk to everyone and anyone on the streets who would listen about her son, and people began to see her as a gadfly.[1]

Both Liu's parents were traditional in their thinking and saw their work as part of the revolution. The revolution was more important than the family. They didn't value their roles as mother and father nearly as much as they valued the esteem of the leaders and colleagues in their cadres. This was characteristic of the Chinese of that era. In addition, they had five children, so the love and warmth each child received was rationed even further.

Liu traveled abroad for the first time when he was just an infant. In 1956 his father was sent by his school to teach at Choibalsan University in Mongolia (now the National University of Mongolia). His wife and he decided to leave their eldest son, Liu Xiaoguang, with his grandmother and take along their second, Liu Xiaohui, and their youngest at that time, Liu Xiaobo, not even a year old.

The Liu family lived in Mongolia for four years. This would be a unique time in the relationship between China and Mongolia.

After Mongolia gained independence, the Soviet Union essentially made it into an unofficial republic of the USSR. When the Communists came into power in China, Mao Zedong sided with the Soviets against the West, in particular the United States. East Asia became a battleground for the two forces during the Cold War, effectively ushering in a new honeymoon between China and the Soviet Union. The Soviets were more than happy to see China court Mongolia so long as it didn't jeopardize Soviet-Mongolian relations.

As a result, China began sending massive amounts of aid to Mongolia in the form of economic, technological, and human capital—the first foreign aid program in Chinese history. This included teachers, doctors, nurses, carpenters, tile layers, chefs, and tailors. Liu's father was one such professional.

Liu Xiaobo lived in Mongolia from age one to four. As the economy worsened at home, his life abroad was ironically comfortable by comparison. When his family finally reunited in China, it would be amid the largest famine in human history, claiming some thirty million lives. Liu's family lived in Changchun, which at the time boasted the highest standard of living in the country due to infrastructure left by the earlier Japanese occupation. Still, raising a handful of boys on such a meager salary was no small feat.

The hardships of his childhood have left an indelible mark on Liu. He has always had an extremely healthy appetite throughout his life. Anyone who has dined with him remembers: when a dish arrives, he is always the first to get some for himself with his chopsticks, without regard for the usual decorum or cultural etiquette. No matter how much food there is, he is always afraid of not getting enough to eat.

Friends ask whether his voraciousness is a habit picked up in prison. He says it is because he often went hungry as a child. The dining table was a battleground, with five boys, Mom, Dad, Mom's mom, and Dad's mom all clustering around one table and chopsticks clanking and clashing against one another. With limited food and even more limited nutritious food, if five feisty, growing boys didn't fight to eat, they didn't eat at all.

Liu writes about those lean years:

> In 1961 just as I was starting elementary school, famine spread across the country. There were five of us boys; food was scarce. My grandmothers often picked grass and cooked it with a little sorghum to make porridge. Each boy got one bowl. That year my big brother was twelve and my second brother was nine. We should have been wild kids, but because we were hungry, after school we had no energy to go out and play. We could only lie in bed and wait for our bowl of grass porridge.[2]

The northeast was known as the "food pantry of China." If those were the living conditions of a high-class intellectual's family, one could only imagine the severity of the famine elsewhere.

* * *

As a scholar, Liu Xiaobo bears no resemblance to his father, Liu Ling. Other than the fact that both were in Chinese language departments, their research had nothing in common. However, as educated parents tend to value the education of their children, Liu benefited tremendously from his background. When he was little, there were always books around; the seeds of his lifelong passion for reading were sown.

The Lius had five sons, with Liu Xiaobo in the middle. His eldest brother, Xiaoguang, has worked for an apparel import-export company and a military sanatorium; his second-eldest brother, Xiaohui, is a historian and assistant director of the Jilin Province Museum; his next-younger brother, Xiaoxuan, holds a biochemistry PhD, chairs the School of Materials and Energy at the Guangdong University of Technology, and is closest to him. In the early 1990s, because of their relationship, Xiaohui was barred from entry into the Tsinghua University PhD program. Nevertheless, he respected and supported his brother's decisions. After Liu Xiaobo's fourth arrest, he represented the family at his brother's trial. Liu's youngest brother, Xiaodong, died young in the early 1990s from a heart attack.

Liu Xiaobo's two older brothers work more closely with the government and disapprove of his life choices. Concerned about their careers, they've kept little contact since Tiananmen with their younger brother and often blame him for the pall he's cast over the family. Sometimes blood isn't thicker than water, and the most intimate strangers are often siblings. Aung San Suu Kyi's brother took her to court for the house their father left behind; it was even rumored he was under the influence of the Burmese military junta. Though Liu's older brothers haven't gone to such lengths, they are still estranged.

Liu Ling was an extremely devout and long-standing Communist Party member and enjoyed the privileges of his seniority. He was considered a top brass official who had made significant contributions to the party. In his younger years, he earned the title "Socialist Construction Youth Activist." He suffered his fair share of raps and blows during the Cultural Revolution, but he still fundamentally believed in the system, with faith in its capacity to self-correct. After Tiananmen, at the Organization Department's behest, he went to see his son in Qincheng Prison in Beijing to persuade him to plead guilty.

A former student of Liu Ling, literature professor Wang Dongcheng, recalls that in the early 1990s, Liu Ling and Liu Xiaobo's stepmother had once traveled to Beijing to take him and Liu Xiaobo out to dinner. The old man had hoped Wang would try to convince Liu Xiaobo to stop criticizing the CPC (Communist Party of China) and to live out his life quietly as an ordinary person. However, Wang didn't believe Liu Xiaobo had made the wrong decision and never tried to persuade him otherwise. Liu Ling became angry with his student because of this.

Even so, simply by being Liu Xiaobo's father, Liu was harassed often. After his son was awarded the Nobel Peace Prize, he was placed under strict orders not to give interviews to foreign press. Retired, he bore his military identity throughout his life, without a moment's rest. Just as they silenced the military doctor who exposed the truth about the army's use of "dum-dum" bullets in Tiananmen and later about the severity of the spread of SARS in China, the authorities denied Liu Ling any public grievance against their treatment of his son.

On January 12, 2011, the seventy-nine-year-old Liu Ling was admitted to a hospital in Dalian for serious liver complications. He could no longer walk and remained bedridden. Even then, the military stationed two officers at the hospital for close surveillance to keep out reporters and others who were not family members. Liu Xiaoxuan told *Voice of America* their father had been in and out of hospitals for the past year, and only family members were allowed to visit. When the reporter asked whether the military personnel were for escort or surveillance, he answered: "I don't know—whatever you think."

On February 20, Liu Ling turned eighty. His sons discussed how they were going to celebrate their father's birthday, yet, in prison Liu couldn't even send a letter or a gift, let alone visit his gravely ill father. Because Liu was awarded the Nobel Peace Prize, his family's visitation rights were stripped away.

On September 12, the day of the Chinese Mid-Autumn Festival, Liu Ling passed away in Dalian. According to the Associated Press and the Agence France-Presse, Liu was granted temporary release in the company of his brothers to attend their father's funeral. As if some great enemy were upon them, the authorities declared martial law. Nearby residents were abuzz, thinking one of the central leaders must be on an inspection tour.

DAYS WITHOUT SUN

When his family returned from Mongolia to Changchun in 1959, Liu Xiaobo enrolled in Northeast Normal University's kindergarten and then in its affiliate elementary school.

NNU Elementary is one of the most prestigious schools in Changchun, situated on the famous scenic South Lake. Follow Freedom Road in front of it eastward, and you'd come upon the Lius' home on the NNU campus. The school was built in 1948 and was China's first open, all-day experimental elementary school. Back then, only children of NNU professors, government officials, military personnel, and other professionals could enroll.

Liu was the middle child, with two older and two younger brothers. Generally it's said that middle children are the most unruly, as it's the only way for them to get attention and prove themselves.

Liu liked to fight, a trait bolstered by the fact there were many boys in the family. He wasn't afraid to ask his brothers for backup, either. Once a neighborhood hoodlum by the name of Pillars stole a brand new pair of black shoes Liu's mother had gotten him for his birthday. They were the most expensive shoes Liu had worn his whole life, and barely a few days went by before Pillars started trotting them around town. Liu spotted them, immediately lunged at Pillars, and gave him a good beating to teach him a lesson. Soon after, Pillars got a band of a dozen or so thugs to surround the dorm where the Lius lived; seeing that things were quickly going bad, the youngest, Xiaodong, ran and informed his brother Xiaohui of the situation. As representative, Xiaohui negotiated with the ringleader, and eventually the thugs disbanded. This was the largest-scale "war" Liu Xiaobo experienced in his youth.

Like all children of his era, Liu lived his childhood under the shadow of ignorance and cruelty, and ignorance and cruelty fed and cradled an entire generation of Chinese. Though they were educated, Liu's parents lived in fear and never thought to voice their worries and doubts to a ten-year-old. It was a time when silence was golden. Even in the privacy of their own homes, parents never discussed politics with their children.

Liu was only eleven when the Great Proletarian Cultural Revolution broke out in 1966. Liu's grandparents had been hardworking farmers who earned an honest but moderately comfortable living, but during the Cultural Revolution they were classified as landlords. After his grandfather died, the full weight of this status was carried by his grandmother, a scarlet letter hanging over three generations of the Lius. In 1966 his grandmother, who had been living with them, was sent back from Changchun to the countryside to be "criticized" by her "peers."

Liu was raised by his grandmother and felt especially close to her, but how could a small child turn back the hands of fate? As his grandmother began to make her way to the bus stop, little Xiaobo ran after her, crying. Each step she took, she would look back and see her grandson, trailing her, tears running down his cheeks. When the bus departed, Xiaobo ran after it until it finally disappeared from sight.

This would be the first time Liu Xiaobo would feel the pain of separation from loved ones.

As a latecomer to the "party" of the revolution, Liu envied his brothers' ability to cut class and travel around the country to "link up" with other youth activists and even meet Chairman Mao himself. A fourth-grader, Liu wasn't yet entitled to wear the red band around his arm like his older brothers and dive headlong into all the tumultuous fervor. Instead, he was cast to the sidelines and became a mere bystander to all the "struggle sessions" (verbal and physical), debates, linkups, and propaganda, to all the beating, smashing, looting, and burning. He could only regret being born too late and missing this golden window in history.

Yet the Cultural Revolution still gave the young Liu unprecedented freedom. For years his disciplinarian father had barely given him any room to breathe; now, either busy "revolting" or exhausted from "being revolted against," he had no time to watch the children. Classes stopped, the older brothers enlisted as Red Guards, Grandma left for the countryside—Xiaobo, Xiaoxuan, and Xiaodong were like orphans in fantastic works of literature, with lives full of fun and adventure.

The boy who had always yearned for freedom finally understood firsthand what it meant: "For a period of time I was able to break away from the tethers of both home and school, develop my own interests, my 'nature,' and indulge in games I created for myself." Later in an interview, Liu said, "I am grateful for the Cultural Revolution. I was a kid then. I could do whatever I wanted. My parents were off 'revolutionizing,' schools stopped, and I was for a time able to be rid of the constraints of an 'education,' to do whatever I wanted to do, to play, to fight. I lived a happy life." This sentiment is very different from the nostalgia that some "leftists" have for the Cultural Revolution and for the Mao era in general.

The majority of perspectives on the Chinese Cultural Revolution focus on adults' experiences; few have delved into the lives of children during the time. Thirty years after the revolution ended, Liu wrote an essay examining this unprecedented historical event from the viewpoint of an elementary school student having his first smoke: the beginning of the revolution also marked the beginning of three decades of smoking for Liu. "As a kid," he wrote, "I wanted to fight back against my teachers (public authority) and my parents (private authority), and smoking turned out to be the starting point of my resistance." He smoked more and more as he grew older. His favorite is the popular Beijing brand Zhongnanhai.

When the revolution began, Mao Zedong put out a call across college, middle, and elementary school campuses for students to "cut class and join the revolution." NNU and its affiliates made an announcement suspending classes for three months, and it would be that afternoon when Liu had his first taste of tobacco.

His first cigarette came from a classmate named "Fatty." Fatty's dad was a high-ranking military general. After their homeroom teacher hurriedly left once the announcement was made, Fatty jumped on his desk, pulled a bright red cigarette pack printed with peonies out of his pocket, and waved it in the air: "Who has the balls to smoke a cigarette? I stole 'em from my dad. Peony brand, five jiao a pack! It's the shit. Who's got the balls? It's on me!"

The few remaining students in the room, Liu included, were all troublemakers. Liu raised his hand first. Fatty lit one for him. A bit timid, he took a small, careful puff. Besides being a little irritating to the throat, it was otherwise a ho-hum experience. Yet it somehow did make him feel more like a man.

Before long he was getting together regularly with his buddies to smoke and learning to lie, cheat, and steal his parents' money and his dad's cigarettes.

Those free and careless days ended with another call to "go back to class and join the revolution." When the students returned to school, they immediately sensed that something was different. "Workers for the Promotion and Propagation of Maoist Thought" had taken over the schools and militarized the administration, now staffed by Red Guards, and body searches were the order of the day. Those found "guilty" with knives, slingshots, pornography, cigarettes, or other "contraband" had to write self-critiques and read them in class or else be subject to struggle sessions. Liu wrote countless self-critiques and underwent struggle sessions numerous times for smoking, fighting, and cutting class. He'd even been placed in "solitary confinement" in the small, dark school storage shed.

His father smoked, too, but considered that to be the prerogative of adults and unbecoming of children. Whenever Liu's parents found him smoking, their solution was simple—screaming or hitting. Corporal punishment was common in China back then, even among educated families.

Liu will never forget the first time he was found out by his mother. She had smelled tobacco on him and found half a cigarette in his pencil box. She first interrogated him and, after his silence, picked up a broom and brought it down over his head a few times; seeing his lack of reaction, she tossed the broom aside and reached straight for a steel pot ladle. In a heated moment, he threw his head against his mother, knocking her down, and fled through the door.

He knew he was in trouble now and was in for a serious beating if he went home, so, stubborn as he was, he decided not to go back. He wandered about in the wind and cold until dark, until he couldn't stand the freezing cold anymore and hid in a crop cellar among the cabbage, carrots, and potatoes. Afterward, his mother said when they found him in the cellar, he was curled up like a little puppy, body under a burlap sack, head resting on a big cabbage, and sleeping like a log.

After that day, every afternoon when Liu would come home from school his mother would empty his pockets and backpack and ask him to open his mouth so that she could smell his breath. But he had a few tricks up his sleeve and would either rinse out his mouth or eat a couple of cloves of garlic, stashing his cigarettes before setting foot in the door.

Later, Liu remembers, when he returned home after being sent to the countryside to work, his father handed him a cigarette for the first time. He remembers feeling finally a sense of complete freedom—as well as, for the first time, in a concrete way, his father's love.[3]

❊ ❊ ❊

Young people back then were, in the words of the title of one of acclaimed Chinese author Wang Shuo's novels, "beasts in the wild." Three years younger than Liu, Wang and he have been close friends since the 1980s, in part because they share similar experiences growing up.

The main characters in *Beasts in the Wild* are a group of teenage boy military brats. In the bedlam at the end of the revolution, they cut class, drink, smoke, fight, and go out with different girls (referred to in the book as "tapping pusses"). Wang says, "In those days you could be sitting at home perfectly minding your own goddamn business when all of a sudden your 'bro' showed up in tears saying so-and-so beat him up, and you stood up, dusted off your ass, and ran out in the world looking for bricks to throw, risking your life whether it was your shit or not." *Beasts in the Wild* was made into a movie by director Jiang Wen, who retitled it *Sunny Days*. Jiang is also part of the "brat pack," shares many of Wang's experiences, and was an associate of Liu in the 1980s. A lot of people have asked why Jiang called his movie *Sunny Days*. Jiang says it's because he misses those simple, free days under the sun.

Nothing was further from the truth. Sunny days they surely were not. Neither were they simple or free. Recalling his school days during the revolution, Liu says the fever infected everyone. The fire of revolution was on every tongue. Cruelty spread throughout society, engulfing every home. People learned about class struggles in their cradles. Struggle sessions at school on top of what they saw and heard every day at home turned little children into monsters who took pride and pleasure in acts of cruelty.

Outbursts of cruelty often go hand in hand with jubilations of summer. People are ramped up, their naked skin and desire exposed under the sun. Liu remembers one particular incident in the unusually hot summer of 1966.

There was an old man, Yi Hai, who lived down the street in his neighborhood, was about the same age as Liu's grandmother, and had watched Liu grow up. The old man had deserted the Nationalist Army after serving a couple of days in the 1949 Chinese Civil War, but he was still branded a "counterrevolutionary" and therefore "untouchable," eking out a living for the rest of his days as a door-to-door barber. There were millions in China like him. The old man chatted with Liu's grandmother and would often cut the young boy's hair.

At the beginning of the revolution, Yi Hai was subjected to a struggle session; his son then wanted a clear boundary between them and kicked him out of the house. Yi lived in a damp, dark shed in the yard out back, originally part of a boiler room, with a rickety bed and not much else. He could no longer cut hair door to door and had to scavenge for a living.

One day when they were out and about, looking for ways to amuse themselves, Liu and a couple of his buddies spotted Yi scrounging around in a heap of garbage. Liu's eyes lit up: *finally, something interesting*! He flagged his friends and tiptoed up behind old Yi. "Hey! Old

Yi! Look up!" he yelled. "Show me your forehead! I wanna give you a few flicks!"

Old Yi was caught completely off guard and leapt to his feet. Once he realized the demand of these children, the expression on his face turned from that of shock and fear to one of pitiful pleading: "San-er [*san* means "three"; Liu was third in his family], please, I'm older than your grandma, we're old neighbors, I've cut your hair and your brothers' hair, please, let me go this time."

Liu shouted back: "No! You old counterrevolutionary! Try to bargain with me? You're getting older and bolder. I have to flick you now. Show it to me!"

The old man begged a couple more times. Seeing he was surrounded by a gang of vicious-looking teens, he probably realized there was no way out and made an offer: "If you really want to flick me, San-er, I'll turn around, and you can flick the back of my head. Will that be good?"

"You old fox, trying to pull a fast one on me?" Liu said. "No wonder you're a counterrevolutionary. I'm gonna flick you hard come hell or high water today!"

The other teens joined in the ruckus, knocking the old man's garbage-filled bamboo basket to the ground, all chiming in one after another: "If you don't let us flick you, you can forget about picking trash anymore!" "Hey old man, you wanna keep living the good life, don't you?"

Hopeless, old Yi stuck his head forward. The sun was bright. Tiny beads of perspiration seeped through the kerchief wrapped around his head. Liu cared only about having fun and didn't know the cost his prank had on the dignity of an old man—an old man, one who was old enough to be his own grandfather, who showed kindness and humor, often telling the youngsters jokes when he cut their hair. But Liu didn't think about how Yi had treated him in the past or sympathize with his present plight. Nor did he feel pangs about poking at an old, defenseless man. It was simply fun; he got a kick out of it.

Liu looked at the man's wrinkled forehead gleaming with sweat, wagged around his fingers a few times, held them in place, and let fly a flick with all his might. *Thwack, thwack, thwack.* At times the thumps were as clear as a bell, at times muffled like a drum; at times they were rapid, at times slower; at times his fingers slipped on the surface, wet from sweat—and if that happened, he couldn't get as good a flick and he had to flick again, twice as many times more, as punishment.

Liu's fingers began to hurt, and they were wet, so he wiped them off on the old man's face. Then he continued until his fingers were numb. Others joined in, too, all flicking at the same time.

When the youths finally stopped, the old man lowered his head right away and didn't dare look them in the eye; turning around, he started picking up the pile of trash scattered on the ground. The kids giggled and then spat a few times on the man's back. "Letting you off easy this time, you old counterrevolutionary." Then they left, secure in their victory.

The tendency to bully the weak is the worst part of human nature. The secret of all dictators is to bring out this tendency in the people. Years later, when Liu returned to Changchun from the country, Yi Hai had died. The end of such a mean life was like a leaf falling to the ground—no one noticed.

With a heavy heart, Liu writes:

> Looking back, I think he must have cried secretly. Tears must have streamed down his old, withered face. And not just down his face, but also into his heart. A seventy-year-old barber who cut children's hair, an old neighbor and friend of their grandparents, was bullied and humiliated by these very eleven-, twelve-year-old kids he watched grow up. If a human heart could bleed, it must have bled the moment my fingers touched his skin.

Most children who lived under the shadow of Mao have done things like that. The strong bullied the weak, the weak bullied the weaker, and the cycle continued. Liu admits:

> I've doled out my share of cruelty and taken pleasure in it when I was young. In this way I was no different from the Red Guards. The lot of us grew up under a savage regime, which cultivated hate, worshipped violence, indulged in cruelty, and encouraged indifference. It made brutality and viciousness part of its people's genes. In a time when lives were cheap and human beings didn't see each other as human beings, no one could absolve their guilt—no one could wipe their slate clean. [4]

THE AGE OF ENLIGHTENMENT

Liu belonged to a group of battle-scarred yet full-of-zest young activists called the Intellectual Youths. The IYs were something of an anomaly in the history of modern China. They were thrown off their life course when their education came to an abrupt halt and they were sent from the city to the country to work, where they lived in the bottommost dregs of society for five to ten years.

In 1966, college entrance exams stopped. Until 1968, many high school graduates couldn't get into college or find jobs. Mao had just done some housecleaning in his regime with his Red Guards and now had to find a way to subdue these revved-up youngsters, so he organized a mass campaign to send all high school graduates to work in various rural villages and gave them the moniker "Intellectual Youths"; in reality, they were barely more educated than the farmers alongside whom they were forced to work.

In 1969, when Liu was fourteen, his parents were classified as landlords and subjected to struggle sessions, and the family was sent to work in a village called Dashizhai in Inner Mongolia until 1973. During this time, Liu was more or less his father's flunky in what turned out to be a "prep course" for his IY days. The difference between the city and the country was night and day. There was no tap water, no electricity, no gas, no heat. If you wanted to eat, you had to grow, and you had to sell what you grew if you wanted to live. The fourteen-year-old carried the burden along with his father of feeding the family, and his young and tender hands grew more and more callused as time wore on.

The landscape of Dashizhai was like that of Outer Mongolia, where Liu had spent his early childhood; "inner" and "outer" were simply political designations. Blue skies, wild plains, desolate deserts, lush forests—Mongolians have ridden and trekked across this land for millennia. However, the standards of living between the two regions and between the two periods in his life couldn't have been more polar. In Outer Mongolia, Liu Ling had worked as a professional as part of a foreign aid program; his family lived in a faculty dormitory, and he earned a decent wage and benefits. By contrast, Inner Mongolia in the late 1960s to early 1970s was a place of punishment and "reeducation" for the same intellectuals; they lived in farmers' mud huts, got up early and turned in late, and toiled for mere subsistence.

Liu has talked very little about this period of his life. Maybe being with his father helped to provide him some material and emotional comfort. Chinese philosopher Chen Jiaying, who was also sent to Inner Mongolia during this time, recalls:

> We came to Mongolia, to farm, to herd, to wrestle with farmers and shepherds, to drink. We hankie-pankied, we rumble-tumbled. We read Tolstoy and Heidegger, under the shade of mud ditches in our fields, under the light of oil lamps by our hearths. We learned Russian, English, and higher mathematics. We sang Russian songs. We listened to Beethoven on vinyl on a 78-rpm hand-cranked record player with a sharpened knitting needle made from bamboo. . . . Some students say to me, "How romantic!" I suppose, compared to prepping for exams and the nine-to-five afterward, sure. At the end of the day of our first harvest, our backs were broken, our hands bleeding and raw. Back at the Youth Point, the girls were in tears. End of next summer, a hailstorm destroyed our crops. The following fall, winter, and spring, three meals a day, it was corn grits mixed with the chili powder we had brought from Beijing.[5]

In 1973, Liu returned to Changchun with his parents. The eighteen-year-old looked much older than he was. The Mongolian sun and cold had darkened his skin, made it coarse. In clothes made from washed-out rags he looked more country bumpkin than city slicker.

But the worst wasn't over. He was back in class no more than six months before being pulled out and sent to the country again under the government's new "Into the Mountains, into the Farms" initiative.

Mao Zedong would die soon, and it was as if the fate of these youths would become inextricably bound up with Mao's very flesh and blood: from education ideologies to labor movements, Mao sought complete rule over his domain. Nothing and no one slipped by him. In other words, Mao had to die in order for policies to change and for millions of youths to regain their freedom.

The village Liu was sent to this time was closer to home and had far better living conditions than Inner Mongolia. San'gang Village was founded in 1961, and was famous for its nine hills, known as the "Chain Link." Locals called it "three thousand hills and three thousand vales, three thousand bumps and three thousand pockmarks." There was even a reservoir with trout. The malnourished Liu and his IY buddies would often sneak into the reservoir in the dark of night to fish. A bonfire, some bamboo skewers, a smear of salt—and it was a midnight picnic with fresh grilled seafood.

In 1976, IYs began returning home. Those with connections left first. The ones remaining in the villages were like abandoned orphans. At the time, Liu Ling hadn't been sufficiently "rehabilitated." His father unable to offer any help, Liu Xiaobo was trapped in San'gang for a time.

Always the firecracker, Liu had gotten off on the wrong foot with the village secretary. The village secretary was the lowest-of-the-low, bottom-of-the-barrel bureaucrat, the peripheral nerve end of the Communist governing body. But to the IYs he might as well have been God, list in hand, deciding who got to leave and who got to stay. Never one to compromise his principles, Liu wondered how he was going to finagle a discharge with the secretary's seal of approval.

Liu's mother was worried sick. She sent Liu the most valuable thing they owned—a Shanghai-brand watch—to give to the secretary as a gift. To give, or not to give? Would the scum sucker change his mind? Gritting his teeth, Liu picked up a cleaver with one hand, held the watch in the other, and went to the secretary's house. "Do you want the cleaver or the watch?" he said to him. "Choose now!"

The secretary chose the latter and drew up the discharge document. Scenes such as this weren't out of a soap opera. This was reality for an entire generation. Compared to human rights activist Hu Ping, who had cut off his left thumb to get a discharge, Liu was a lot luckier.

The Cultural Revolution ended in 1976. That November, Liu returned to Changchun. Without any connections, Liu ended up doing plasterwork for Changchun Construction. He made friends quickly, worked hard, was a quick study, and was well liked all around. The pay wasn't much, but Liu was able to make a decent living as a single young man who didn't have to worry about mouths to feed like his coworkers. He'd often buy cigarettes to share with everyone.

Liu had made a big step up the Communist social ladder from farmer to construction worker. But, he thought, is this what I'm going to do for the rest of my life? As the sun went down he sat under the awning and watched the skies gradually darken. He felt lonely and bleak, like someone had robbed him of his life. He was afraid of living, living just like this, growing older, older, and older. It would be worse than death.

Nietzsche said, "To live is to suffer, to survive is to find meaning in the suffering." Being a farmer and construction worker and sinking to the bottom of society grounded Liu, nourished him with the salt of the earth and the air of common, everyday life. It shaped for him a way of thought and a way of life completely different from those of lofty and self-satisfied intellectuals. This difference would become more and more apparent as time went on.

✻ ✻ ✻

Liu's education began officially during his time in the country. He has thanked the revolution in his writings later for the freedom it had given him.[6] Though his father was a literature professor, there were no "banned books" at his house. Like most young people in his day, he had read only the likes of Marx and Lenin. "Like all Chinese youths, I passionately, devoutly believed in Marxism. The belief was in part due to ignorance and naivety, and in part due to the vacuum of knowledge created by a kind of cultural fascism. Looking back, I was living in a wasteland of culture. Those in power decided for their ideological successors—us—what we should and could fix our eyes on: Marx and Engels, Lenin, Stalin, Mao, and all their exegetes and apologists."[7]

He read *The Communist Manifesto* at fifteen. The conviction with which the authors held their beliefs moved him. In high school he read the selected writings of Marx, Engels, and Lenin and in college some forty volumes of their complete works, being able to recite passages at length from memory. Marx became not only his entrée to Western philosophy but also his first bridge to the world.

His writing career began in this period, too. Liu recalls: "My affair with words began in the seventies as an Intellectual Youth. The unbridled revolutionary sentimentality of the times was built on blind passions and empty slogans. We were sincere in telling the lies from our little red books." They were suckled on the teats of wolves. "In this wilderness generations were fed nothing but hate, violence, pride, not to mention deceit, corruption, cynicism. The toxins remained in us long after even our supposed emancipation. Mao's language and thought became part of us. The process of detoxifying our souls—that would take a lifetime."[8]

Suffering is a catalyst for awakening. Liu's time in the country not only didn't turn him into an unthinking slave, it gave him the courage to look the reality of his people's lives in the eye and the compassion to want to make them better.

If they had not been sent to the country, youths like Liu would not have experienced the reality of the majority of Chinese people's lives firsthand. Mao had failed to consider this. "In the fields, in the mines, at the borders, at the frontiers, the young got the shock of their lives. The worsening of the agricultural economy, the ineptitude of the mining management, the poverty of the workers, the tension between the administration and the people, the utter failure of the policies—they not only lived through them but had to also bear their consequences. Belief and reality were in constant clash against each other."[9]

Compared with tightly monitored cities, the country was more out of the regime's reach, which gave IYs more space and time to develop their critical reading and thinking skills. Famed Chinese author and former IY Ah Cheng says, "To most people the seventies in China was the decade of repression. So why was thought so vibrant? It's because adults were too busy playing their power games. No one paid any attention to what young people in city corners and country fields were doing and thinking."[10] IYs often went on long errands together and talked about all sorts of things on their minds.

Spread throughout Heilongjiang to the east and Yunnan to the west, from Hainan Island in the south to Baiyang Lake in the north, even to Mongolia, under the pressure of politics and the heavy workload of their daily lives, the youths found an escape in reading, thinking, and talking to one another. They formed study circles, and Liu was a member of one. They learned about the world by whatever means they could, such as eavesdropping on enemy radio broadcasts. Often a chance encounter would lead them to discover they'd been reading the same banned books, just under different covers.

❈ ❈ ❈

Three things happened in the 1970s that changed Liu's life.

The first was Mao's 1971 ousting of his would-be successor, vice premier and Red Army field commander Lin Biao. Mao and Lin's relation had soured, and en route to his defection in the Soviet Union, Lin's plane crashed in Mongolia under mysterious circumstances. For many, this was the turning point in their faith in Mao. Lin's death shattered the halo around the supreme leader's carefully crafted cult of personality. The monolith razed, the communist ideological edifice and people's belief system scattered to the winds; there was no longer a coherent ruling narrative. At sixteen, Liu would see through the hypocrisy and cruelty of the regime and take the first step in a journey of no return toward dismantling its power.

The second event was Mao's death in 1976. At long last, the red sun had set. Many mourned; even more heaved a sigh of relief. Liu was among the latter. In the night that followed, Liu was one of many who looked up and saw the light of stars.

The third life-altering event was the reestablishment of college entrance exams in 1977 after Deng Xiaoping took power. It is estimated that more than half of the twelve million test takers and 700,000 enrollees were IYs ranging in age from sixteen to forty. Everyone applied in the short span of three years. They were an army trying to cross a river on a single wooden log. Opportunity never knocks on the doors of the unprepared. Liu had had only about a year's worth of high school, but he never stopped studying, even when he was in the country or when he was making a living, taking to heart his father's words that knowledge would never fall out of fashion. As a result, he got into his first choice of schools at Jilin University.

BIG MAN ON CAMPUS

On March 13, 1978, the freshman arrived on campus for his first day at Jilin University. Like other Chinese-major freshmen, he reported to dorm 7. The next morning, they ate their first breakfast together—wheat biscuits, cornmeal porridge, fermented tofu. Everyone always ate the same things from one big pot in the cafeteria. Along with 1,205 other students in the class that started in 1977, Liu sat in the school auditorium for the opening ceremony. The curtains finally parted for a college life long due.

Teachers also returned, many like Liu's father having been forced to abandon their posts and research for years. They were eager to get back to their jobs and impart their knowledge to the next generation.

What these students lacked in knowledge they made up for in life experience in abundance. Hungry for learning, they wanted to get back every second they had lost. Each of them had a story, a wealth of real-life experiences, and an arsenal of questions fired by their curiosity. A golden age of knowledge had dawned on China.

Jilin University had a long history and high reputation, and the Chinese Department was a veritable who's who of contemporary Chinese literature. Individuality and intellectual rebelliousness were not only encouraged but required.

Liu studied hard and strove to be number one in everything. He took especially to philosophy and aesthetics and read all the German classics. One of his classmates recounts: "I remember he stuttered a little. Rumor was he had a memory like a steel trap and was able to recite Hegel's *Aesthetics* in total. He was an overachiever: if somebody else wrote poetry he had to write poetry; if somebody published a short story he had to publish short stories; if somebody was studying aesthetics he had to memorize Hegel."

Dorm 7. Ten at night, lights out. Flicks of switches, students cursing—all faded into the darkness except a single light in the stairwell dividing the boys' and the girls' floors. Phantoms haunted here—students catching up on studying, catching a whiff of the fragrance drifting down from the girls' abodes above. The lanky Liu was one such student, drawn to the light. They read by the reflection of the snow and the glow of the fireflies. A dim and distant beacon shined on their future.

Liu slept on a top bunk in room 202 with eleven roommates. Staying up all night and telling stories was a favorite pastime, and soon everyone got along famously. Many of his bunk buddies went on to esteemed careers in their own right.

❖ ❖ ❖

Classes began March 23. There were seventeen classes in total—four in politics, three in general studies, ten in other specialized areas. The foreign language requirement wasn't English but actually Japanese—a sign of improving relations between China and Japan. The campus atmosphere was thick with politics. Everything was politicized. Topics such as "Does class consciousness exist in art?" were often tossed around in class. Even extracurricular activities consisted of spirited political debates. Liu and his classmates were once shown an anti-Mao movie; the whole class broke into applause.

Dances were popular, too, following the lead of the Communist Youth League of China, a CPC-run program for youths fourteen to twenty-eight. Liu often went ballroom dancing in his spare time. Undaunted by his two left feet, he would never be one to miss out on the newest, latest, and biggest thing.

China was spiritually famished after the austerity of the revolution—especially the young, who soaked up anything and everything new, almost without discretion. What changed Chinese people's, especially young people's, attitude most during this time was popular culture, from the pop songs of Teresa Teng from Taiwan to poetry publications such as *Today*. These "sounds of decadence" and "voices of dissent" (as labeled by the government) thawed the humanity previously frozen in political ideology and plunged Chinese civilization headlong into modernity.

In Liu's memory, Teresa Teng conquered an entire generation of Chinese with her voice. It stirred up a long-buried gentleness in people. Her love songs felled the steel-framed rhythm of the revolution and laid its ironclad will to waste. They softened hearts hardened by hardship and cruelty and shed light on desires cast to the darkest corners of the mind. Long-stifled emotions finally found an outlet. Behind closed doors, students huddled around a radio codenamed "the Brick" and listened to the well-played songs again and again, singing along in their bedrooms, in the hallways, in the cafeteria. Whoever had possession of "the Brick" enjoyed enormous celebrity and star power themselves.

People also got their first taste of foreign film, literature, and art. Japanese movies were the most popular. Audiences never tired of films such as *You Must Cross the River of Wrath, Love and Death, Sandakan Brothel No 8, Eclipse, Proof of the Man, A Distant Cry from Spring*, and *The Yellow Handkerchief*, and TV shows such as *Judo Saga, Astro Boy, Red Suspicion, Moero Attack, Oshin*, and *Ikkyu-san*, and their theme songs could be heard playing throughout millions of households. Directors such as Akira Kurosawa, Kenji Mizoguchi, and Yasujiro Ozu had a profound influence on avant-garde Chinese filmmakers of the Fifth Generation and later. Liu himself found a wellspring of inspiration in Japanese literature and art.

Meanwhile, news of a wall in Beijing being plastered with poetry and posters criticizing the government began trickling into the ears of young people five hundred miles away.

✿ ✿ ✿

It was a golden age of literature. Students with the best grades wanted to major in Chinese. They believed literature could open people's minds and change the world. Becoming an author was their dream. Literary clubs sprouted up across campuses like mushrooms after a spring rain. With books no longer banned, people suddenly got a big piece of their history back, sparking in them a fascination with their own literary and cultural heritage.

One of the biggest clubs was Jilin University's poetry club, True Hearts, with an eponymous semesterly, which received more materials than it could print and was read as widely as the popular *Today*. The club consisted of seven core members: Liu was last to join. During winter break, everyone left, and the dorm was empty. Liu and a friend each took a twelve-bunk room and read whatever they wanted all day long; when it was time to eat, they'd hang out and talk, spending the entire winter like this. To a couple of poor student poets, it was paradise on earth.

Every issue of *True Hearts* was a collective labor of love. From reviewing, to proofing, to printing, it was a completely DIY operation. Club members worked afternoons and nights, gathered around an old mimeograph, fixing the wax, mixing the ink, cranking the roller, counting and loading the paper . . . it was like a game, as if they were running an underground rag. Pranks, of course, ensued, and Liu was the ultimate prankster. Seldom did anyone walk out of the press not covered in ink. Binding was the most fun. They laid the pages in order in piles around the table, lined up, and walked around it one after another, picking up the pages as they went. Once everyone had walked in a full circle, seven issues were made.

The club lasted three years. After college, they all went their separate ways, with Tiananmen as a sort of threshold and all the highs and lows and ups and downs that came with making a mark and making a living in the coming sea change. On their thirtieth graduation anniversary, the class that started in 1977 held their reunion online. Other than one who had passed away, the only graduate who couldn't attend was Liu. The old friends decided to put together a "Collected Blog Writings of Class of 1977 Chinese Department Graduates," but someone was missing. Some people remembered Liu, who was in prison, and posted online: "Maybe ask Liu Xia to write a few words for the book?"

After thirty years, friends became strangers; some didn't even want to be mentioned in the same breath as Liu. Someone immediately shot back: "Liu Xia is under heavy surveillance. Forget it." Another posted: "Why not? We're just reminiscing about old times, nothing more. We're even including people who are dead. There's no reason to exclude people who are alive." Another posted: "This is for the class of '77 only. Liu Xia is not a part of it." Someone else: "Exceptions can be made. Aren't other people writing for those who have passed?" There was even one: "I vote no, or I'm out. I'm not afraid of anything, I just don't want to cause any trouble."

Still, more warmth seeped through than cold. In December 2009, after Liu was sentenced to eleven years' imprisonment and two years' deprivation of political rights on charges of "inciting subversion of state power," many old friends expressed their outrage and sadness. Wang Xiaoni said, "We're classmates in college. In the twenty-some years after those unforgettable four, all I've seen is the frailty and helplessness of the individual. . . . I am pessimistic." Xu Jingya said, "As part of the same class, as part of the same generation, I feel for Liu Xiaobo! I don't want us to live under the shadow of 'Criminal Speech' forever!" Wei Haitian said, "I am proud to be Liu Xiaobo's classmate, and I am ashamed for not being on the frontline with him fighting the good fight. From now on, we stand together."

Not long after the news of Liu Xiaobo's receiving the 2010 Nobel Peace Prize broke, a post appeared on the class of 1977 reunion board, along with an old photo of the seven founding True Hearts poetry club members. The subject of the post was: "Alumnus Wins Award." Everyone had signed the photograph except one, designated only by the letters "L-X-B."

So little said, so much understood.

2

BEIJING STORIES

THE WIDE-EYED GIRL

He loved to read but was never a good student, at least in his teachers' eyes. He had a high IQ and would learn things before the teachers even taught them. He was a troublemaker and a clown. He corrected his teachers frequently and loudly. And so he was always sent to the back of the class. He never took tests seriously, which his grades clearly showed.

Then one day, everything changed.

That day after class, just as he passed the school gates, he caught sight of two girls walking and talking in front of him. A peal of laughter burst into the air. One of them laughed especially loud. His curiosity was piqued.[1]

The pretty girl with the loud, clarion laugh was named Tao Li. She was the number one student in her class. Before he introduced himself, Liu Xiaobo thought: "If I'm gonna have a shot in hell with this girl, I need better grades first." He put the pedal to the metal, and his academic records soared. Then he found an opportunity to borrow a book from this girl—cliché, but tried and true nonetheless.

And true it was. The girl, nicknamed "Wide Eyes," was the daughter of renowned Northeast Normal University professors and scholars Tao Dezhen and Pu Manting. Tao Li was an artistically gifted and frail girl. The laugh that caught Liu's ear was a rarity. She was usually alone and rarely socialized or paid attention to outside things. Her paintings and calligraphies were extraordinary, but she seldom showed them. Her solitude and air of mystery drew Liu in even more.

The mood at the Tao home was completely different from that at the Lius', with one precious boy and two lovely girls amid a sweet and serene, almost aristocratic atmosphere rarely seen in Chinese households; the two girls were especially beautiful and talented, like a pair of blossoming peonies whenever they went out together. A close friend of Tao's recalls:

> Mrs. Tao was always so warm and welcoming. This renowned scholar of children's literature cooked for us and treated me like her own daughter. It was around that time I found out "Wide Eyes" had a heart condition. She was an extremely thoughtful girl, very frail physically, and very quiet, with this alluring way of looking at you. Her dad was always reading, doing research, and rarely talked to us, but he always let us read his books. I still remember the musty wood smell of their cramped little study. The little boy was also very handsome and, because of all the political hardships they suffered, had a weak constitution like his sister as well.

Liu began chasing Tao with dogged determination. Slowly, they formed a bond. The young woman discovered in the young man a wildness and set out to tame him.

During that period, Liu liked spending time at Tao's, experiencing an elegance and a warmth there he had never before known. The Taos liked the well-read, talkative young man. They smiled at each other knowingly: this boy was going to be somebody someday.

Liu and Tao decided to go for it and took the college entrance exams together. Compared with Liu, Tao was much better prepared and frequently tutored him at her place after he got off work.

Like many young people, Liu wanted to flee the nest and got into his first choice of Jilin University, whereas Tao enrolled at NNU. With the two campuses relatively close, Liu and Tao saw quite a bit of each other, going to the movies, dancing—it was the most carefree time of their lives.

Liu graduated in 1982, and the pair soon married. It seemed like a dream come true. But Liu had never given any thought to how to be a good husband. Big in ambition and wild at heart, he had a hard time staying tied down by his gentle and sensitive wife.

In 1979, Tao's parents joined Beijing Normal University's Chinese Department, and Tao went to work at BNU after graduation. The newlyweds were now five hundred miles apart. Liu decided to apply to graduate school there in the Chinese Department.

Beijing was the place to be for literarily and artistically minded youths in China. It was the political, artistic, and cultural epicenter of a formidable empire, much like Paris in the Belle Époque or New York in the 1920s. Those looking for fame and fortune or to otherwise fulfill their dreams flowed from the rural provinces to the capital like pilgrims to Mecca—notwithstanding its awful weather and awfully high price tags.

Come lately as he was from circumstances beyond his control, Liu had sworn to himself he had to go to Beijing. He had to get into BNU. BNU ranked second only to Beijing University and was notoriously difficult to get into. But Liu was confident, and he was accepted with flying colors.

That summer, a suitcase in each hand, he took the train from Changchun bound for Beijing. He felt he couldn't get there fast enough. Tao had been waiting for her husband at the station; she had put on a bright floral-print dress just that morning, hoping to stand out more in the swaths of people passing through Beijing Railway Station. As soon as Liu stepped out of the platform, he spotted a young woman like a fresh lotus in a muddy pond. The two ran to each other and embraced under hundreds of ogling eyes. Tao was already familiar with the campus and helped Liu register for classes. A fantastic homemade meal by his in-laws awaited him. He was in heaven.

Founded in 1902, the School of Chinese Language and Literature at Beijing Normal University had been a bed for the May Fourth/New Culture Movement. Famed writers such as Lu Xun and Shen Congwen had all taught here. The school rose to even greater heights in the 1980s, its halls then practically a walk of stars.

At school, Liu stood on the shoulders of giants. The professors, stars themselves, provided him the background to shine even brighter.

The following year, Liu's son, Liu Tao, was born. At the time, Liu Xiaobo was focused on his studies and career and often left home early and came back late. He wasn't winning any husband- or father-of-the-year awards and certainly wasn't prepared to be a husband and father. Tao Li's own parents frequently came to the rescue.

After getting his master's degree, Liu stayed on to lecture while pursuing his PhD. Sharing a dorm for young faculty with others, especially without a private kitchen or bathroom, was a pain in the neck to say the least. But Liu and Tao were happy. After all, it was home.

In the 1980s in China, those with an education barely earned more than those without. PhD holders were thought to be posthole diggers, especially those in the humanities. Tao enjoyed the unassuming life of a scholar and wished the same for her husband, but in a time of cultural and political upheaval, competition among factions, and young people's fight for expression, Liu couldn't stay quiet.

Tao had published some literary criticisms but never expressed her own political views in her writings. Like the famous fourth-century BC Chinese philosopher Zhuangzi, she preferred a "free and easy" personal style that broke from and rejected the world at large. She wrote Liu once: "Xiaobo, you appear to be the prodigal son of the world. In truth you never left it. You recognize yourself in society. In turn it recognizes itself in you. It will tolerate you, accept you, forgive you, encourage you, even as it rails against you. You are the embellishment in its underlining. As for me, I am nobody. I ask for nothing from society. I don't even blame it. You don't understand me. I have no place in the world. Even with you."[2]

The young man didn't know how true those words would ring until much later.

THE RIGHT-WING PUPIL

Liu was appointed to the coveted post of lecturer at BNU after receiving his master's degree in 1984. Still, he needed a doctorate for further career advancement, and the mid-1980s saw a return of doctoral education in the humanities. When he decided to pursue his PhD, his wife gave him her full support: "You do the dissertation, I'll do the dishes."

A news article once described Liu's academic career, not without some exaggeration: "He opened the course catalog, flipped to a page, saw the unusual name 'Huang Yaomian' in the literary theory section, and decided to try to get into the program. He got in, smooth sailing."[3] In truth, Liu put much thought into choosing his mentor.

Huang Yaomian was the most senior professor in BNU's Chinese Department and had been personally branded as "right-wing" by Mao. Liu admired his courage to speak his mind despite his having fallen ill over the years.

Some weekends the teacher invited the student to his house, chatting about history, about politics, about life. The student loved especially hearing the professor talk about the old republican China, about how corrupt and repressive the Nationalists were yet how left-wing writers at the time could also run their own papers and magazines, playing hide-and-seek with the censors. These stories carried the young man away to a lost time.

Huang was a standing committee member of the CPPCC (Chinese People's Political Consultative Conference) and regaled Liu with many tales of bureaucratic foibles and buffooneries, to which the latter listened with equal parts rapture and novelty, frequently injecting clever comments that provided bellyfuls of laughs for the old man.

A number of the young man's classmates later went to work for the government. The cream of the crop became secretaries to party leaders and rose further from there. But Liu had decided then and there never to set foot in a bureaucracy. It was simply not fit for human life in his view.

Huang doted on but could not help worrying about his diamond-in-the-rough pupil. Liu was the first doctoral student he personally had taken under his wing. Though the regime had loosened its grip somewhat, Huang, a veteran of the times, had seen enough to know it was merely lying dormant, not dead, and could pounce on the foolhardy any moment and tear them to shreds. Thinking his teacher had lost his edge, the young man let the old man's advice and admonition go in one ear and out the other.

In the end, the teacher couldn't do anything but sigh—ah, let him be. Let him find his own way. Maybe Huang was worrying too much, anyway. All great men in history were foolhardy in some way. That was precisely their greatness.

As a young man himself, Huang was self-taught. Though respected, his own career was cut short by the Cultural Revolution, so he had little to offer Liu in terms of actual scholarly knowledge and expertise. Huang later published a memoir, just on the eve of his death in 1987. He titled the memoir *Turbulence*. It makes one wonder, though, had the teacher seen the next twenty years of his prized pupil's life, including being awarded the Nobel Peace Prize, what he would have thought. It's all relative, perhaps.

After Huang passed, Liu's secondary advisor, Tong Qingbing, became his supervisor. Less political but more open, Tong prized Liu all the same and later defended him against a host of jealous persecutors and standpat detractors: "Some people think he's an extremist, a show-off, posturing for the sake of posturing and provoking for the sake of provoking. They misunderstand him completely. As his mentor and colleague, I can vouch for the absolute integrity and genuineness of this man."

When Liu was released from prison in 1991, he had already been expelled from BNU. The course of his life had been derailed and set down another path—the luminous, yet thorn-lined path of a heretic, a dissenter. From the 1990s on, student and teacher gradually lost touch. Still, in 2008 when Tong heard the news of Liu's second arrest, he sent a brief but touching message to Liu's family: "Please ask him to take care of himself."

THE WINGED STEED

The young scholar was already making a name for himself in the mid-1980s. His first work, "On Art and Intuition," was published in 1984, shortly followed by a piece on the Chinese philosopher Zhuangzi. In truth, Liu owed his induction into the literary hall of fame to two short-lived publications in the 1980s—*A Hundred Schools* and *China*, particularly *China*, then known as a starting gate for dark horses.

China was the coda to famed Chinese author Ding Ling's legendary life. One of the first modern feminist writers in China, she made a splash in 1927 with her debut, *Miss Sophia's Diary*, where a young girl living in a tuberculosis sanatorium describes her thoughts and feelings on love, sex, and self in unusually frank terms. Later criticized for her exposé of living conditions in the city of Yan'an, widely celebrated as the birthplace of Communist China, she was nevertheless protected by Mao because of their hometown connection. In 1951 she won the Soviet Union's Stalin Prize for literature with *The Sun Shines over the Sanggan River*, the most prestigious award for Chinese writers at the

time. Yet just four years later she was classified as a counterrevolutionary and sent to the country to be reeducated through labor for twelve
years and then jailed again for five years during the Cultural Revolution. Ding was exonerated in 1984. She was eighty years old. Abandoning her long-awaited novel and memoir, in her last years she decided to
put all her energy and effort into creating a mass literary publication,
which she called *China*.

Poet, editor-in-chief, and Liu's personal mentor, Niu Han, had this
to say about the publication: "In the spirit of Lu Xun and May Fourth,
China existed in service not to politics, but simply to readers and writers. Never a mouthpiece for politicians or a megaphone for sloganeers,
China was nonetheless a voice for freedom, a plea for democracy."[4]

Two younger editors, Zou Jin and Wu Bin, also had connections to
Liu. Zou was one of the "Seven True Hearts" at Jilin University with
Liu Xiaobo. Wu's wife was the poet Liu Xia.

No one knew what was going to happen at Tiananmen Square a few
years later.

No one knew Liu Xiaobo and Liu Xia were going to fall in love.

China was always in the midst of the storm, logistically and financial-
ly. At the end of 1985, Ding Ling was admitted to the hospital. A
meeting was held in a hospital wing, wherein the magazine's leaders
decided to expand its scope. An exciting new wave of up-and-comers
rolled through the pages of the periodical, but the fact didn't escape
Ding that *China* was going to either cease or change after her death.

It was during this time that Liu began writing for *China*. He wasn't
particularly fond of Ding, as in some ways she was a flag bearer for the
Left, but her "one book" philosophy, which proposed that every writer
should write at least one book that will live through the ages, found in
Liu's individualism a kindred spirit.

He wrote only three pieces for the magazine, in 1986—a critique of
the self-portrayal of intellectuals in recent works of fiction, a polemic
against the contemporary Chinese philosopher Li Zehou, and a set of
poems titled "This. . . ." The first two were hotly debated and gave rise
to strong feelings on both sides. In the fourth issue's "Reflection without Escape: The Picture of the Intellectual in Recent Fiction," Liu
panned influential writers and filmmakers for airbrushing intellectuals—themselves—and making them up as Christ figures; instead, he
wrote, they are apish and self-pitying. In the tenth issue's "Conversa-

tions with Li Zehou: Self and Sensibility," he challenged the rationalist philosopher by placing emotion and the individual above reason and the collective, an opposition as much philosophical as generational.

By the end of 1986, *China* was forced to shutter its doors. In a farewell message, the editors wrote: "The *China* our comrade Ding Ling has poured all her heart, soul, and life into, that has been supported by our allies in the Party, that is beloved by our readers and writers, has reached the end of a leg in its journey. We don't want it to. Here we quote a line from a poet who died at the hands of those who did him wrong: I proclaim, we are innocent, and then we wither." The issue was secretly printed in the faraway city of Xi'an.[5]

Hearing the news and knowing the truth about the regime's hand in *China*'s demise, Liu was furious. He couldn't understand the editors' sitting-duck mentality and tried to get writers across the country to sign a petition, calling and writing around the clock. Few dared. Though the campaign was a wash, the young writer gained valuable experience in grassroots organization and open-letter circulation.

A few months later, Liu published his first book, *Critique of Choice*. *China* had published the first part of the book, and Liu thanked the magazine in the acknowledgments, saying, "Though it has withered, once upon a time a flower bloomed in full brilliance, from which a thousand winged hearts drank. That should be enough."[6] And though he would move further and further away from the life of a literary critic, *China* would be an important step in the young man's journey and career.

❊ ❊ ❊

As in the story of the Ephesians or "Little Briar Rose," the Chinese after a long night of chaotic feverish dreams suddenly found themselves awake, and in the mid-1980s China enjoyed a renaissance of sorts. Philosophy, art, politics, poetry, fiction, films from *Yellow Earth* and *Red Sorghum* to Westerns, literature seeking roots as well as those seeking to break from them, modernism, rock 'n' roll . . . in the words of author Ah Cheng, "All of a sudden people had contact overseas. All of a sudden there were translations. All of a sudden there was this theory and that theory, this piece of knowledge and that piece of knowledge. People changed, and they changed fast."[7] It was the age of trauma, it was the age of recovery, it was the epoch in which China opened its dust-sealed doors to a whole new world, it was the epoch in which people challenged old ideas with new ones, it was the season of turbulence, it was the season of life.

Everywhere were salons, forums, gatherings. Not many people had phones, and news passed directly from mouth to ear. Even if it took an hour by bike to get to a gathering, even if the gathering was just a few friends chitchatting, it was both gratifying and fortifying. Liu went to his friends' places often but more frequently hosted in his own home. Your home was open to all your friends, and all your friends' homes were open to you.

Even then the young writer was known as "a dissenter among dissenters." He felt like a fish out of water with intellectuals and would rather hang out with students and ordinary people. He wasn't a schmoozer and had no gift for brownnosing and so wasn't exactly *persona grata* in scholarly and writerly circles. His friend Geremie Barmé pretty much sums it up: "Liu Xiaobo has been a loner, and although popular enough with audiences of university students who flocked to hear his lectures, he has never been an accepted or even welcome figure in the Chinese intellectual establishment."[8]

He was merciless in his criticism, even of those "on the same side," exposing their vanity and hypocrisy. He took leading thinkers Jin Guantao, Li Zehou, Fang Lizhi, and Wen Yuankai to task for their "negative influence on young people"; he even raked over the coals the popular 1988 television documentary *River Elegy*, on the decline of traditional Chinese culture, for its die-hard Maoist, pious tone. This put the "emperor's tailors" into a tizzy. Even those who liked to call themselves "even minded" avoided Liu like the plague. His behavior, which could be construed as abrupt and rude, his stutter, the colorfulness of his tongue, and his unsentimental honesty, not to mention his heretical pronouncements, all served to isolate him in the literary arena. He was an individualist to the core, convinced he had pulled himself up on his own, not through any networking or nepotism, and so he showed no mercy to those around him or to himself—burning bridges both behind and ahead of him.

Friend Liao Yiwu recalls that the young man was always looking for a fight. Once at Wu Bin and Liu Xia's house, the author Xu Xing asked whether Liu would write a review of his new book, which had caused some stir in the literary world for its newfangled way of storytelling. Liu shot back: "Why should I write a review for you? I can't write a review for you just because we're buddies." Xu explained that the work was important. Liu countered: "Isn't it basically *Catcher in the Rye*, Chinese edition? What's so great about plagiarizing other people's work? Why would I write a review for a secondhand work like this?" Xu was trying to remain polite, but he had been pushed far enough and joined in the ripostes. A shouting match ensued, and before long, shirts came off. "Come on, talk is cheap. Put 'em up!" They went out into the hall and were about to fight when people pulled them apart.

People found Liu overbearing and unforgiving. "Live and let live" was not one of his mottos. Liao, for instance, was from Sichuan and had a hard time with Mandarin. Liu couldn't understand him, so he chided Liao for not speaking properly. Back then he was a dyed-in-the-wool rebel who had absolutely no consideration of other people's feelings.

The 1980s were the "expressive stage" in China's development. Honesty was its most salient characteristic. Though it still imitated the language of the Cultural Revolution and fed on limited knowledge of the past, with sights still narrow and thoughts somewhat shallow, it had an unwavering focus on reality and the conditions of everyday life. Liu thought he had already wasted many years in the revolution and was now throwing away even more as a longtimer in the boondocks of academia—why not get famous quicker? Provocative, ambitious, in search of an audience, in 1986 he took off, landing one heavyweight publication after another.

But if you thought he was merely a sensationalist, you would be wrong. If he had not been so original or penetrating, people would not have gravitated toward him so much. His influence stems from his thoroughness: he has the ability and the audacity to think everything through to its end, to its conclusion—even if he or others might not like what they find there. Some believe he has staked his name on attacking "celebrities," but then why are young people so drawn to him? Because he dares go to the extreme in thought and feeling. There are no totems or taboos, no paper tigers or sacred cows, in his head or at the end of his pen. People are yearning for a better world, and his popularity proves that we still have a long way to go.[9]

☼ ☼ ☼

In early September 1986, the Institute of Literature at the Chinese Academy of Social Sciences (CASS) held a conference called "A Decade of New Literature." Most participants were established authorities on Chinese literature with one exception—the babe newly out of the woods, Liu Xiaobo. The conference was supposed to be a capstone on the past ten years in the arts with nothing but positive spin and official lines, perfectly even keeled and decidedly inoffensive, commonplace among such semiformal academic gatherings.

People spoke in order of seniority. As the powers that be recited their lines and put the audience into a stupor, Liu, a shaggy-haired young man with his sleeves rolled up, was moving his lips excitedly in the corner, as if mumbling to himself. As the senior figures were out of politeness gesturing to each other to speak, the man suddenly charged onstage and grabbed the mic. No one knew who he was. Everyone stared in shock. Some elderly statesmen frowned. At these events, politeness was paramount. Why was this person so rude? Who invited him?

As a murmur fell over the crowd, Liu began to speak. The title of his talk was "The Crisis of New Literature." Seemingly impromptu, the presentation was actually painstakingly prepared and memorized. The young man had long dreamed of setting the literary world ablaze on this day. Disheveled, stuttering somewhat, he spoke with a passion and a conviction rarely heard inside the cold, bare walls of the ivory tower. This was no run-of-the-mill grist—every word hit like a bullet; every sentence cut like a knife.

Holding it up to the bar May Fourth writers such as Lu Xun had set, Liu declared all postrevolutionary literature "worthless." On hearing such a frank, no-nonsense assessment of the current state of affairs, some nodded in agreement while others glowered in disbelief. The young man had turned a cause for merry celebration into a forum for sober reflection. The brain trust was infuriated by this violation of the unspoken rules but could do nothing to take back the floor. The authorities had to sit and listen.

The points Liu touched on were these: intellectuals resist change more forcefully than ordinary people; chained up by rationality and morality, there is no individuality in Chinese literature and hence no life or longevity; and without breaking with tradition completely, smashing it to pieces like the May Fourth writers did, there is no getting out of this crisis. He wasn't the first one to think these thoughts, only the first one to say them.

As it turned out, the biggest topic of discussion at the conference that year was Liu Xiaobo. No one cared about Professor So-and-So and Dr. Such-and-Such. The theme of the conference changed. The speaker finished his speech to thunderous applause. It was as he had predicted. A smile touched the corners of his lips.

Word of mouth reached beyond the conference. People imitated his accent and stutter: "Mo-modern Chinese literature is no-nothing but a pale copy of cl-classical Ch-Chinese lit-erature," giving him the moniker "the dark winged steed of the literary world."

Coincidentally, a college classmate of his was also at the conference. Xu Jingya was a reporter for the watchdog paper *Shenzhen Youth Daily*. Impressed by the speech, he printed it in the daily's October 3 edition across the front pages.

"Crisis! Literary World on Verge of Collapse" moved like hotcakes. The price of the paper jumped from four fen, to one jiao, to two jiao. Mostly college students snatched it up. It was promptly reprinted in other papers. The world—at least China and Chinese communities abroad—was indeed on fire.

Liu owed his success as much to himself as to the times. There was no one like him before, and there would probably be no one like him after—not for a want of talent but because harsher laws and a less-forgiving public would not permit it.

He asked the literary luminaries: "How can you stand the emperor's new clothes?" In a time when no one rocked the boat out of fear or complacency, he capsized an entire fleet, crew, passengers, and all, with one pry of a paddle. He told an interviewer in Hong Kong two years later: "What I want to say is there's no good mainland Chinese literature. Not they're not allowed to write any, but they're not able to write any. . . . I have a double standard when it comes to judging literature, one for Chinese literature, one for world literature—even the best of the former isn't on the same ground as the latter." Needless to say, he made few friends and many enemies. But he never looked back. Pats on the back, self or mutual, were not the way he worked.

From the start, Liu never critiqued literature just to critique literature. He was not popular or notorious simply because he was a critic.

He studied art and aesthetics, a hot topic in 1980s China and interdisciplinary by nature. Sensitive like an artist and profound like a philosopher, unlike many scholars, he thought outside the box. His real target was both traditional Chinese culture and the withering of that culture at the hands of an Orwellian regime. As a writer, one must write either what people want to hear or what they want to say, and Liu was the people's Sancho Panza. This was the real reason for the "Liu Xiaobo phenomenon," especially in intellectual circles and on college campuses. "Crisis!" wasn't just about the narrow world of literature: the crisis facing works of the new period after the revolution was one facing "not just a people, but the whole of humanity itself." A thinker first, already Liu had begun his escape from ivy-laden halls to become a warrior for freedom and human rights.

THE ROCK STAR

It was spring of 1988. A doctoral student was going to walk a year early. He had just finished his dissertation, titled "Beauty and Freedom."

A hundred thousand words, zero citations. Usually professors read these things *starting with* citations. It was thought the dissertation would receive a surefire F. To the student, however, more citations didn't mean more knowledge or thought—just a lack of independence and originality. He chose a more direct approach: "It suits me. The tradition of annotation upon annotation throughout the history of scholarship is archaic and pointless. It's 'citation paranoia.'"[10]

Later, not only would the dissertation get high marks, it would also become a best seller.

The book puts forward two main ideas. One, beauty comes from conflict. "Life is full of contradiction, suffering, conflict. . . . Human beings are always teetering from one moment to the next on the edge of flesh and spirit, desire and morality, sense and sensibility."[11] The principle of harmony lauded through thousands of years of Chinese history does nothing but stifle individuality and creativity.

Two, freedom comes from beauty. Freedom, previously taboo, became a rallying cry in 1980s China. It is, and has always been, the word Liu lives by. And the very embodiment of freedom, he believes, is beauty. Through the creation and recognition of beauty, human beings transcend a coldly rational world, they transcend greed and self-interest, they transcend social dictates and pressures, and they transcend themselves. But this transcendence can be only momentary, elusive. It is both life's joy and its tragedy.

In summer 1988, Liu finished classes and was getting ready to defend his dissertation. Aftershocks of the government's "Anti-Bourgeois Liberalization" campaign against Hu Yaobang and his ilk were still being felt. The State Education Commission had blacklisted Liu as a "bourgeois liberal" but, while originally barring him from the dissertation defense, finally caved under the university's pressure. Universities in China then still had a degree of freedom and independence.

The time for the student's oral defense, which happened to be the first doctoral defense in the history of BNU's Chinese Department, finally came. It was like a rock concert—standing room only. Something like this would never happen again inside the walls of academia.

The morning of June 25, 1988, was a hot one. Hundreds of students swarmed into the BNU main building, crowding inside one tiny, poorly ventilated conference room. Crowds spilled out the door into the dimly lit hallway.

The flyer on the door simply read: "'Beauty and Freedom,' Dissertation Defense, Literary Theory Doctoral Candidate Liu Xiaobo." It wasn't exactly a hot topic. It wasn't overtly political, nor did it have anything to do with current affairs. There was only one reason for the crowd—the name "Liu Xiaobo."

The defense committee members looked out onto the throngs around them, shocked: they'd never seen anything like it! They had barely anywhere to sit. More people continued to trickle in. Then the president of the university made an unprecedented decision: change of venue. The defense was moved to the four-hundred-seat ballroom on the eighth floor of the main building. The narrow stairs drew streams and streams of people up, and the ballroom was quickly filled, delaying the defense by well over an hour.

The committee lineup was impressive: chaired by BNU's own and leading Confucian scholar Wang Yuanhua, it consisted of an arsenal of big guns from other schools such as Beijing University, Sichuan Normal University, Fudan University, and Renmin University. Liu was particularly close to Renmin's Jiang Peikun and knew his son Jiang Jielian. In a twist of fate, Jiang Jielian would be shot and killed a year later in the Tiananmen Square massacre, of which Liu was a part.

Wang saw potential in the contentious young man who never thought someone of Wang's stature would agree to sit on his dissertation defense committee. Still, the State Education Commission (SEC) found the committee too "bourgeois-liberal" and insisted on adding four "hardline Marxists"—from BNU, Renmin, CASS, and East China Normal University—to the mix. At the last minute, Fudan's Jiang Kong-yang suffered a fracture and had to send in his comments, leaving nine members standing. The SEC was still unsatisfied and sent two more auditors on the big day. You could cut the tension with a knife.

The committee members asked a series of questions and made a host of comments. Liu gave a unified response at the end. His stutter was gone. There wasn't a peep from the room until the end, when the audience, mostly college students who hadn't a clue what Liu was talking about, burst into applause.

Without further objection from the nine members or two auditors, the student was awarded his doctorate. The vote was unanimous.[12]

❂ ❂ ❂

A reporter once wrote: "Professor Liu Xiaobo didn't dress like a professor. He dressed more like a train driver or railroad worker." Liu read it and laughed: "But I *am* a construction worker!"

He didn't look like a professor on the outside, but the knowledge inside him could fill the heads of all the students in the Chinese Department. He was the most popular professor at BNU, not only because of his originality and erudition but also because he acted like one of the students. A big kid himself, he never put on airs or distanced himself from those he taught.

He hung out in student dorms often, shucking peanuts, chugging beer, playing poker, even wrestling in the sandpit in the field. When he lost, his students would stick a note on his forehead with "LOSER" in big letters or make him tunnel under desks as punishment. Any boundary between teacher and students disappeared. They could say his poems stank, play pranks on him and poke fun at him, ask whether his stutter derailed his train of thought—the kind of scenes found only in the *Analects* of Confucius that have been all but lost otherwise in institutes of higher learning today.

Just over thirty, the hale young professor was an expert wrestler. Even most students were no match. When he won, he boasted. "Professor Liu beat you fair and square!" He loved sports and watched soccer with students, even joining the team. His kick left something to be desired, but he was the only faculty member running on the green. Spectators thought he was one of the students. Scholars have always been thought to be unathletic—not Liu. He was a "jock." Instead, music was his Achilles heel. As tone-deaf as a cauliflower and with a stammer more severe than that of George VI, whenever Liu began singing his teammates ran straight for the hills.

He treated students he liked as brothers, and the ones he didn't— the precocial, officiary, obsequious ones—he never minded telling flat-out.

Once a student showed him a work of calligraphy by famed calligrapher Qi Gong, bragging: "Look, Master Qi made this for me."

This ticked off Liu, and he yelled in the student's face: "Master-this, Master-that, the only thing you know is how to stick your nose up other people's asses!"

An awkward moment for the student. He tried changing the subject: "I read *Critique of Choice*. Brilliant, absolutely brilliant!"

"Did you finish it?" Liu asked.

"About half," the student replied.

Liu immediately shot back: "How do you know it's brilliant if you haven't even finished it?"

"I can still talk about it a little even if I've only read half of it, right . . . ?" The student's voice grew meeker.

Liu replied: "We have to be on the same footing if we want to discuss something seriously. You only read half the book. How can you talk about it with me?"

The student persisted. "Then can you mentor me?"

"Hell, no!" Liu shouted. "You don't deserve it! I don't want a student like you. What's in it for me? Nothing. Not even a glimmer of hope. Everything about you turns my stomach. Get out of my face! Now!"

One of BNU's youngest lecturers, he keenly smelled the rot in the state of education today. "The Chinese have perfected their system of turning human beings into slaves through education. In this respect they are unparalleled in the world." He wrote: "Ninety-five percent of college graduates are garbage. Ninety-seven percent of master's graduates are garbage. Ninety-nine percent of doctoral graduates are garbage."

Some people are born with the gift for teaching, and Liu was a natural in the classroom. A student recalls: "Before beginning each class, he would write a classical poem or lyric up on the board, and simply spend some time savoring it with the students."[13] There is something unusual about his stammer: its severity seems to decrease with the increasing size of the audience. One on one, he stammers like a gramophone during an earthquake; give him a roomful of students, and he can spin sentences forward and backward faster than you can spit them out. He loves teaching. For twenty-five years since Tiananmen, however, he has not been able to set foot in a classroom even once.

Liu was often invited to speak on other campuses. Before Tiananmen, schools had more autonomy; students had more say. The more radical speakers were, the more popular they were with the college crowd. After Tiananmen, drastically increased censorship and bureaucracy all but sucked out the fermenting atmosphere from universities, squelching any life left in the mind of society.

"Liu Xiaobo fan clubs" had started popping up everywhere. Some fans, such as Zhang Qianjin, a Beijing Language and Culture University student who joined the Tiananmen protests in 1989 and was later jailed at Qincheng maximum-security prison in Beijing, can still picture clearly their long bike rides to BNU to hear Liu Xiaobo talk. Speakers were a dime a dozen; the true prime real estate was students. Whenever Liu gave a talk and other speakers were scheduled for the same time and date, they usually bowed out of their own accord. No one was stupid enough to gut his own audience.

Zhang still remembers Liu's rally to students to "embrace life naked," to lift the mask of hypocrisy and unplug the ears of cowardice. In sharp relief against most intellectuals and scholars, who didn't deign to talk about the green stuff, Liu had an extremely healthy attitude toward money. He never shied from talking about payments for his speeches, and he didn't give speeches without setting a mutually agreed-on price beforehand. "Why do I give talks? One, I like giving them. Two, I get paid for them. If I don't get paid enough for them, I don't give them." His rate was forty yuan an hour, higher than the pay of the entire senior faculty.

Once, he got to a lecture, and a student rep told him they couldn't pay him because the school had cut their activities fund. Enraged, he was about to get up and leave—never mind the rows of his fans already in their seats, waiting with bated breath for hours—when the reps pulled out their own wallets in a panic, pooled their money, and handed it to him. He took it without a second thought and gave them their lecture: "Do you know what a social contract is? If you violate one, you have to pay!"

Saintly vows of poverty and hypocrisy in the guise of charity do not sit well with Liu. He likes to say that if there's a five-dollar bill on the ground, a construction worker will pick it up, whereas an intellectual will step on it first, look to see whether people are around, and then snatch it up on the sly, hiding it in his pocket.

From a lecture of his:

> The task of youths today is to rehabilitate yourselves, to decalcify the arthritic form of thinking inculcated in you since childhood. I achieved what I achieved today ultimately not because of others but because of myself. I think we don't need to feel such a sense of responsibility, of duty toward others—all that really matters is we remain true to our visions, realize our potentials. The faith we have in ourselves must equal that of believers in their God, without squabbling over much else.

Cassette tapes were popular among the young in China at the time. They even used them to learn English. Some recorded Liu's talks on cassettes to pass to and share with others. There was no "intellectual property." Many couldn't come from far away to hear him talk; this was as close to the real thing as they could get. Even without the live energy, the "rock star's" passionate words rang deep in the hearts of thousands. Beijingese started giving the tapes as gifts to out-of-town family and friends. Pre-Facebook, pre-Twitter, this was how ideas went viral in 1980s China.

Even private companies like the IT magnate Stone Group wanted him to come speak.

He did.

They were sorely disappointed.

CEO Wan Runnan recalls: "Xiaobo knew some people at Stone. They wanted to bring him in as an inspirational speaker. I agreed. I went to hear him speak. Honestly, I was let down. He wasn't very good, and he stuttered. When he got really excited, he was practically incomprehensible. I know people who stutter tend to be very smart. Their mouth simply can't catch up to their brain."[14]

Spring came early to Beijing in 1989, and it was a beautiful one, sand of the Gobi seeping in notwithstanding. Some say April is the best month to visit the Forbidden City, with moderate climate, transparent blue skies, and showers of peach, pear, cherry, apricot, and crabapple blossoms. Yet in the gently swaying, lulling spring breeze, there's wind of a storm brewing.

A distant thunder sounds of a torrential rain to come.

3

THE BLACK HAND OF TIANANMEN

A HOP, SKIP, AND A JUMP

On August 24, 1988, Liu Xiaobo arrived in Oslo, Norway, to present a guest lecture on modern Chinese literature at the University of Oslo.

It was to be a three-month gig as part of a symposium on modern China. Others, such as poet Bei Dao, artist Mi Qiu, and filmmaker Chen Kaige, were invited as well. Liu delivered a series of five lectures and donated his notes to the archives.

The University of Oslo is Norway's biggest and oldest university. Compared to Beijing, Oslo was a small, quiet town. Little did Liu know at the time this wouldn't be his last or only tie to the city. With a light workload, he had plenty of time to think and write.

Of course, it didn't take long before his first run-in with his host and chair of the department, Bonnie McDougall.

McDougall had hoped to place Liu under her control. Liu, on the other hand, had no interest in office politics and certainly wasn't going to be anyone's lapdog. He started hanging out with Mi Qiu, who wasn't exactly on McDougall's good side—much to the latter's chagrin.

McDougall called Liu into her office. "You are the first Chinese I've invited who doesn't listen to me! How dare you talk to me this way? Do you want to stay or not?"

Liu responded: "Don't be so full of yourself. Not everyone's going to kowtow to you for a visa. I've no intention of staying long. I'm leaving as soon as the gig is over. But remember: if you want to study modern China, you can't not study me."[1]

Geremie Barmé has this to say: "His indelicate style was a shock to sinologists more used to the superficially respectful and cooperative intelligentsia of China." But to Barmé, Liu's critical tendencies applied to not only others but also himself.[2]

Liu later points out the perverse relationship between what he calls the "thoroughbreds" (the Chinese intelligentsia) and the "wranglers" (the Western experts who study them): on one hand, the wranglers have a strong desire to tame and own the thoroughbreds; on the other, many thoroughbreds obey and bend over for the wranglers just for a chance to trot abroad, even race the international circuit. The Chinese government has always tried to paint a picture of Liu as a "traitor," a "sellout" who blindly worships everything Western for personal gain. Nothing is further from the truth.

University of Oslo culture studies and Oriental languages professor Halvor Eifring, who has translated Liu Xiaobo as well as the 2010 Nobel presentation speech into Chinese, was a graduate student then and recalls his professors not thinking much of Liu other than as a young scholar from China with potential. Liu was radical and rebellious and shot from the hip, not just at the Norwegians; he was an equal-opportunity "hater." After Tiananmen, Eifring thought Liu gained more "cred" and became serious about changing the Chinese political landscape—and paid dearly for it.

Liu didn't enjoy his time in Oslo, which wasn't helped by his opinion of the people at the university. After the stint, he journeyed to the University of Hawaii at the behest of theater professor Elizabeth Wichmann-Walczak, where he lectured on Chinese philosophy and current politics. During this time he finished his bombshell *Contemporary Politics and Intellectuals in China*, which wouldn't be published until 1990 in Taiwan.

In Honolulu, just south of paradise, his creativity and productivity erupted. "I was stunned myself," he said later. "I was a speed demon. I was afraid I was churning out inferior work." Like Oslo, Honolulu was a world apart from Beijing. An intellectual soldier used to the battlefield of the classroom, he felt a little like a fish out of water amid the tranquility of sun, sand, and sea.

After Hawaii, he wondered, what next? He wanted to see more of the world. He disagreed with some writers' stance that you had to be rooted in your home soil to produce great works. "It's an excuse. It's an exit strategy. It's a hallmark of the weak. Life is everywhere, before your eyes, under your nose, at the tip of your fingers, beneath your feet. It's every minute you breathe. As long as you can face yourself and stay open, you can write. No matter where you are."[3]

He had planned on going to California but received an invitation from Andrew Nathan at Columbia University for a one-year visit.

Liu landed in New York just as it was bidding farewell to the bitter winter of February 1989. This heir to Athens, Alexandria, and Persepolis was again a world apart from Honolulu. Liu had never seen so many brilliant, vibrant colors, smelled so many disparate yet mingling scents, heard such a symphony and cacophony of voices and noises. He touched his finger to the city's pulse and finally knew what "freedom" felt like.

He had a lot of free time, and in a strange city he quickly found his kind, including James Tu, who would later become publisher of Taiwan's *Apple Daily*, one of the biggest papers in Asia. After Liu's fourth arrest in December 2008, Tu came out and said, "Liu Xiaobo could have chosen compromise, like many do, in the face of power. Like many do, he could have chosen wealth, status, safety, security. But what he chose was to go to prison, time and again. To run in place, in life, to squander away his gifts—so the people of the world would realize the people of China are not second-class human beings."[4]

Unlike many Chinese scholars abroad, Liu didn't mind hanging around civil rights groups and activists. Part of it was the more lax political atmosphere at the time. Even so, he had tried seeking asylum from the American embassy. But then he changed his mind.

Then chair of the China Alliance for Democracy (CAD) in New York and editor of *China Spring* magazine Hu Ping remembers Liu wasn't interested in organizations but was interested in publications and magazines. He wanted to work for *China Spring* with an ambitious vision in mind. "He hit the ground running and was here every day, making phone calls and soliciting manuscripts. We never really settled on a title for him. . . . He wanted to be editor-in-chief and pushed for a separation of the magazine and the alliance, or for the alliance to offer him a job."[5]

He was on the job a grand total of two weeks while things were still in the works. Then something happened that would change his life—and the lives of a billion Chinese—forever.

A MOTH BACK TO THE FLAME

On April 15, 1989, former CPC general secretary and controversial reformist Hu Yaobang suffered a heart attack in Beijing and died. Known for his liberal views and critical stance toward his own party, Hu had been forced to resign just two years earlier. Public outcry forced the Chinese government to give Hu a state funeral, with students petitioning to have the verdict that led to his resignation reversed.

On April 18 in New York, Liu Xiaobo, Hu Ping, and several others released a list of demands to the Chinese government, asking for a retraction of the state's 1983 Anti-Spiritual Pollution and 1987 Anti-Bourgeois Liberalization campaigns, a repeal of Deng Xiaoping's Four Cardinal Principles, and revisions to the People's Republic of China (PRC) constitution, among others.

Hu's memorial service was held four days later in the Great Hall of the People, at the western edge of Tiananmen Square. A hundred thousand students poured into the square. Student representatives knelt down below the national emblem to deliver a petition letter to Premier Li Peng but were refused by government officials. A call for indefinite strike was declared. That very day, Liu and others issued an open letter to the students, urging them to "stay organized," "publish their communications," "strengthen their ties to various sectors," "maintain dialogue," and "preserve freedom on campus." The end of the letter read: "We have a feeling China is on the edge of change. We are shaping history. And we are shaping ourselves."

The demand list and open letter were posted on every corner at Beijing University. Liu was labeled "the black hand" behind the Tiananmen student protests by the state. Accepting the charge from CAD, he doubled back to Beijing. Originally scheduled to stay at Columbia until 1990, he was already at the square by May 1989.

He wore the label "black hand" like a badge of honor. At the beginning of a hunger strike on the night of June 1, on the front steps of his alma mater BNU, he proudly proclaimed: "The government keeps saying a vocal minority, a handful of bad seeds, are behind this. They're probably talking about people like me, people who aren't students. But as a citizen, I have a duty to speak out. What I'm doing is neither unlawful nor unreasonable. I'm not afraid to be a black hand. I'm proud and honored to be a black hand!"[6]

He didn't care much for Hu Yaobang and thought the dogs made their master out to be more of a hero than he really was. But the student movement and its aftermath kept him up nights. "It's a rebellion on every level, a lash against the iron cage of tyranny. It's unprecedented. How could I just sit back and watch? I had to do something. It's the difference between playing center and sitting on the sidelines. I had to go back."[7]

Family and friends thought he was crazy. "He can't resist playing the hero," "Liu Xiaobo rushes in where angels fear to tread," "He's drawn like a moth to a flame." His friend Bei Ling recalls that an air of calm came over Liu after he made the decision. "W-we can't just st-stay in N-New York right now," he stuttered. "Ha-haven't we been pre-preparing all our-our lives for this moment?"

We choose history as much as history chooses us. Throwing caution to the wind, Liu Xiaobo went home.

He had planned to fly out May 1 due to a prior speaking engagement in San Francisco at the end of April. However, when he called, all tickets to China for April through May were sold out except for one the very next day. He didn't want to give himself an excuse to stay or delay. So he bought it. Ticket in hand, he called his hosts in San Francisco to tell them he was not coming and left for home the next day, without taking time to even say goodbye to colleagues and friends.

That plane ticket changed Liu Xiaobo's life forever.

Tu, who drove him to Kennedy Airport, remembers: "On the way, he would be suddenly talkative, and suddenly quiet. I asked him what he was going to do back home. He just said he wanted to be with the students, but couldn't say anything more concrete. As I saw him off and waved goodbye, I had the distinct sense he was headed off on a one-way journey."[8]

That day, Deng Xiaoping published a piece in *People's Daily* denouncing the student protests. They were "antiparty," "anticommunist," and he was ready to use all necessary and appropriate force to control the "riots." Sunset in New York was sunrise in Beijing, and Liu didn't see the paper or catch the news of the massive street demonstrations in response until he arrived in Narita for a layover.

In the airport lobby, Liu noticed many Chinese and white faces anxiously awaiting outbound flights, like refugees fleeing the judgment of Sodom. His heart began to race, his stomach in knots. *What am I doing?* he thought. *Am I doing the right thing?*

"Flight to Beijing. Final call."

He bit his lips and walked through the terminal.

Before Liu left, friend Chen Jun called Stone Group in Beijing to pick him up at the airport and instructed them if Liu was arrested on the spot to call CAD immediately. Fortunately, the police had their hands full with the demonstrations that day. Liu passed through customs quietly. The arrest wouldn't come until deep in the night of June 6.

The forty-two days between April 26 and June 6, he would later say, felt longer than the entire thirty-four years of his life. Every time he recalled those days, they yawned more into an endless stretch of abyss, impenetrable yet weightless. "They are a wound in my soul that doesn't heal. A scar that doesn't fade with time, but becomes fresher, bloodier. As if my life came to a standstill. They are a grave, swallowing a thirty-four-year-old me, and giving birth to a me I don't recognize yet."[9]

* * *

It was eleven at night when the plane landed in Beijing. He stayed in his seat until everyone else had deboarded. He was the last one off.

At the exit, he saw his wife and an old friend, Zhou Duo. Tao Li had lost weight and looked a bit pale. Anxiety was written completely across her face. She had tried countless times over the phone to dissuade her husband from coming home, to no use.

In the car, Tao and her sister told him everything that was happening. They drove past BNU. All the streets were blocked off. Though it was past midnight, hundreds of thousands still swarmed the steps of the university.

"I AM LIU XIAOBO!"

Liu hated crowds.

An individualist above all, he especially despised those easy-come, easy-go demonstrations that were glorified block parties at best, mindless mobs at worst.

At first, he just wanted to observe. Tao told him that because of the open letter, he was being watched. No good would come of his joining the protests. Liu promised his wife he would stay out of it for now. And he did for the next two weeks.

On the morning of April 29, he went to BNU to check out the bulletin boards. Posted were mostly emotional ramblings, with nothing particularly concrete or insightful. On the wall of the boiler room by the student dorms, he spotted a "breaking news" memo: "Liu Xiaobo holds press conference in America against China's closing of *World Economic Herald*, donates thousands of dollars supporting student movement." Angry, he ripped the posting off the board.

Right then a group of students walked by and saw him tearing down the poster. They surrounded him, asking whether he was with the public security bureau; a few men even tried to grab hold of him. He shouted: "I am Liu Xiaobo!" The crowd hooted and jeered. "Liar!" "Fake!" "Fraud!" "Professor Liu has long hair! Do your homework!" Liu didn't know whether to laugh or cry; he had just gotten a haircut. It was only later that a couple of students from the Chinese Department came by and verified who he was.[10]

That day the government sent a handful of officials to talk to the student representatives. The officials' haughty and patronizing attitude disgusted Liu, who was equally disappointed with the students' impulsive shallowness. He had a thought: How about polling the students on what they thought about the talk between the officials and the reps? He got a graduate psychology student to work on the survey, but they only managed to send out a few hundred, with little response.

Liu was invited to a "New May Fourth Declaration" colloquium held on the evening of May 3 in a Beijing University dorm. There he met student leaders Wuer Kaixi, Wang Dan, and Wang Chaohua. Afterward, he got home around 1:30 a.m. and got a call from a student saying Wuer Kaixi would like to see him again right away. They met under BNU's March 18 Massacre Memorial monument. Liu didn't want to

continue the mass demonstrations. He told Wuer the large-scale parades missed the point of democracy, and students should go back to
campus and practice democracy "at home" first. The students would
think he was a wet blanket.

Liu and Wuer became close after the meeting. Students would later
proclaim: "Wuer Kaixi is our leader in action. Liu Xiaobo is our leader
in spirit." Wuer himself states: "No other person has had greater influence on me than Liu Xiaobo." In his "June 2 Hunger Strike Declaration," Liu would write: "Kaixi and I are friends. In political life, we are
equals. We are citizens first, though in the classroom I am the teacher."

The next day, May 4, was the seventieth anniversary of the 1919 May
Fourth Movement. Party general secretary Zhao Ziyang spoke to students and praised their patriotism. Mass rallies started up again at Beijing University. Liu and Tao got on their bikes and followed the parade,
which was stopped three times by the police. Husband and wife were
separated at the Liubukou intersection by the crowd. Marchers reached
Tiananmen Square at 4:00 p.m. Wuer, Wang, and others reread the
"New May Fourth Declaration." Liu later said it was "full of passion and
slogans and not much else."

Many intellectuals at the time sat at home and waited for students to
come to them for advice. Liu sought out students and asked for their
opinions and offered his own. Student leader Feng Congde remembers:

> A young-looking, professor-type man was waiting for me by the door.
> He said his name was Liu Xiaobo and was a lecturer at BNU. . . . He
> had just come back from America and heard I was chair of the
> Beijing Students' Autonomous Federation. He said he hoped we
> could have an exchange of ideas. Just very modest. I was embar
> rassed and told him I'd actually just resigned. He seemed stunned
> for a moment, muttered something softly to himself, and just turned
> around and left.[11]

Trust between intellectuals and students was a major sticking point in
the Chinese civil rights movement of 1989.

Three days later, Liu drafted "Our Demand: Free Speech in Classrooms," in which he pointed out first the student movement's failings—
"words over actions," "democracy in name but not in practice," "ignorance of the law," "sights too high, sways too wide," and so on. Then he
called for a series of initiatives to promote democracy on campuses—

"freedom of expression," "student autonomy," "dialogue between administrators and faculty and students," "faculty and student evaluation of administrative leadership," "discussion groups on the democratization of China," and so on. He posted it on the bulletin board. It was ripped down the next day.[12]

Students had started trickling back to school after Zhao Ziyang's speech, but his push for rule of law and issue-based dialogue was met with resistance from the Li administration, which still offered protesters nothing concrete, triggering a spate of scraps and scuffles between the state and the people.

May 13, 4:00 p.m. Three hundred hunger strikers, all students, escorted by two thousand of their classmates, entered Tiananmen Square. At 5:40 p.m., the strike began. It had been planned to coincide with Mikhail Gorbachev's visit to China two days later.

Hours earlier, the CPC's United Front Work Department (UFWD) had requested a meeting that evening through Zhou Duo with Liu, Wuer, other intellectuals and student leaders, and representatives from the Communist Youth League. Sixty attended. CPC Central Secretary Yan Fuming expressed his wish for students to leave the square before Gorbachev's arrival. Liu got to the point: the government must no longer call the protests "riots."

Zhou recalls Yan's face "darkened" as soon as Liu walked in the door. Liu remembers differently: "I felt he had an openness, generosity, and modesty rarely seen in party officials." It was the government's first show of willingness to dialogue with the people in any way, shape, or form, he thought, and that's what was important. It was a start.[13]

Liu encouraged the government to revise its previous published stance on the protests and rebrand them as "acts of patriotism" and encouraged the students to leave the square by May 15. He stressed the students must learn how to compromise to gain party moderates' support. Responding to Liu's last point, Yan smiled: "Xiaobo, don't be too transparent."[14]

Student leaders wanted the meeting broadcast live but were denied. Yan still dallied on the retraction of Deng Xiaoping's piece. The meeting ended up a wash.

After it was over, at 3:00 a.m., the UFWD escorted Liu and Zhou home. On the way, Liu suddenly said, "No, I have to get back to the square." Later, Liu blamed Zhou. If they hadn't wasted so much time at the UFWD meeting, he might have had a chance to convince the students to leave.

Before sunrise, Liu saw the students throw several government officials and party members out of the square. State-protester relations were becoming more and more tense. He stepped onto a platform and started speaking: "Don't cloud this place and your heart with hatred. Go back to school. Start democracy there." The words fell on deaf ears. "The dark horse has become a sheep!" "Coward! Get off the stage!" It would be the first time in Liu's life he was booed off any stage.

At 5:00 a.m., tired and hungry, he took the number 22 bus home. Dejected, he swore never to be part of any student movement again, and was going to head straight to the embassy to renew his American visa. The phone rang when he got home. It was a friend watching the news overseas. "You took a huge risk going home, Xiaobo, and now instead of being arrested by the government you're thrown out by the students." This restoked his fire. "I know how difficult my role is, and I know only I can play it well. There is one Liu Xiaobo, unique and inimitable."[15]

A few hours' rest later, he attended a communications briefing by invitation at the Beijing Social and Economic Research Institute. A declaration by the intellectual community was read. Liu had different ideas. He thought the language—"liberation," "proletariat," "long live the people"—was timeworn and riddled with moth-eaten communist ideology. Others urged him to change it; he refused. He decided to steer clear of intellectual organizations and activities altogether: "Students already despise us. The more we theorize from the armchair, the more we keep up this charade of intellectual pretension, the less credibility we have. If we want to be a part of this, we have to be with the students."

He went home to sleep that night.

Next day, 4:00 p.m. *Knock, knock, knock.*

"Professor Liu!" A student called outside, out of breath. "Wuer Kaixi sent me to take you to the square right away! Please help him convince the strikers to leave!"

They ran straight for the square.

It was no use.

At last, he gave up. Passion won over reason. He began collecting daily necessities for the students and lecturing to the onlookers. Students wept at his words. They wrote on a large piece of white canvas: "Prof. Liu, Thank You."

The fever at the square infected him. He lost all reason and judgment and decided to live and die right then and there with the students. He wasn't immune to the power of the crowd.

The second day of the strike, Liu told students they must still drink liquids and estimated that the government would send someone to talk to them after seventy-two hours. Students began waiting. Seventy-two hours later, they had not heard a peep from the officials. Stumped, Liu declared: "They're worse than the South Africans!"—thinking of Nelson Mandela's imprisonment and the African National Congress protests at the time. "This-this fucking gov-government"—angry, he cursed up a streak again—"is-is fucking ri-ridiculous!" Students began imitating him for fun.[16] A mere thirty-four-year-old lecturer with far less prestige, experience, and connections than many of his colleagues, Liu nevertheless became a key figure in the movement because he put his money where his mouth was, didn't put on airs, and took a stand with the students until the end.

In the CPC, Li's hard-liners were gaining an upper hand over Zhao's moderates. Use of force was imminent on Deng's go-ahead. On the protesters' side, the square became command central with a merry-go-round of leadership. Whoever was loudest and fanned the hottest flames took over. A peaceful end seemed more and more remote.

May 16, evening. Liu went to speak for the first time at the Voice of the Student Movement, a broadcast station set up by Tsinghua University students at the base of the Monument to the People's Heroes. When people know they will be seen or heard by others, their egos balloon accordingly. Liu was no exception:

> Perhaps the whole of China, the whole of the world, knew on that day, at the moment, somebody named Liu Xiaobo was speaking at Tiananmen Square, in Beijing. My heart was pounding, my words were tripping over my tongue, my face was beet-red, for sure. My eyes must have been wide open, gleaming with excitement. . . . When I said my name, the high of those three characters passing through my lips is something I'll never be able to forget.[17]

May 17. The strike entered its fourth day. Students were fainting. Civilians and students organized a million-man march, drafting another declaration targeting Deng Xiaoping. Liu thought this a grave tactical error. That afternoon, Deng decided to mobilize the armed forces. It was Zhao's curtain call. He went to see the students at the square at night. It was his last public appearance.

May 20. Martial law was declared. Tension was at an all-time high. Liu became one of only a few intellectuals who remained at the square.

May 23, morning. Liu drafted a proposal titled "Our Suggestions," signed it "Beijing Normal University Autonomous Student Union," and distributed it across campuses. It asked for, among other things, investigation into then-Shanghai municipal committee secretary Jiang Zemin's role in shutting down the *World Economic Herald*, an influential reformist paper. Jiang rose to power in the 1990s and always regarded Liu as a thorn in his side, eventually placing him under what would be two decades of strict state surveillance.

May 27. Wuer and Liu went to a Federation of All Social Sectors in the Capital (FASSC) meeting. Liu brought up the idea of a "people's spokesman" and Lech Wałęsa in Poland as an example. The people needed a hero, he said, and nominated Wuer. The audience was stunned, especially Wuer's detractors.

Attendees voted by a show of hands on whether to pull out of the square. The decision was unanimous: yes. However, Chai Ling, commander-in-chief of operations, had a change of heart on the way back: "I felt it would've been a mistake to go ahead with this without the students' vote. We had vowed to stay until the end. I had a responsibility to those who put their trust in me. If we had just proceeded like that, it would've been a betrayal of the very democratic principles we'd sworn to uphold."[18] In those days, everybody talked about "democracy," but nobody knew exactly what it meant.

The vast majority of students voted to stay. The die was cast, the official party line declared—"til the bitter end"—with the FASSC backing out.

The last flame for peace was snuffed out.

THE FOUR NOBLEMEN

May 29. Another meeting. This time to talk about maintaining order on the ground. The meeting itself was as disorderly as could be. Liu suggested that the protesters take a moment for self-reflection and that they hold another vote for leadership. He was shot down.

At the end, Liu leaned over and said to a friend, Wang Juntao, "This is pointless. I'd rather go join the strike."

Wang responded: "What's the point in that?"

The offhand remark was driftwood to a drowning man. Morale was low, but protesters, most of whom at this point were students from outside Beijing, stood their ground. Joining the strike might just be the thing to revive the flagging campaign.

Liu went home, sat down, and began writing a manifesto for the hunger strike. Tao asked him to come to bed. He lay, staring at the ceiling, unable to sleep. He remembers:

> I felt a sense of relief after making that decision. Like I was walking on air, almost. Now I was justified in looking down on other intellectuals and the masses who went on strike on May 13, because I chose to do so after the fact, after martial law was declared. It wasn't power in numbers. It was the power of one. I wasn't hiding behind any cloak of the collective. I was my naked self. I thought it was very Christ-like. I didn't do it just for my people, but for all of mankind. I saw the fresh blood on the cross, dripping, beckoning the conscience of man. Through starvation, I sank to the bottom of humanity, found myself for the first time, and was able to wash away all my sins. Death would cleanse me, make life light. It's a flash of lightning, shearing through the unbroken darkness, the infinite nothing.[19]

Dense and tangled, his web of thought was at once Christian and Nietzschean, nihilistic and life affirming, selfless and egomaniacal.

While other intellectuals were back-pedaling, Liu was looking for others to ride the crest. He called Zhou Duo first. Zhou was on the fence and asked him to put it off until they could talk face to face.

May 30. They met. Liu said, "Even if you're not, I'm going." Zhou replied: "Then I shall cast my lot with the nobleman." They went to the square and announced their decision. Only Wuer and Professor Chen Xiaoping voiced their unconditional support.

At 3:00 p.m., Liu, Zhou, and ex-*BNU Weekly* editor Gao Xin began drafting a "Hunger Strike Declaration."

They needed more hoopla.

Liu thought of singer Hou Dejian. Hou was the face of the seventies Taiwanese college folk-pop scene and had immigrated to China in 1983. He and Liu met three years later. Hou writes in his memoir: "I knew Liu because he criticized me, out, loud, and proud. He said because I came from a traditional intellectual background I had no heart for good pop songs. After we were introduced I caught him off guard by agreeing with and thanking him for his criticisms. He was shocked to learn I penned some of his favorite songs like 'Wine Bottles for Sale,' and made a partial peace offering. We've been tight ever since."

That day, Hou was performing at the Concert for Democracy in China at the Happy Valley Racecourse in Hong Kong to benefit the Tiananmen student movement. Liu called him in the middle of the night and asked whether he wanted to join the strike. "Hunger strike?" Hou said. "I'm too skinny!" Liu, Zhou, and Gao picked him up at the airport the next day and showed him the declaration. Moved, Hou signed on.

Liu asked Chen Xiaoping and Wang Juntao to be the "Four Noblemen's" liaisons to the media. Wang refused at first but later read in the declaration: "We have no enemies. Don't let hatred poison our wisdom." "This was what we wanted to say all along, from the bottom of our hearts," Wang remembers. Finally he said yes.[20]

June 1. Children's Day. Liu and Tao dropped in at the BNU kindergarten to spend the morning with Tao-tao. The father had other things on his mind. Tao tried everything she could to stop her husband from going, but Liu was like a top, spinning faster and faster, out of control, with no turning back.

The American network NBC interviewed the Four Noblemen that afternoon. Liu returned to the steps of BNU in the evening and announced: "We're going on strike for three days. For seventy-two hours, we're striking, we're protesting, we're pleading, we're repenting. We're protesting the administration's use of force against the student patriots. We're repenting and giving the intellectuals back their backbones!"[21] Millions were moved by these words. Liu didn't want just to change the government: he wanted to change it by changing people's hearts first.

June 2. The Four Noblemen entered the square. The strike began. They made four proclamations: "*One.* We have no enemies. Don't let hatred and violence poison our wisdom or the democratization of China. *Two.* We must reflect. We are all responsible for the state we are in.

Three. We are citizens first. *Four.* We are not looking to die. We are looking to live!"

As usual, Liu didn't let up on the students, either. He pointed out the inconsistencies of their words and actions; their divisiveness, inefficiency, and waste; their lack of reason and knowledge; and even their sense of entitlement. His call for a moment of collective reflection didn't sit well with a number of student heads.

The square was packed to the gills. A relay was in the offing at the end of the seventy-two hours. Liu and his cohorts were half-led, half-dragged to their tent past the teeming hordes. The tent was completely surrounded by picketers. The inside was "pimped out"—fresh blankets on the ground, four single army cots, new pillows, woolen beddings. It was much better than the student tents, anyway.

Liu felt he'd turned into a kid or a pet. Everyone was praising him, protecting him, tending to him: all eyes were on his every step and move, especially the medics, who hovered around the tent around the clock as if it were an ICU ward. It took a lot to convince them to approve Liu's and Hou's cigarettes.

Time and again picketers would hand in a piece of paper, a baseball cap, a t-shirt—for autographs. Liu recalls how he felt: "At first I was stoked and full of myself, like every stroke of my pen was being etched in history. I even thought my handwriting wasn't good enough and wished I could've been a great calligrapher like Huai Su. Then I grew numb. An autograph? Okay. Sign here? Sure. Almost mechanical. Finally I hated it. I wanted to scream: 'Leave me alone!'"

June 3. China Central Television broadcast the strike. People flocked here for a whole new reason: "See the Goddess, hear the Monkey." The Goddess of Democracy was a thirty-foot statue made in four days out of foam and papier mâché by student artists for the protests, erected between the monument and the gate, facing Mao Zedong. "Monkey" was Hou Dejian's nickname. At 9:00 a.m. Chen held a press conference. Liu lost himself amid the commotion: "Looking down from on top the Memorial, I saw thousands of yellow faces, and beyond, masses of black hair. They were screaming, chanting, cheering, waving their flags, banners, arms. Those closest to us reached out pieces of paper for us to sign. Countless cameras flashed from every angle, and tape recorders were held up high."[22]

The press conference was busted up by the crowd as soon as it started and had to be rescheduled for 1:00 p.m. at the foot of the Goddess. Crowds were clamoring for Hou. Nearby some students hoisted up Wuer to speak. Within minutes the square turned to complete chaos again, and the foursome had to be escorted back to the tent. Chen asked where they should reschedule the conference. Liu responded: "Forget it. Holing up in our tent is about the only thing we can do now."

THE NIGHT OF THE MASSACRE

The sun set over a cloudy sky at 7:34 p.m. on Saturday, June 3, 1989. Suddenly, the atmosphere at Tiananmen Square grew tense. The People's Liberation Army had entered Beijing. News of clashes between troops and civilians kept drifting in from every street corner.

The Four Noblemen quickly issued a call for peace and nonviolence. They knew the students were no match for the soldiers. They wanted to talk, however slim that chance might be.

Liu got up onstage. Barely had he said a word before being interrupted. "Coward!" a student shouted. More heckling followed. He had to stop.

At dusk, troops closed in on the square from every direction. Millions of civilians tried to form barricades.

At 9:00 p.m., the first shot was fired. The massacre had begun.

Tanks rolled through the streets, blessing the people with showers of bullets. A path to damnation was opened. Men and women, young and old, fell to their knees in legion.

If you did a Google search today (outside China) on "Tiananmen Square," other keywords would pop up, like "West Chang'an Avenue," "Muxidi Bridge," and "Xidan Road." You can also simply hop on Beijing subway line 1, which runs from Pingguoyuan to Sihui East under Chang'an Avenue and bisects the city through Tiananmen Square, and trace the tracks of the tanks a quarter-century ago in under thirteen minutes. You won't see any memorials, though. And you won't see the blood-red color of the Beijing sky lit up bright by gunfire as it was that night.

Four hours later, troops arrived at the square, joined by others already stationed amid tens of thousands of protesters. At 1:30 a.m., a state of emergency was declared through megaphones. People scattered like birds. Students sitting close to the memorial sat in a little closer. According to Liu's memory, "The lights went out. In mere moments the Square was empty, except for those still close to the Memorial. Then sounds of gunshots echoed."

They were like firecrackers heralding the news of the dead. People panicked. The broadcast station nearly collapsed.

Suddenly a picketer ran to say he saw a gun on the south side of the memorial. A couple of construction workers had mounted it. Liu and others made a beeline. They saw a machine gun mounted at the very top of the memorial on the southwest corner, under a blanket, muzzle sticking out, aiming west, guarded by the workers. They kept striking the gun with steel pipes and shouting at people to stay back.

Hou walked up and put his arms around a boy, about twenty, and introduced himself: "I'm Hou Dejian."

"Brother Hou!" the young man cried out, and began to sob.

Hou comforted him and pulled him away, leaving Liu with the rest. He begged, pleaded, and beseeched through his stutter. The students were China's future, he said, and they had to protect them. This set the workers off: "So only you college kids' lives are worth something? Our lives are worth shit? Why should we run into the line of fire? You're fine. But what about us? How many of us have to die for you!?"

After much wheedling, the workers finally handed over the gun they had swiped off an armored car. A second worker handed over another one hidden in a tent nearby. Afterwards, many suspected the PLA had leaked the few arms to civilians.

Liu and others went back to the north side. Holding the gun up high, Liu brought it down against the rail around the memorial. It wasn't as easy as he thought. The force of the recoil sent a shooting pain through his chest. He smashed and smashed the gun until it broke into bits.

Most of the media had retreated to the Beijing Hotel except for one reporter from Spain's TVE who got the scene on tape.

The Four Noblemen called for protesters to put down their clubs, bottles, and rocks. Liu said, "Beijing has begun to bleed, and it's bled enough. The world is beginning to see. Drop your weapons. They're not weapons. They do more harm than good. Don't give the state an excuse.

Don't destroy the image and spirit of the movement. Those with guns must turn in your guns." In a moment of chaos and confusion, Liu made a lucid decision.

❖ ❖ ❖

In the tent at three in the morning on June 4, a picture began to emerge in the minds of those huddled in the chilling air: this was a planned attack, a premeditated act of mass murder. They could no longer cling to false hope. They must stop the bleeding first and plan a withdrawal. Two doctors from the Red Cross suggested Hou and others take the ambulance to go talk to the troops.

Now the question was who should go. Liu raised his hand first. Zhou thought Hou and he himself should go. If Hou shouted "I'm Hou De-jian!" to the troops, they probably wouldn't open fire. Hou told Liu: "You've got a fuse shorter than an ant's knob. If you blow, we're all done for. Zhou looks less like a thug. We should go."[23]

Off the Four Noblemen went to see Chai Ling. Headquarters refused to send a rep along. "Whatever you all want to do is up to you," Feng Congde said. "If you want to go talk to them as a third party, sure, but don't claim to speak for the students. Whatever you and the officials decide has to be voted on by the students, too."[24]

Half an hour later, Hou, Zhou, and the doctors rode an ambulance out the east side of the memorial. The military agreed to leave a safe path for protesters in the southeast corner of the square, under one condition: the square must be cleared by 7:00 a.m.

At 4:30 a.m., the lights came back on. Hou and others returned to the station to persuade everyone to leave. "We're not afraid to die!" he shouted. "But our deaths can't be meaningless! We don't want to die. What we want is to truly live!" *"Boo!"* The crowd jeered. *"Pushovers! Quitters! Wimps!"*

Liu grabbed the mic, stuttering: "Students, I'm-I'm Liu Xiaobo! Pl-please have faith in us! Our mission is peace and nonviolence. You've bared your hearts. Now you must cool your heads. You've made great sacrifices. We can't let you make more. The best thing you can do for your country right now is to survive!"

Headquarters held a voice vote—"yea" for staying, "nay" for leaving. "YEA!" "NAY!" Both sides shouted equally at the top of their lungs. Feng declared: "The nays have it! *Let's go!*"

Two hours left—do or die. The foursome split ways to help the remaining few who refused to leave.

As soon as the decision was announced, the military ramped up its game. It blasted out the station speakers. Three tanks rolled from the Great Hall east to the south side of the memorial, firing shots into the air.

Liu went to see whether Chai Ling and others were still there. He bent down and peeked into the tent. Empty. He straightened up to a cold, hard muzzle against his back. Shoved, he almost fell off the platform—not due to the force of the shove, but because his legs gave out in fear. Student Wang Yuehong grabbed hold of him.

Suddenly he remembered: his passport and documents were still inside. He flew back up the steps and was only halfway to the tent when a soldier pointed his gun straight down at him.

"Get down!"

"I forgot my passport!"

"Passport? What do you still need a passport for? Get down! Or I shoot!"

Facing the barrel of a gun, Liu felt a chill down his spine. He backed down instinctively. Some students tried to help. "Do you all want to die, too?" the trooper yelled. They backed down as well.

Liu pushed against the wave of exodus to look for his companions. He spotted Hou on the arms of a couple of students. Nervous and famished for the past two days, Hou looked like he was about to pass out. Liu took him from a student whose own leg was bandaged and helped carry him on.

By now most protesters had left. Troops blockaded the path leading from the memorial to the Museum of Chinese History, cutting off the southeast corner. Liu and the two or three hundred students remaining were herded to the Red Cross first-aid station in front of the museum, corralled by three rows of troops. Expressionless, the troops looked like animals.

The terror reached its peak.

The sun came up. The sky turned light. Liu saw troops stab trash left in the empty square, lift it up, and toss it into a pyre. A tank rolled in from the north and over the Goddess, which had been knocked to the ground.

The doctors negotiated with the troops to let the last batch of people through a gap in the southeast corner. In ranks of four, as they made their way, gunfire rang out. The procession stopped; everyone hit the ground. It was the guards in front of the Beijing Municipal Public Security Bureau firing at civilian residences nearby. After it died down, they continued.

Liu had on a white short-sleeved undershirt, soaked through by then in sweat, filthy and rank. A coldness ran through him. He started shaking uncontrollably.

Behind him, the Gate of Heavenly Peace drew closed.

CAUGHT

The tired, poor, huddled masses made their way through Qianmen East Street, then Wangfujing Street, toward the Peking Union Medical College Hospital. Hou Dejian lay on a stretcher carried by eight hospital staff in turns. When they passed Chang'an Avenue, Liu saw abandoned buses and armored cars on fire.

The hospital was like Beijing Station during New Year's. Everyone was looking for his family, her children. Hong Kong journalist Cai Shufang reported: "We asked staff what the toll was. They told us dozens dead, hundreds injured. The hospital was packed. The wounded lay wall-to-wall on floors in hallways. The staff was completely overrun."[25]

Doctors took Liu, Hou, and Wang Yuehong into a small shed with a table and a bunk in what looked like a call room. They brought them bread, sausage, soda, watermelon. Hou seemed finally to be getting his color back. The doctors urged them to rest. Liu and Hou crashed and slept like logs.

A staccato of knocks made them jump out of their beds. It was only Wang. It was past 1:00 p.m. Word was that troops were searching hospitals. They were in danger.

Liu said, "We can't stay here. I want to go home."

Hou said, "We can't go home. The streets aren't safe. Your house is probably being watched. We have to stay low."

Liu: "Where?"

Hou: "A diplomatic compound."

Liu: "Our families don't know if we're alive or dead. We have to let them know."

Hou: "We can call them."

Wang chimed in: "It's too dangerous. I'll call."

Liu and Hou gave Wang the numbers, plus the number of a foreign friend. Wang came back shortly. "I told Tao Li and Cheng Lin not to worry, that you're safe. Your friend will pick you up at 3:30."

They paced nervously around the room not much bigger than a coat closet, wondering what had happened to Zhou and Gao. The two doctors stayed with them.

At 3:25 p.m., the doctors led them out the hospital front gate. They had put makeup on Hou and dressed him in a white coat and hat. Crowds continued to gather at the gate, with many anxious faces searching for loved ones.

A red sedan with a diplomatic black plate pulled up ten minutes later. They got in. The driver spoke some inarticulate Chinese to Hou. Suddenly, they were surrounded. "Hou Dejian!" someone pointed and screamed. The driver put his foot on the gas, and the sedan sped away.

Only after they got on the Chaoyangmen overpass did Hou finally give his friend a smile. "You are the bravest driver in Beijing!" The man didn't respond, staring straight ahead solemnly. East Second Ring Road was bumper to bumper with armed vehicles. Liu looked out the window. *What if we get stopped? What if they shoot at us?* He ran through a list of questions like a Rolodex in his head. In ten minutes the car entered the Jianguomen Diplomatic Residence Compound. He finally could put his mind at rest.

The driver signaled them not to speak as they waited for the elevator. The door opened. The operator, a middle-aged woman, looked the three of them up and down. Liu got nervous again. He'd heard stories of DRC workers being government spies.

As soon as they got in the apartment door they hugged the driver, thanking him profusely. "You *are* the bravest driver in Beijing!" The man finally introduced himself. His name was Jimmy Florcruz. He was *Time* magazine's Beijing correspondent.

The apartment belonged to Australian cultural counselor Nicholas Jose. Liu was just here a few days ago with Barmé. He had even washed and changed here. The apartment looked exactly the same—bright, open living room; warm-toned carpet and sofa; wine and tea on the shelves; music . . . everything seemed a world away from the hell on earth outside. Yet there was a strange feeling, as if it were hollow and unreal.

Liu thought a shower would calm him down. As jets of hot water splashed down, he ran his hands over his skin. It was as if he were trying to wash something else off besides the grime and dirt. His body was somewhere far away. It didn't feel the water; it didn't feel the heat; it didn't feel the touch of its own hands. The shower was full of hot steam, but he couldn't stop trembling. Maybe he hadn't left the procession; left the animal-like, expressionless stares; left the muzzle, gleaming. He later wrote: "The dead departed / But there was no seeing off / In the tub of luxury / Floated a petrified corpse / Its skin by water eroded / Its soul forever damned."[26]

The doorbell rang. Hou and he looked toward the door. It opened; in walked Nick and his friend Linda Jaivin. The four embraced deeply. Linda cried.

The atmosphere relaxed somewhat. Liu tried recounting the day through the pounding of his heart, making little jokes. Hou was as cool as a cucumber. He described his gurney journey: "I died once already. There was even a parade."

After what seemed like the most delicious dinner of their lives, they talked about what they were going to do now. Linda suggested that Liu go to the Australian embassy; Liu didn't want to. Hou thought Liu could stay at his house in Guangzhou in the south; Liu said no. His response was: "Until I see Zhou and Gao, I'm not leaving." On the other hand, he urged Hou to go to Hong Kong. Hou refused. Liu said, "One of us has to make it out alive to tell the world the truth. You're the one to do it. If you stay, the world will probably never know." Hou nodded reluctantly.

Liu tossed and turned all night. The phone rang. It was Barmé calling from Australia. He saw the carnage on TV. Liu felt guilty. "If I hadn't launched the strike, the protests wouldn't have come to a head. If the protests hadn't come to a head, the regime would've waited for them to fade out and not cleared them out by force; if the regime hadn't had to clear them out by force, many people would still be alive today." After getting out of Qincheng Prison, he told a lot of friends this same thing. Though they tried to tell him the government had long planned

THE BLACK HAND OF TIANANMEN

the deed, that it had nothing to do with the Four Noblemen's strike, he was never convinced. And he could never forget that, in some way, he was an accomplice to this mass murder.

It was the middle of the night. Gunshots echoed outside the window, at times dense, at times sparse, at times near, at times far. A couple of people seemed to spend most of their time by the windows. After each gunshot, they would lift up a corner of the curtain and gingerly peek out.

Gao Xin arrived shortly. Hou wanted to draft an emergency petition to the world under all four of their names, a plea to every government and every citizen who cared about justice to censure and sanction the Chinese regime for its fascist, brutal acts. Hou suggested they get the petition on tape: "If I can get out, I'll play it around the world. If I can't, then give it to Linda or someone who can." Liu and Gao hesitated because they didn't know what Zhou Duo would think. Hou said, "Don't worry. When we withdrew, we were acting as one. We still are. Human rights have no personal or national boundaries. Under the shield of the United Nations, we have nothing to fear." Liu and Gao agreed.

Liu penned the first draft. Others thought it too long and not succinct enough. Hou cut it down and cleaned it up, citing part of writer and translator Yang Xianyi's BBC interview. Liu gave it the final once-over, and the petition became roughly as follows:

> The Democracy Movement that grew out of Hu Yaobang's death and made up of mainly university students is absolutely constitutional. Its guiding principles have always been reason, peace, and nonviolence. Yet Li Peng's administration saw fit to use tanks, armored vehicles, military trucks, planes, and troops in full gear to put down completely empty-handed students and civilians. It is a throwback to fascism, a brutality whose range and magnitude exceed nearly everything we have seen in this modern decade.
>
> Now, as the massacre drenches the entire city of Beijing in blood, students and civilians are holding fast to their principles of peace and nonviolence. This shows the consciousness of democracy has awakened in the people of China. This awakening cannot be suppressed by the blood-soaked hands of a regime.
>
> Beijing has not seen a blood spill this size in the entire modern history of China—not by the Beiyang Clique of the Revolution of

1911, not by the Nationalist Government of the Republican China, not even by the Japanese fascists of the Sino-Japanese Wars. But the Communists—they've gone and done it. Neither heaven nor earth shall suffer such grievances.

For this, we call on every state, every citizen, every steward of democracy and human rights in the world, every protector of justice, peace, and nonviolence on this earth, to sanction the fascist Chinese regime economically, politically, diplomatically, and morally, and to help and support the Chinese people's project of democratization and the victims of June 4, 1989, in every way, shape, and form possible.

Petitioners: Tiananmen Square Hunger Strike Participants
Hou Dejian, Gao Xin, Liu Xiaobo, and Zhou Duo
June 5, 1989, Beijing

After it was finished, Hou and Gao each read it once into the tape recorder.

Liu stayed at Jose's until June 6. At 7:00 p.m., Gao and Wang showed up to talk about the next steps. At 9:00 p.m., Jose came home and said he'd been ordered back to Australia the next day. "Let's leave right away," Liu said. "Take my car," Jose said. "It's safer." On the road, Jose spoke up: "Xiaobo, do you want to go to the embassy?" "No," Liu replied. They passed the embassy. Jose asked again: "Xiaobo, do you want to go in? This is your last chance." "No, thank you," Liu responded. Then he picked up his things and got out.

He got hold of a bicycle and was going to bike home. He thought he could see his family once before the arrest. Barmé thinks: "Liu's suicidal decision not to leave Beijing and in fact to court disaster by traveling around the city openly on a bike echoes the tragedy of individualistic and heroic Chinese intellectuals of the last century."

A dragnet was cast over the capital. The DRC, as Liu thought, was heavily surveilled by the Ministry of State Security. Plainclothes officers sat right by the entrance and had their eyes on Jose and Liu the moment they stepped out the door.

Two hours later, on June 6 at 11:00 p.m., Liu Xiaobo was placed under arrest. It was a scene out of a highway robbery: on his way home on bike, a van came out of nowhere on one side and knocked him and his bike to the ground. The door opened, and a couple of burly guys jumped out, twisted his arms behind his back, gagged and hooded him, and dragged him inside.

Every human being has known fear at some point. Chinese martial arts writer Gu Long says, "Fear is human beings' basic weakness. They're born with it. Unless they're completely numb, or dead, they'll always feel it." Liu later said that when he was taken, fear became almost like a reflex. "If they'd come for me at home, I would've been a little calmer. It was just so sudden. I couldn't stop shaking for fifteen minutes. My first thought was: *I've been caught.* Then: *Where are they taking me? Are they taking me somewhere secluded? Are they gonna kill me right then and there?* But after fifteen minutes my fear died down. They ungagged me. I still had the hood on. Then I asked for a cigarette."

In those fifteen minutes he came to a realization: So what if he was going to die? So many students and civilians had already died much worse deaths. Yet he couldn't stop worrying about his frail wife Tao Li and six-year-old son Liu Tao.

On June 24, *Beijing Daily* published a long piece under the name of Wang Zhao called "Grabbing the Black Hand of Liu Xiaobo." It contained a litany of charges against Liu, quoting him in an interview as saying, "We must organize armed forces with the people." The article read: "If certain kind-hearted people still doubt the conspirators' intention in inciting counterrevolutionary riots, please have them read that conversation."

In fact, Liu had always stood fast by the principles of reason, peace, and nonviolence. In the interview, Liu was actually talking about "the power of the people to self-organize," but when it was translated into English, "power" was translated as "forces," and when it was translated back into Chinese, it was mistranslated as "armed forces." A mistake in translation almost cost a man's life. An August 8 *Wall Street Journal* article introduced six dissident Chinese intellectuals currently detained; only under Liu Xiaobo it read: "He could face the death penalty."

Hu Ping and others overseas were worried sick. They put a head shot of Liu on the cover of *China Spring*, trying to get the world's attention. In August, Hong Kong's *Contemporary Monthly* put out a report called "Rescuing Liu Xiaobo." Scholars in Oslo organized Liu Xiaobo focus and support groups. Columbia University professors in New York wrote Beijing Normal University letters expressing their outrage and concern. In Sydney, Jaivin started a petition for pardon signed by forty-one activists and intellectuals, including four Nobel Prize winners.

Around the same time, Norwegian intellectual circles made a nomination to the Nobel Committee of Liu Xiaobo for the Peace Prize. This would be Liu's first nomination for the Nobel Peace Prize.

It was something he wouldn't receive, however, until twenty-one years later.

4

START FROM ZERO

THE CONFESSION

Liu was soon moved to Qincheng Prison.

The prison, in Qincheng Village in the Xingshou Township in the Changping District of Beijing, is the most well-known prison in China.

In 1960 it was originally housed in four three-story gray-bricked buildings numbered 201, 202, 203, and 204. Hip-roofed, each building had a different layout with a washroom and foot-pedaled flush toilet. Later, two four-story red-bricked buildings were added and numbered 205 and 206.[1]

Each cell in each building had a three-foot by three-foot window facing up and opening out on a slope sill with the glass painted white. It had three layers—screen, bars, glass. Each prisoner had a tiny piece of the sky, which, when overcast, made the window seem more like a rectangular opening to a deep well.

The only furniture in a cell was a foot-high bed. An elementary school desk was moved in only when prisoners were ready to "make admissions." Probably for safety, there were no chairs or stools. You had to sit on the bed to write. Nothing had sharp corners; everything was sanded down.

At intake, prisoners were first led to a small bungalow, where they left their shoelaces and anything else prohibited, changed into black uniforms, and got standard-issue towels, toothbrushes, basins, toilet paper, bowls, spoons, and so on. Except for enamel water cups, everything was plastic.

Liu recounts: "They took away my belt, shoelaces, the elastic band inside my thermals, even the band in my briefs. Two guards cut through the briefs with a pair of scissors and pulled it out section by section." He'd never felt so humiliated, and suddenly, in a fit of hysteria, he started screaming at the guards, at the top of his lungs, the most vicious and vile names he could think of. "My nerves shot up like springs, I was flailing around like a fish, my hands grabbed on to the briefs like they were the end of a rope hanging off the edge of a cliff. It's as if I were staring death in the face and struggling hopelessly. Within a minute or two I was spent." The guards reassured him they wouldn't hurt him; then he calmed down.[2]

There were class divisions among Qincheng residents. Some were in solitary, others on the main block. Meal qualities varied greatly. Food cost for "high-class" prisoners was 120 yuan per month, that for "low-class" prisoners, 30 yuan. Students were among the latter, while "black hands" like Liu were among the former. Renmin University student Liu Xianbin recalls: "Our meals were terrible, a steamed corn bun and bowl of corn gruel for breakfast, with pickles, and a bun and bowl of vegetable soup for lunch and dinner, every day."[3] Obviously, 30 yuan per month couldn't fill the tiniest of stomachs, while 120 yuan was the living expense of a typical middle-class family at the time.

❖ ❖ ❖

Guards delivered food three times a day (twice on Sundays and holidays) to cells. Come mealtime, trays were passed through slots a foot off the ground. Prisoners showered between once a week and once a month, thirty minutes at a time. Men and women were not allowed to latch doors and had same-sex guards just outside.

Political prisoners at Qincheng didn't have to perform labor. Your routine—turn out at seven on whistle, turn in at nine on whistle. No staying in bed outside bedtime. Thin, standard-issue sheets. Less deluxe rooms had straw. Lights stayed on when you slept. No hands under the covers. No facing away from the peephole or you could be awakened and yelled at anytime. No vandalism. No writing or drawing on walls. No speaking loudly. No singing. No turning your back to the cell door.

Et cetera. Round-the-clock surveillance. If you stood in a corner or stepped out of the guard's direct line of sight, your door would be thrown open and your "home" searched at once.

For the first six months, though he wasn't tortured, Liu lived in torment. No newspapers to read, no radio to listen to, no one to talk to, besides the arraigner, in his room. Not to mention that his sentence still hung over him. He would talk little about his time in Qincheng later on.

All the "black hands" were put in Building 203 in solitary. The only place they could meet was the yard. Two rows of recreation areas were walled in by fly-ash bricks (FABs) in the middle of each horseshoe ward. They were cells without roofs. A hundred square feet each, they were connected by a walkway on top of which guards patrolled and surveyed from on high. When they weren't paying attention, prisoners could pass notes back and forth.

Fellow prisoner Chen Xiaoping says, "For a while we imitated the loudspeaker alarms in our rooms out of boredom, out of loneliness. We even bore holes in the yard walls and stuffed them with note after note."[4] Liu was no model prisoner. He passed notes, talked to others through drains, screamed and yelled, and pulled pranks. For a time he was neighbors with young China University of Political Science and Law lecturer Liu Suli. They talked by tossing paper balls. In the "black hand" ward, paper was for writing "admissions" and letters to family. Liu Xiaobo and Liu Suli would write notes in their rooms; during yard time, they would crumple the sheets of paper and, when the guards weren't looking, throw them across the partition. Eventually they were caught and separated during yard time.

Chen was Liu's neighbor next. They pretended to practice English aloud and communicated this way. Eventually they were found out and kept apart, too.

Next was China Society of Economic Reform chair Yang Guansan. To introduce himself, Liu wrote his name with a twig on a cement board and threw it over the wall when the guards had their backs turned. Yang did the same. After release, when they met for the first time, Yang said to him loudly, "Xiaobo, you're really something. I was jogging, and all of a sudden a big piece of cement fell out of the sky, barely missing my head. It hit the ground and broke in two. I squatted down, trying to piece it together and figure out the message on it.

Finally I realized it was just your name. Funny, the communists didn't do me in, but you almost did."[5]

Liu also saw the dissident Bao Zunxin. Weathered by wind and rain, the FAB walls dividing the yard turned brittle and crumbly. Liu found a soft spot in the mortar and poked at it with a twig. A few days later, he succeeded: a small hole was made. He put his eye up to it and saw the upper half of Bao, who had his back turned and was stretching his legs. Liu wrote a note when he got back to the cell, hoping to get the low-down and Bao's take. The following day, he knocked on the wall first, wrapped the note around a twig, and passed it through the hole. Bao saw and took it. Liu was thrilled, expecting a response the next day. But after a couple of days, nothing. He was disappointed. After they got out, Liu asked Bao why he never replied; Bao no longer remembered the incident.

On Chinese New Year's Eve, 1990, Liu saw family for the first time in six months—his wife and in-laws. They told him about the pain and suffering he had caused them. They told him about his six-year-old son and asked what was going to happen to him, now that his father's future was so uncertain? His father-in-law, Tao Dezhen, was a nice, mild-mannered man who had never been through anything like this. Worry was as plain as day on his face, but it was frail Tao Li's tears that felt like a knife in Liu's heart. He didn't think he had done anything wrong, but now was not the time to argue. He remained silent for the first time in his life.

In early October he was taken to Banbuqiao Detention Center to visit his father, whom he hadn't seen in a year and a half. That day, his father was dressed in full military garb, with a large bag in each hand. The expression on his face was complex—hopeful, distant, scared, sad, all under a cloud of anxiety. He brought his son food and clothes, made and packed by his mother.

His father briefly updated him on things at home and then got to the point: "Admit what you're supposed to admit, plead what you're supposed to plead, and the party and administration will handle your problem properly. You have to trust the party and administration's practical way of dealing with things." When he got to the subject of his wife, his tone softened, and his voice lowered: "Your mom wanted to come. She was screaming and crying. I had to try hard to talk her out of it. If you stay in here another eight, ten years, I'm afraid she won't make it to see you get out alive." His voice broke, and tears streamed down his old, withered face. This was the first time Liu in the thirty-five years of his life had seen his father cry. "I finally understood then what fatherly love is," Liu reflects, "and how precious the relationship between a father and a son is." His father's tears began to soften his heart, as well as his stance on confessing.[6]

❋ ❋ ❋

After the massacre, the government was lenient toward intellectuals and students but severe toward civilians. Dozens were put to death. Some were given life sentences, others sentences as long as twenty years.

When the administration revealed Liu's arrest, there were more Chinese news reports about him than any other prisoner. He was given another "laurel": in September, Chinese Youth Press published the book *Who Is Liu Xiaobo?* specifically denouncing him. The appendix included a number of his articles and interviews in full—his most "Socratic" and shocking ones, like the three pieces on Hu Yaobang's death, "Our Suggestions," the "June 2 Hunger Strike Declaration," and a host of incisive critiques of communism and one-party rule. Seemingly condemned, these works were nonetheless made available to the public. One wondered whether there weren't some subversive intent on the publisher's part.

On Zhou Duo's release, a warden showed Liu the news. "There's hope for you yet," Liu recalls him saying. The sympathetic warden had told him once: "When it comes to these things in China, there's much thunder but little rain." And wouldn't he know it—Hou and Gao were shortly let out, too.

But there was one condition—they had to confess. Writing a confession in exchange for his freedom was something Liu considered for a while in his empty cell. This "freedom fundamentalist" by turns stood fast and teetered, was both seduced and threatened, and finally decided to compromise. "I wrote it in November. Strange I was so torn before, and then I wasn't. Nothing's more dear or costly than freedom. So what if I was a hypocrite? Wasn't China one big hypocrisy, anyway?"

The government worried he'd recant. The day before court, the judge paid him a visit in prison. "You can't take back your confession in court, or we're going to have a problem here. Do you understand?"

Afternoon, January 26, 1991, the People's Republic of China v. Liu Xiaobo. Liu was caught completely off guard when he heard "Time served." He thought he would be sentenced to at least two to five years. Instead, he was released immediately. Hou had already started planting peaches and apricots in his yard, figuring they'd be ready and ripe in three or four years for his friend when he got out. Liu was so overcome with joy he wanted to shout from the top of the Himalayas. He did not, however, cry, contrary to reports by the likes of *Beijing Review* and *Wen Wei Po*.

Not one to act cagey, as soon as he stepped out of the courtroom Liu leapt into the air as if no one were around, snapped his fingers, and yelled, "I've gone and done it again!" The two escort officers grabbed him by the arms and whispered: "This is not the place, Mr. Liu. You'll have plenty of time to celebrate later."[7]

They went into a room. The officers, courteous and deferential, smilingly handed Liu a cigarette. Judge Tan Jingsheng and BNU professors Liu Qingfu, Wang Xianda, and Huang Zhixian came in shortly. Tan laid out a series of documents—"Beijing Intermediate People's Court Criminal Verdict," "Beijing Intermediate People's Court Decision Regarding Bail Pending Trial," "Guarantee of Recognizance," "Proof of Release." Liu Qingfu signed the "Guarantee of Recognizance," and Liu Xiaobo signed and fingerprinted all necessary documents. Liu wanted to see his wife and child at BNU, but Tan said it wasn't a good idea for him to stay in Beijing for the time being and suggested that he go to his parents in Dalian for a while.

That evening, Liu ate dumplings with the people from the court. "It was the first time we sat to eat with the accused at the same table."[8] At 10:00 p.m., they dropped off him, Wang, and Huang in front of the sleeper car of a train bound for Dalian. The latter two were to accompany Liu. At 11:37 p.m., train number 229 left Beijing Station. Outside the windows, it was black. A wave of mixed feelings rushed past Liu.

Along with him, Liu's four brothers made it home to the Dalian Military Academy from Changchun and Guangdong, and the family reunited for the New Year's celebration. There was an air of mirth, like being among survivors of a disaster, yet Liu's heart was heavy. He refused to see Zhou and Gao and spent time only with his family. Because he avoided all outside contact, rumors spread that he was tortured in prison and had become a vegetable.

Three things about Liu Xiaobo's imprisonment and release during this time have been topics of controversy.

One. On January 26, 1991, the day of Liu's release, Xinhua News Agency, China's state press agency, published the news bulletin "Rioters sentenced separately: Wang Dan, four others receive prison terms; Liu, two others times served," pointing out that "despite the seriousness of his crimes, Liu's guilty plea, remorse, and meritorious act granted him release." "Guilty plea" and "remorse" referred to his confession; "meritorious act" referred to the Four Noblemen persuading protesters to leave the square. Liu says if history gave him a second chance, in no way would he sign the confession. "My confession was a true lie. I didn't believe it; I had to say it to save my life. I caved in to the lies of others, to violence. . . . I signed it out of weakness. I didn't hold out until the end."

The confession has entered the pages of history, preambling a lifetime's reflections and regrets for a man. He has never shied from pointing out this stain in his life: "When I sold out my own dignity, I also sold out the souls of the dead. I had notoriety; many cared about me. What about the many who died? Who lost the ability to live? Who are still sitting in a dark cell to this day? Who knows them? Who remembers them? Who cares about them?" He had made up his mind: "The only way to redeem myself is to resist, to go back to prison. It's the only way for me to realize my beliefs, my ideals, my integrity."[9]

Two. Liu agreed to a postrelease government TV interview lasting forty minutes in which he gave an eyewitness account of the square clearing, saying, "No one died at Tiananmen Square." He caught a lot of flak from peers.

He'd said no to the interview twice. Of course, he knew why they wanted to talk to him. For truth? More like for publicity. They got him to say exactly what they wanted him to say, even though he told the truth. "I knew if I said yes, I'd agree to be their tool."

But the arraigner showed him Hou's interview with People's Daily, saying, "If you didn't see anyone die at the Square, why not come out and say it?"

So Liu found three reasons to do it. First, he didn't see anyone killed at the square. The right thing was to call them as you saw them. He was disgusted with Wuer and others' lies about the carnage at the square. Second, Hou caught fire for speaking out. Liu thought as another witness he could back Hou up and share the burden of the backlash. Last, he wanted to explain, though no one died at the square, many were shot and killed or injured elsewhere in the city. That was a stone-cold fact. And no one was killed at the square not because the government showed mercy but because people backed down.

In his 1993 book *A Survivor's Monologue*, Liu still maintained the interview was not a mistake: "To this day I'm glad and proud of my honesty and frankness in the interview." But in time, he realized the extent of the negative side of the whole thing.

Nothing is wrong with truth, but there is a time, place, and audience for it. Journalist Su Xiaokang: "The state wanted to tell the world through his lips it didn't kill anybody. I don't know if he had a choice, but he really didn't see anyone get killed at the Square. How was he supposed to say West Chang'an Avenue was washed in blood? He lent his voice to the perpetrators; now the victims will never forgive him, and he's ridden with guilt. While history waits for vindication, Liu's changed, his arrogance turning to humility."[10]

Three. In *Monologue*, published in Taiwan, Liu took a scalpel to himself, the students, and the democracy movement.

Fellow writer Zha Jianying says, "[H]e may be the only Tiananmen leader who published a book exposing the movement's moral failings, not least his own. . . . Liu detailed the vanity, self-aggrandizement, and factionalism that beset the student activists and their intellectual compadres. He put himself under a harsh light, analyzing his own complex motives: moral passion, opportunism, a yearning for glory and influence."[11]

Monologue is an imperfect book to say the least. It overemphasizes the errors of the protesters' ways, playing into the government's brainwashing campaign. Dross of the era's romanticism and narcissism float between the lines. Liu thus took the opportunity to further "reflect" on his "reflection."

Friend Chen Jun says, "He doesn't write about politics from a political perspective. He writes about human nature from an ethical and aesthetic perspective, like Jean-Jacques Rousseau. He's a narcissist, like most people into philosophy and literature, believing they can see what others can't. Liu's an extreme case. His self-criticism becomes self-admiration, his self-admiration becomes self-fanaticism, and people take him to task on it."[12] He told Liu this when they met again in the States in 1993, and Liu seemed to have taken it in.

As June 3 turned into June 4 in 1989, "[a] foolish old man / Is turning an ancient city / Into another Auschwitz."[13] Within two or three days the blood was wiped clean, as if nothing had happened. Right and wrong made way for politics and economics. The last line of poet Liao Yiwu's "Massacre" shouts: "Whoever survives is a goddamn son of a bitch!" Liu adds: "We're worse."

THE DIVORCE

Liu and Tao divorced in August 1990. The papers were delivered to Liu in prison. His signature looked like any of the countless autographs he'd signed, but his heart felt different. Eight years of marriage were over and about to become a mere memory.

On the day of his release, January 26 of the following year, the government sent Liu straight to Dalian. He couldn't see his wife and son before he left. He wrote Tao, asking her to come with little Tao-tao to Dalian for New Year's, but he never heard back. He knew Tao had given up. You cannot fix what is irreparable.

Two months later Liu returned to Beijing. The BNU dorm he'd called home was empty. With nowhere to go, he stayed at Hou's vacant place.

In the 1980s, career-wise, Liu seemed to have it all, but at home he was failing as a husband and father. Northeastern men tend to be chauvinistic, and Liu was more the exemplar than the exception. He took after the American Beats and boned up on postmodernism. The sexual revolution paved another way for his pursuit of liberty. Married, he nonetheless had countless affairs with no consideration for his wife.

Tao was a promising scholar of Eastern and children's literature, taking after her parents. She sacrificed her career for her husband and son. Writer Xu Xing remembers Liu and Tao biking across the city to his compound and, even after his falling out with Liu, has this to say about Tao: "A rowdy bunch of us would tie one on, the seven, eight of us crammed into the Lius' one-bed flat. I felt bad about Tao cooking for us and all, the frail state she was in."

Tao was a good wife. She not only took care of the house but was also her husband's sounding board. Liu admits to her influence in many of his writings. She of course supported the student movement but worried about her husband's involvement. In tears, she tried to dissuade Liu from joining the strike. "I have to do what I have to do," he simply responded. "This is me. Nothing can change my mind once it's set, even if I have to do it alone." When she heard Zhou was joining, she said to them, "I feel better. At least Xiaobo listens to you."

It was as if they were going on a suicide mission. Family and friends trickled in and out of the Noblemen's tent all day long on June 3, practically turning it into a hotel lobby. The fragile Tao came to see her husband. She cried when she saw him and continued to cry for more than an hour without saying a word. Liu recalls: "I didn't know what to do, how to calm her down. Before she left, she just put her arms around me tight, like she wanted me to go home with her."

But even then, Liu was unfaithful. Soon after Tao left, a girlfriend of his arrived and stayed until 11:00 p.m. Even during a revolution, he found time for hanky-panky.

Only Hou had no visitors. At the time, Hou and his singer girlfriend Cheng Lin were breaking up. While Liu was carrying on with his paramour, Hou finally couldn't stand it anymore and yelled: "Xiaobo, you bastard, you want me to starve myself, or are you just trying to tease me? I'm gonna kick you out!" It was then that Liu realized what he was doing was wrong.

Tao was still in love with Liu. When Liu and others were hiding in the DRC, they sent a message to family through students. Gao gave Liu the rundown at home: "Got to BNU at noon, went to see Tao, had lunch, then came home. She wants you to stay low. If you can get out of the country, do it, don't worry about her and the kid. Here's 3,000 yuan she told me to give you." Three thousand yuan was their life's savings at the time. "As soon as the first shot rang out last night, she ran to the BNU east gate to wait for you, from 11:30 to sunrise, until all the students went back to school. She couldn't find you and thought the worst. She cried her eyes out."

Only through this baptism by fire and blood did he realize how much he'd hurt his wife: "No matter how horrific the events turned out to be, no matter how much I suffered, it had nothing to do with Tao. It was all on me. I deserved it." And what did his wife deserve? Pain? Fear? Anxiety? Disappointment? Bedridden and tormented by illness, she nevertheless had to raise their son with help from her parents.

Liu admits his wife and son never entered his mind as he looked out over the cheering masses. Not once did he think about his wife's suffering as cameras flashed and mics were held up to his face. He was blind to how her heart bled as his eyes wandered to other women. "I was a bad—terrible—husband. Not that I was a lazy good-for-nothing. But I was unfaithful. Our bond was all she cared about. If I couldn't honor that, then everything else I did was a sham and only added to her pain. I was a monster."

The realization came too late. When people blamed Tao for not sticking by her man in his time of need, Liu stuck up for her: "I wronged her in our marriage, and I wronged her in our divorce. I hurt and disappointed her with my political embroilments and philandering ways. She lived almost every day of our marriage in fear and sadness."[14]

Close friend Zhou Zhongling believes Liu had learned something. He treated his second wife, Liu Xia, well, Zhou thinks, to make up for how poorly he treated his first wife, Liu Tao. And not just Liu Xia, but all women, for how poorly he'd treated women in general. "Half of him began to think like a woman. He became extremely gentle and considerate, a one-eighty from his former self-righteous and devil-may-care ways."

As he grew older, he'd often say, "A man who doesn't love his wife and children, no matter how he appears in public, is not a man worth knowing." A lot of public intellectuals whose private lives are less than unimpeachable try to justify themselves by saying personal action is not a prerequisite for great thought, bringing up examples of Rousseau, Zola, Russell, and others. It was what Liu believed back then, too, that loose didn't mean lewd. He had come to realize that such an attitude was extremely selfish.

In the mid-1990s, Tao moved to the States. She disappeared from the public eye, and no one was able to interview her when Liu received the Nobel Prize. One wonders what she thought. Their marriage was far from perfect, but they still shared a precious time together in their lives. He is no longer who he was, and she is no longer who she was.

Could she have forgiven the "dark horse"? Maybe even wished him well?

CONVERSATIONS WITH DEAD PEOPLE

To be, or not to be—that was the question of Shakespeare's northern prince. To stay, or not to stay—that was the question facing China's democrats after June 4, 1989.

In 1991 Geremie Barmé invited Liu to Australian National University as a visiting scholar. During this time he was also invited by Harvard and Berkeley to speak; it would be his second trip to the States. The Chinese government was for it. Its attitude: out of sight, out of mind.

He caught up with Hu Ping and other old pals in a jaunt to New York and gave an interview to *China Spring* editor Ya Yi. The interview is included in Ya's *Interviews with Exiles*, yet Liu has never been an exile.

Ya asked whether he regretted going back to China in 1989.

Liu responded, each syllable clear and distinct: "I have always believed if you want to descend into hell, then you can't complain about the darkness. Besides, going home was hardly going to hell." He didn't go home on a whim, on an impulse, he stressed to friends; it was a careful and deliberate decision. Of course, he would always add that he could've done a lot of things better.[15]

Chen Jun drove Liu and Hu to Boston on Du Weiming's invitation to speak at Harvard. Filmmaker Carma Hinton also interviewed Liu for her and Richard Gordon's controversial 1995 documentary *The Gate of Heavenly Peace*.

Afterward, Liu went back to Australia and from there back to China. This trip home wasn't nearly as melodramatic and sensational as the first; still, a free man freely chose to live an unfree life. "I didn't know what was going to happen in China. The administration is unpredictable. It doesn't play by the rules. You don't know when it's going to change again. I didn't know if they'd let me out again, ever."

Once officials realized Liu was not going to stay out, they took his passport away. In 2000 he tried applying for one again in his hometown, Dalian. The immigration officer took him aside to another room and said, sheepishly, "Pardon us, Mr. Liu, we can't issue you a passport. The order came straight from the top. Our hands are tied." Even the officers knew it was a legal and constitutional violation to refuse a free citizen his passport, but they had to follow orders to save themselves. Like many dissidents at home, Liu has lost his right of exit. Those in exile, on the flip side, are stripped of their right of entry. China has become an immense prison: some can't get in, and others can't get out.

An advocate for complete Westernization, Liu had little lingering attachment to Chinese culture, and unlike many, he wasn't nostalgic for "China the Beautiful" or some such idea. Other than a language problem, he was like a fish in water in America. If the protests hadn't happened, he probably would have stayed. He had been a scholar, a literary critic, an intellectual—all professions that traveled. It wouldn't have mattered where he was. After the protests, however, he had a "career change" and became a human rights activist, a political critic, which meant he actually benefited more from staying in his home country.

Ya asked in the interview: "Did you think it was more useful to go back to China than stay in the States?" Liu replied: "I don't know about 'useful.' I didn't think about it that way. I went wherever I was comfortable. It wasn't a question of democratizing China for me. Of course you can say doing something small but concrete at home is more useful than organizing a hundred democracy advocacy agencies abroad."[16]

He knew what awaited him at home. It might not be hell, but being constantly watched, followed, harassed, and at the officials' beck and call, enduring the home searches and house arrests—the stress was as much psychological as physical, and most people would crack in three to five years. In a letter to Hu Ping after being released from prison for the third time, Liu wrote: "People seem so busy in China these days. Being in prison for three years, after I got out what shocked me was how rich my friends got. I like it here less and less. But memories of hard times won't let me leave. Am I a masochist or what?"[17]

Liu has lived more than twenty years like this. The abnormal is now normal; the exceptional is now everyday. Outside, he is a Chinese who has given his life for the democratization of his country; inside, he is a man of the world, without a care for geographic or political boundaries. Thomas Mann said, "Wherever I am, Germany is." To Liu, wherever he is, freedom is.

✿ ✿ ✿

The blood of martyrs not only failed to draw up and make pure the spirit of a people, it made an entire generation of intellectual elites who appointed themselves "the conscience of the people" lose their compass. "Why," Liu asks, "in a movement led by students and educated elites, were most of the people who died ordinary, common folks? Why were all the people who got the most severe sentences ordinary, common folks? Those who paid dearly had no voice in history and remained in silence, while those with little to lose continue to talk and talk and talk." It was time for the living to shut up. It was time for them to listen to the dead.

But how? "Let us feel the full weight of our shame and guilt. Let us reflect. Let us fight against the repetition of history. Let us learn to care about everyone near and far without bias or prejudice. Let us learn to live with dignity and with humanity." He stresses: "Do something for the victims and their families. Be unsparingly critical of yourself. Hold onto your humanity. Acknowledge and cherish the moral capital countless people have amassed and traded their lives for."[18]

To speak to the dead under the Gate of Heavenly Peace, Liu used poetry—the supreme language, the tongue of angels. Liu Xia says, "I never thought of Liu Xiaobo as a political person. From beginning to end he's really just a simple-minded, hardworking poet." Most people see only the political side of Liu Xiaobo, but Liu Xia says, "Liu Xiaobo the activist and Liu Xiaobo the poet are inextricable. On the one hand with the passion of an activist he keeps saying to the dictator, 'No! No! No!' On the other hand with the tenderness of a poet he keeps saying to the souls of the dead, to me, to his loved ones, 'Yes. Yes. Yes.'"[19]

Poetry, the ancients say, is perfect when it's "sad but not distressing, plaintive but not rancorous." But in the face of a massacre, Liu couldn't do it anymore—he couldn't hold it in. His feelings erupted and flowed like lava, as if he wanted to sear the iris of those looking upon his words. His poems sadden and distress, are full of anger and lined with bitterness, spewing straight out of his veins and pores.

Every anniversary, on June 4, he'd write at least one article and one poem. For him, it's a day more important than any other. "Under terror and oblivion / The day is buried / In courage and memory / The day lives on / The undying gravestone / Can shout / The evergreen cemetery grass / Can fly."[20] In summer 2009, with help from friends, Liu Xia gathered all of Liu Xiaobo's poems commemorating the massacre into an anthology, *June Fourth Elegies*, set to her oil paintings and photos from her *Ugly Babies* series. A small run was printed in Hong Kong and given to friends as a token of remembrance and thanks.

Words of mourning can keep the poet alive in his poems. In one, since intellectuals are thought to be useless, Liu imagines himself a dumb wooden plank on which bodies can be laid: "A wood plank / Can't shield against grinding metal wheels / Still, I want to save you / Dead or alive, with a single breath left." The plank can also be made into a coffin: "Come, O Youth, strong and firm as water / By your loves' consent / Make me a pauper's grave of wood / That I shall be with you interred in my home and roots deep / Side by side, eyes open / Waiting / Till they seal over, and / Sprout a forest."[21]

If poetry can't heal the wound, it can at least document the pain. Poet Jiang Lipo: "In my eyes Liu is an outstanding poet. His poems lend an often cake-faced language back its dignity. His punishment is a scourge to the Chinese people, an embarrassment to the Chinese language."[22]

In the twenty years since the massacre, the group Liu has cared about most has been retired professor Ding Zilin's Tiananmen Mothers. Liu admired Ding's speaking out about her son's death at the hands of the People's Liberation Army (PLA): "When Ding built a shrine to her seventeen-year-old son Jiang Jielian and appeared in public for the first time, the whole world saw her indignant face, heard her harrowing story, felt her burning tears. Yet she was no longer afraid, because she knew, they knew, bowing down to terror and lies amounts to spreading them yourself."[23]

Albert Camus said, "I believe in justice, but I shall defend my mother above justice." Liu vowed, too. As soon as he heard of Jiang Jielian's death after his first prison release, he went to see former mentors Jiang Peikun and Ding Zilin. That day he saw Jiang Jielian's photo on the altar, "seventeen, marching in the '89 parade, a red scarf around his head and a red flag in each hand, young, sharp, full of life."[24] Jiang and Ding told him what happened; he excused himself, came back half an hour later with a bouquet of flowers, walked up to the altar, and fell to the ground, crying. The next day he went up before the shrine again and read a poem, "For Seventeen," he'd stayed up writing the night before. His voice broke. He couldn't go on.[25]

In 1993 Liu published an article, "We Are Defeated by Our Justice," in Taiwan, dressing down the student movement, to Ding's dismay. She passed on the message to him not to visit anymore. Nevertheless, in summer 1996, after his second release, he went to see Jiang and Ding to explain himself. From a letter: "I knew what they'd thought of me, but I truly respected and admired them, and never harbored an ounce of resentment against them. I knew I could gain their understanding and trust if I was sincere. The spirits listen and guide us: if our hearts are pure, we will eventually meet on the same path."

In 1999, on the last day of the last year of the second millennium, after his third release, he went with his new bride Liu Xia to see Jiang and Ding again. They handed him a book. It was the list of the 155 known victims of June 4 and their stories. "My eyes grew wet on the first page. I read the book to my wife in tears, stopping every sentence—I forget how many times. Each pause seemed pregnant with the breath of the dead, weak, helpless, whimpering, heartbreaking." On this joyful eve of the new millennium, the four of them held a wake for the spirits of that day.

In the nine years before his fourth arrest, Liu became Jiang and Ding's closest confidant and the Tiananmen Mothers' staunchest supporter. At the end of 2003 Jiang had a heart attack and was on the slate for major surgery. Liu got to the hospital at dawn and pushed Jiang on the gurney himself through twists and turns to the operating room a floor below. He then sat with Ding in the waiting room until it was over. Finally he pushed Jiang all the way to the ICU himself again. Doctors and nurses thought he was Jiang and Ding's son.

Liu has helped the Tiananmen Mothers with everything from drafting and revising publications to going door to door to get in touch with victims, brokering meetings with ambassadors and media, and delivering donations. On the eve of the fifteenth anniversary of the massacre, the police illegally detained Ding and other Tiananmen Mothers; Liu published a number of articles right away calling the world's attention to the group and its plight.

Liu has never had a hand in the group's administration. "They do a fine job already. . . . If you want to help, leave your money on the table, and walk away." Ding remembers: "He's always agreeable. He never saw us as something to invest in and later reap profits from. He knows we only care about what's right. There's no politics. We're just an old, frail, illness-ridden, handicapped bunch. There's nothing in it in helping us other than taking on a share of the burden. Xiaobo and we work well together, easily and seamlessly. This is something we're proud of."[26] For Liu, standing with the mothers is akin to standing with the children.

And whitewashing the massacre was tantamount to repeating it. The fact that its executioners not only escaped judgment but were rewarded proved it had not even ended. Ten years later at the Dalian Labor Reeducation Camp, Liu watched the flag-raising ceremony at the square on television, writing: "After a decade / Well-trained troops / In the most dignified postures and precise movements / Continue to guard the Big Lie / The five-starred red flag dawns / Flying in the morning breeze / The people are standing on their toes, stretching out their necks / Curious, awe-struck, devout / A young mother / Lifts up the tiny hands of her child / To salute the lie covering up the sky." Meanwhile, "[a] white-haired mother / Plants a kiss on her son's photograph / She uncurls each of his fingers / And washes off the dirt and blood under his nails / She can't even find a fistful of earth / To lay him to rest / She can only hang her son on the wall."[27]

You may think Liu Xiaobo is tilting at windmills. But what he really wants is to put an end to this intergenerational transmission of trauma. Ding writes: "Over twenty years we've searched for the truth, turned every stone lest justice be right around the corner. The road is long and hard, but we won't rest. We're still walking, still looking." Along the way, souls of children will grow, blossom, nourished not by their mothers' milk but by their tears. Su Xiaokang points out:

There had never been a tradition of witnessing in China. Killings, wars, revolts happen over and over; we're walking round and round in circles, as if we're still stuck in the Dark Ages. Beginning with the Tiananmen Mothers, China has shown it will no longer be blind, deaf, or mute. This is what we got in return for the lives of Jiang Jielian and others. As mothers help shut the eyes of their children for the last time, a civilization opens its eyes for the first.[28]

A BRAVE NEW WORLD

Under a dictatorship, if you want to be a dissident and uphold the truth, the first thing you have to do is give up any sense of a normal home life.

Liu Xiaobo has been the living embodiment of this truth for more than two decades.

When he got out of prison for the first time, he wanted to head to the square. He wanted to get down on his knees before the memorial and kneel there for days. He walked to Xidan, turned back, walked there again, back and forth. He was afraid—afraid to face the dead alone, to face his memories. He choked back the tears.

Once he and Liu Xia were in Hou's Mercedes, and the driver took East Chang'an west. At first he didn't notice, chatting with Liu Xia. As they were driving past the square, he happened to look out—there it was, the memorial. Suddenly a force came over him like a tidal wave; he was pinned to the seat, trembling. It was as if someone had stuck a knife through his chest and twisted the blade. He tried looking down but couldn't, his gaze nailed to the monument, its gravitational pull drawing him out the window. Tears trickled down his face. All of a sudden he let out a cry and began to wail uncontrollably. Liu Xia and the driver couldn't get him to stop. According to Zhou Duo, "That's who he is. He's always sinking heaven and raising hell; that's how he lives. He's always reflecting, repenting, like a saint, never reconciled with himself."

❊ ❊ ❊

In just three years after Tiananmen, China had gone through unprecedented changes. "Everybody goes into business" was the cry of the early 1990s. Nine out of ten revolutionaries donned new clothes and became mercenaries; mill-grinding workhorses became mice-catching fat cats. Liu reflects:

> People found a way out in Deng Xiaoping's policies. They found a way out in the economy. When you can't change the world around you, you want to be able to at least look out for yourself. No one wants to lead a piddling existence. . . . Money can be a form of self-worth. When you have money, even if you don't have freedom of speech, your money still speaks to, to an extent, your life's worth. [29]

But in this high-paced, fast-changing brave new world, is there still room for a Liu Xiaobo?

Liu has nothing against money. In the 1980s he was one of the first intellectuals to make money a topic of open and serious discussion: "Money is a good thing. When you've got a certain amount, your world opens up to a certain degree." From a lecture: "Our eyes ought to light up when we see money. It can broaden our horizons." He thought some intellectuals should get into business. Power relations should be replaced by economic relations, freeing people to pursue their interests. In the 1990s money became the opiate of the Chinese masses, yet Liu himself never set foot in the den. Ensconced in its at once scintillating and numbing fog, thought stagnated, even in ivy halls. There were no longer great thinkers of the era, but there were great businessmen.

Democracy was out; authoritarianism, nationalism, and postmodernism were the fashion of the day. The shot heard around the world on June 4 also divided it in two, the passionate 1980s and pedestrian 1990s. After the white terror came the gold rush. Under the guise of communism, capitalism fell into full swing.

After prison, Liu was part of the "three-no" class—no job, no income, no insurance—a world of difference from his winged-steed days. He became an "enemy of the state," an unshakeable "black hand." Former acquaintances avoided him like the plague. Yet Liu became even more resilient. Zha Jianying says, "I first met Liu Xiaobo at the beginning of 1991 at a little hotpot place to celebrate his release. He was making fun of the hoity-toity literati. He told a young guy there the critic who raved about him was a sheep and an idiot."[30] Some things never change.

Liu was also part of a "Qincheng gang." These "graduates" were three-no's like Liu. Life was hard, but they stuck by one another. Together they worked, talked, ate, played mahjong, and went out. Fired from university, Chen Xiaoping recalls: "We were watched after release. Xiaobo, Bao Zunxin, Liu Weihua, me—we became each other's pillars, each other's rocks. We spent almost every weekend together, in our tiny apartments. Who cares we're being watched? We gobbled up roast chicken and rabbit stew, fought over every fen on the mahjong table. Before sunrise we rode the van on the Third Ring Road home, telling each other our stories."

According to writer Jiang Qisheng, in the early 1990s, he, Liu, Bao, Chen, Zhou Duo, Wang Dan, and Liu Nianchun hung out a lot, talked about current affairs, and wrote open letters. On the sixth anniversary of Tiananmen, they met at a restaurant near Liu's to come up with a declaration of sorts. At the time, activist Wei Jingsheng was arrested again, and they talked about the possibility of his getting the Nobel Peace Prize. Liu said if Wei did, it would be a great boon to China's democratization.

Liu made other friends on and because of June 4. Take, for instance, writer Ye Fu, who went from pig to jailbird because his rage at what was being done to students "made his hair stand on end." After he got out he went into independent book sales and took Liu out to eat a lot. "I get it. I've been through it. Face is important especially to people in dire straits. They'll often refuse charity. Besides, we were all poor. It's not like any of us had an extra arm to give. All we could do was throw water at rocks, and treat each other to a meal or a book, things like that."[31]

Ye Fu and friends Wang Shuo and Zhou Zhongling were going to help Liu publish a book under an alias. When he was released from prison the third time in 1999, Liu hadn't a penny to his name. Wang, whom he'd known since 1986, went to see him, often bringing food and necessities along. Wang mentioned to a friend in publishing that he wanted to help Liu but thought Liu wouldn't take cash. The friend told Zhou Zhongling; Zhou agreed and suggested another way—publishing a book for him. Wang's books were doing well; if they put out a dialogue-style book with Wang, and Liu under a pseudonym, it would surely be a bestseller. Zhou told Wang; Wang was for it and brought it up to Liu the next day at Zhou's.

Liu was sitting on the couch. After hearing the idea, the first thing out of his mouth was: "My name can't appear in public in China. If I can't use my name, then I refuse to write anything."

Zhou tried to convince him: "I'm a businessman. I want to put out a good product. Help me make some money. I'll consider it a favor."

Liu was silent a while. Then he said, "Let me think about it."

A day later Liu came back. The first thing out of his mouth this time was: "Tell Wang, let's make some money together."

Since they couldn't use his name, he assumed one. When the book came out, on the cover next to "Wang Shuo" was someone named "Old

Xia" (inspired by Liu Xia), which in Mandarin also sounded like "Old Warrior," the name of one of the conversants in the book.

In November 1999, over four days, in a room in Wanshou Hotel by Liu's home, Wang and Liu talked. Liu remembers: "I mostly prated. Wang mostly prodded. . . . Zhou took the tape afterward and gave me the transcript. I gave my edits to Wang. Finally we put our names on it, Wang his real one, I my fake one, and crossed our fingers."[32] Wang had made the final edits and taken out some sensitive material.

Zhou hoped to make the yearly Beijing National Book Distribution Fair in January. The manuscript and cover were pumped and primed, and advances were pouring in at the fair, but they still didn't have an ISBN. For the first half of 2000, Zhou was running around knocking on every publisher's door. Still no number. Wang thought the material was still too sensitive. They needed an old hand and found *Guangming Daily* editor Xu Xiao, who revised it further. Months later, Ye Fu managed to get them an ISBN and published the book together with Zhou.

Ye got Changjiang Literature and Art to sign with Wang in Beijing. Wang's rate was usually 12 percent and a 200,000 first run, but considering the risk, Changjiang offered 150,000, and Wang stipulated a single payment within one month. The deal was sealed.

Book title was next. Wang said the less it had to do with the book, the better. Ye Fu suggested one of Lu Xun's doggerels, "The beauty slipped me a roofie." The motion passed *nem con* amid roaring laughter. The publisher was curious about who the "old warrior" in the book was. Wang replied: "It's an old master of mine who had just come down the mountain after an extended retreat."[33]

When Ye got the lump-sum payment, he asked Wang how they should distribute it. "Get an account for Xiaobo under someone else's name," Wang said, "and transfer it all in there. I don't want to see a single cent." Ye was shocked. Wang could finally replace his rickety rickshaw of a car with half the money. But Wang said it was the only way he could help Liu. "Wang's a real friend," Liu would say years later. "Everybody knows it." And, with this paycheck, he bought his first, very own, state-resumable house.

5

ONE MAN'S WAR

"GNASH IT OUT"

When the Four Noblemen started their strike, Liu overestimated its impact on the protest movement and the whole course of events. Under the memorial, megaphone high in the air, he shouted into the crowd: "Let's gnash it out with Li Peng!"[1]

"Gnashing it out" is a northeastern phrase, meaning not giving up, latching on and not letting go. "Gnashing it out" described Liu at the square; it also describes his rapport with the Chinese regime over the past twenty years. Like the calf against the oak in Solzhenitsyn's story, he never let up, never backed down, never gave in, never ran out.

China entered a new silent era in the 1990s. The fall of communism in Russia and Eastern Europe had more or less to do with Tiananmen, but China turned the whole thing on its head: unlike its comrades to the north and west, it became even more reactionary and repressive. Worse, it was becoming depoliticized: people were turning all their attention to the economy. If you can't be free, at least you can get rich.

Those who spoke up were treated like heretics. In 1992 Deng Xiaoping went on tour in southern China pushing economic reform. Old dog, new tricks—the emperor was as zealous as ever and ruled with an iron fist, handcuffing and taping the mouth of anyone and everyone who dared let out a peep. The economy hypertrophied; everything else atrophied. The task of rehabilitating a civilization fell on a smattering of discontents' shoulders.[2]

The administration had the media and universities in the palm of its hand, effectively erasing Liu and others from public life. Liu continued writing open letters drumming up noise and support for political and human rights reform. To be safe, he and others stopped communicating by phone and mail. Instead, he rode everywhere, a lone bicycle amid millions, in Beijing. He did it all. Getting laughed at and having doors slammed in his face were par for the course, but he had no time to worry about that.

On February 20, 1995, Liu and others published a "Proposal against Corruption: To the Third Plenary Session of the Eighth National People's Congress," outlining eight suggestions for short-term reform: (1) institution of independent oversight by the National People's Congress (NPC) of the ruling party and governing body, and establishment of an NPC Anticorruption Committee; (2) special legislation by the NPC against waste and fraud in the use of national resources; (3) implementation of judicial lifetime tenure; (4) enactment of civil service examination; (5) legislation for public official assets declaration; (6) legislation prohibiting commercial business operation by officials while in office; (7) freedom of public opinion and supervision; and (8) passage of media laws—and five suggestions for long-term reform: (1) lifting of ban on political parties; (2) separation of powers; (3) establishment of an independent constitutional court; (4) freedom of press; and (5) constitutional amendment guaranteeing the lawfulness of private property ownership.

Even now, this document is ahead of its time. None of the short-term goals have been reached, and only the last of the long-term goals has. And though the PRC Constitution provides for both private property and real right laws in theory, practice is altogether something else: forced relocations in cities and violent enclosures in the country are common sights and have spurred everything from appeals to riots. The relationship between the government and the people is only becoming tenser.

Liu and Chen Xiaoping also put out a petition on the Tiananmen sixth anniversary, "Lessons from the Bloodbath: The Progress of Democracy and the Rule of Law," in which they again called for freedom of press, freedom of association, other human rights and freedoms, and the establishment of a constitutional high court. "The Chinese people," they wrote, "have suffered long and hard on the road to a modern democratic society. June 4 will forever be remembered as a day of such suffering. But if we have the conscience, the wisdom, the courage, the confidence, and the perseverance to look into our bleeding wounds, then suffering shall be a gift. A people that has suffered shall be prosperous and profound. They shall be a people of hope."

In August 1996, Liu met veteran activist Wang Xizhe in the southeastern city of Guangzhou. They wanted to send a joint recommendation to both the Communists and Taiwan's Nationalists on the fifty-first anniversary of the Double Tenth Agreement, signed by Mao Zedong and Chiang Kai-shek on October 10, 1945, in which the two parties would recognize each other as legitimate governments. Wang drafted the "Double Tenth Declaration." Wang had chauvinist leanings; Liu didn't. The administration found out about the letter, which had to be written in a hurry, and Liu did not have time to revise it. His name ended up on the paper, but the work wasn't his.[3]

Remember, this was all before the Internet. The series of letters could only be published abroad and passed around in small circles at home. The majority of Chinese had no idea. Impact was limited; signers grew few. If resistance was futile, why did Liu even bother?

Liu went to Zhou Zhongling's once, and they ended up talking all night. Zhou asked him flat out: "What's the point of all this? Isn't it better to offer concrete help to concrete individuals, like Liang Xiaoyan is doing for farm kids pulled out of school?"

Liu said he admired Liang, but there were other things to do, too. In society, different people play different roles with different responsibilities. Personally, he wanted to see more change on an institutional level. "Change on an institutional level can benefit everyone. This is the direction I want to go." He didn't want to stop just one Tiananmen; he wanted to stop all Tiananmens.

Finally, he said, he felt guilty. To alleviate this guilt, he had to keep going; else he would be betraying the Tiananmen victims twice. "Others can stop. I can't."

Zhou told him he wore his heart on his sleeve, he didn't have a political bone in him. He didn't belong in politics.

"Of course I know that," Liu said. "And I'm not interested in politics. I'm interested in human rights. One day Tiananmen will be vindicated. On that day a lot of people will want a piece of that cake. I'll excuse myself then. I don't want a single piece, a single crumb. No, because my heart will finally be at rest, and I can go back to teaching."

The conversation lasted until dawn. Liu mentioned that if it weren't for Liu Xia, he wouldn't be here and would probably still be in prison. "Being a prisoner is my destiny. I'll be one again someday. And when that day comes, I'd appreciate if you could take care of Liu Xia for me."

"Don't mention it," Zhou replied. "We're all family." He knew Liu was right, but he never imagined when Liu was imprisoned for the fourth time that it would be for so long and under such cruel and unusual terms.

Liu is Sisyphus, rolling his boulder up a hill, only to watch it roll back down, again and again. He may never reap what he's sown. Despite the democracy movement of 1989, the collapse of the Eastern Bloc, and sanctions by the West, the PRC has managed to not only survive but also, riding the crest of globalization, turn its economy around on the blood, sweat, and tears of its people, baptizing them in a new economic fundamentalism. In this world, opposing the one-party rule amounts to fighting a losing battle. Yet Liu Xiaobo is still "gnashing it out."

PEN

The most important thing Liu Xiaobo did in the first decade of the twenty-first century was founding and leading Independent Chinese PEN (PEN).

PEN was founded in 2001 and approved with majority votes to be a member center at PEN International's Sixty-Seventh Congress in London that October and has sent representatives to the congress every year, becoming one of the most active member centers in the organization.

At its founding in 2001, PEN consisted mostly of Chinese writers in exile. The year 2003 was a turning point for the center. That November it held its membership assembly online for the first time. Online elections turned out to be the tiny group's first step toward practicing and realizing democracy. Liu: "Democracy on the Internet was new. We had no experience and learned by doing."

Bylaws were voted on, and a board was elected, led by a president. Liu won by a landslide and wrote an inaugural address: "I ran for and accepted this position because of irreconcilable differences between my belief in freedom—freedom of speech, especially—and my country's lack of it. Freedom of speech is a linchpin of modern civilization. Fighting for that freedom and against censorship, and creating great works, are my own goal and goal for PEN."

Liu had his finger in every pot. The center was humble in size, but all the parts were there: Liu spent a lot of time running and overseeing things high and low, big and small. His wife, Liu Xia, complained: "He's the CEO and the PTA." But love's labor's not lost, and his accomplishments were indisputable: membership went up threefold in his first term, drawing influential writers at home and raising the group's reputation in professional circles.

In October 2005, the assembly was held online again. Bylaws were ratified, and a new board was elected. Liu posted to the center's internal forum addressing the members: "I've never been involved in any organization, but somehow I became the president of this one. After two years, my term is up. While I didn't achieve anything spectacular, I kept the center going and did what we set out to do." He looked back: "My tenure was spent in argument, dialogue, negotiation, and compromise. For the greater good, all disagreements in the open, no matter how strong, were well worth disagreeing over. Either we found common ground through compromise, or we let go personal differences through majority rule. If it weren't for these open clashes of views and ideas, the center wouldn't be what it is today."

Liu was reelected; Yu Jie and Chen Kuide were elected first and second vice presidents, respectively.

Liu chose not to run in 2007. PEN was now strong enough on its own. He continued serving on the board until his arrest on December 8, 2008.

In Liu's four-year tenure as president, PEN turned from a duckling into a swan. As the center was run directly by the president, the job was no small feat. PEN was bankrolled by the US National Endowment for Democracy and small individual donations; compensation for department heads and the webmaster was nominal. Liu gave the most and got the least: he forwent it altogether, becoming "head volunteer." PEN was going to get him a work cellphone. Liu kept telling them to get the cheapest one. Short on money, he said, they had to squeeze every nickel and pinch every penny and make helping writers in prison top priority.

His passion for the job wasn't an ego trip. He wanted to learn how nongovernmental organizations (NGOs) worked. The weak point among Chinese intellectuals has always been "big on thought, small on action." This was partly why protesters had a hard time getting organized at the square in 1989 and why popular resistance was slow to grow after 1989. Liu strove to be the change he wanted to see. Not content being a thinker and writer, he wanted to be a doer and organizer. His personality mellowed and matured as a result, and his ideas grew sharper and clearer.

PEN was a huge learning opportunity to Liu and others as public figures. Before, Liu played by his own rules and didn't care at all what anyone else thought. He debuted in the literary world like a bull in a china shop. Up front and straight from the shoulder, his communication style was unique, at least among the Chinese. It was his boon and bane, irritating folks left and right along the way. Word on the street was "Liu Xiaobo is not a people person."

Even in the 1989 movement he rarely took part in collective activities and signings by intellectuals and instead reached out to students like the Lone Ranger to Tonto. He looked down on those brick-in-a-wall writers and intellectuals. Even the spiring "Four Noblemen" was cobbled together on the fly. The four weren't that close, nor did they see everything eye to eye.

For a long time he refused to be labeled, refused to belong to any group; that way he could maintain complete critical freedom. But especially nowadays, for public intellectuals to have any effect on society, they must pull together and present some sort of united front. They have to associate and organize, and lone wolves that they are, they still must learn to hunt with the pack. As president, Liu had no choice but to adapt. He told friends he took on the role, so he had to play by the rules, even do things he didn't want to do. As far as NGOs went, PEN with one to two hundred members was bush league, but with its full cast of characters and egos, any little disturbance could develop into a full-blown category-five Prosperian maelstrom. Playing the lead demanded savvy and finesse, to say the least.

Liu and company created a secretariat and Freedom to Write, Writers in Prison, Internet Working, and Literature Exchange and Translation Committees. With the setup of a website and online archive and

Freedom to Write and Lin Zhao Memorial Awards, PEN encouraged its members to write freely, bravely, and passionately.

In terms of freedom of speech, the most "radical" official communist publication is meaningless next to the most "reactionary" independent and popular one—Liu has long held this belief since the 1980s.[4] He worked with writers Yu Shicun, Liao Yiwu, and Yu Jie to try to get PEN publications reviewed by an editorial board and printed quarterly, but with increasing state scrutiny they were never able to get it off the ground. *Freedom to Write* exists now only online.

Liu is a night owl. Midnight in Beijing is midday in the United States and Europe, so it worked out: through the web, he was able to talk, by voice and text, with colleagues across continents and oceans, across geographic and political boundaries. He used to spend at least two hours a day, every day, for four years doing work for PEN.

There were plenty of other wheels to turn and lots more gears to grind. Writers are generally not a gregarious bunch—mix them all in one bowl, and you're likely to end up with egg on your face. Liu had been an "egg," too, but as president he hardened his shell amid all the give-and-take. Added to his duties as "master of the house" and "maid" were "referee" and "peacekeeper." This drained a lot of his time and energy. The Internet was a blessing and a curse: he could be reached by anyone, anytime, anywhere. It was a ruthless invasion of privacy.

Yet writer and later PEN president Tienchi Martin-Liao describes: "Like many extremely brilliant people, Liu is quick on the draw, with his thought as with his pen, and he stuttered. Often he's chatting with me online, and through the microphone I could hear him smoking, sipping tea, eating. Or typing. Or talking with Liu Xia."[5] The Internet roped in PEN pals, many of whom had never met, from all over the world.

Liu was also able to get in touch with old friends and recruited a lot of them. It was the fast and cheap way of choice to communicate. Writer Meng Taoer remembers Liu typing on the screen once: "There's nothing in the world I fear anymore."[6]

* * *

Liu's focus at PEN was writers in prison. He established the Writers in Prison Committee in December 2003 just after taking office.

China had not wanted for dictators throughout its history, and as long as there had been dictators, there had been censors and those who fought back. Language is power, but also in language is truth.

"'Writers in prison,'" says poet Jing Wa—"what a deplorable phrase! . . . In a country of more than a billion, there's no strength in numbers, but there's strength in determination. These writers are determined to fight, to challenge a violent regime and the masses still living in the dark ages. Their words spell the crisis of Chinese culture and governance."[7] China sends more writers to prison than any other country in the world. It's the shame of the nation, a sign of disdain for freedom. The numbers keep climbing, and PEN's Writers in Prison Committee is the busiest in the world.

The committee hit the ground running and started compiling information on imprisoned writers and comparing notes with Reporters without Borders, Committee to Protect Journalists, Amnesty International, Human Rights Watch, Dui Hua Foundation, and other human rights groups. For the list of seventy-four they began implementing a "Plan to Support Writers in Prison," including international pleas and protests, establishment and maintenance of archives, website creation, publication support for writers and families, inmate visit and correspondence assistance, legal aid, and fund-raising and solicitation.

They also set up honorary memberships and a Writers in Prison Award (renamed Liu Xiaobo Courage to Write Award after Liu's own arrest). Of forty-two honorary members inducted since 2005, twenty-nine are still in prison. The award was created in 2006 with member Yang Tianshui as its first recipient.

Liu couldn't deal with each case personally; still he poured his blood and sweat into the project. Having been a writer in prison himself, he knew, behind the fly-ash brick walls, every word of encouragement, every last ounce of support from the outside counted.

Many prisoners have never interacted much with him or even met him—yet friends love at all times, and brothers are born for adversity. He channeled as much of the center's resources as possible toward the cause, even donating money from his own writings. Family members of many, if not all, incarcerated writers have gotten a personal call or e-mail from Liu. He even met and took them out to eat on his own dime. He felt especially for wives of prisoners, made clear in his essay "Women Imprisoned in Their Hearts," because his own family was a ship without a mooring in the ocean.

In 2005, poet and journalist Shi Tao was sentenced to ten years for posting to the New York–based Democracy Forum under a Yahoo account a memo revealing the CPC Publicity Department's blackout of Tiananmen coverage. Before then, Shi and Liu had no direct contact. When Shi's mother visited him in prison, he whispered to her: "If anything happens, go find 'Bo.'" The words, though few, spoke of absolute trust and respect, feelings invoked in friends and colleagues toward Liu without exception.

Liu didn't disappoint. Using the center's platform, he shined the spotlight on Shi before the world. He fired a fusillade of charges such as "Shi Tao Has No Secrets," "A Scream for Shi Tao," and "An Open Letter to Jerry Yang, Chairman of Yahoo! Inc., Regarding the Arrest of Shi Tao." Especially in the last one, Liu thoroughly analyzed and unequivocally condemned Yahoo's complicity in the affair for turning over records to Beijing, asking the company to stop before it's too late and not help the Chinese government "mend its collapsing 'prison of the soul.'" The letter caused an international stir and was reprinted by various media.

Meanwhile, the committee found an attorney in Hong Kong and, with the Laogai Research Foundation's help, drew the US Congress's attention. Congressional Human Rights Caucus cochair Tom Lantos summoned Yang to testify. Yang apologized to the victim's family, and Yahoo agreed to a substantial settlement and established the Yahoo! Human Rights Fund supporting political dissidents imprisoned for voicing their views online.

Liu was taken by the police from his home on December 8, 2008. From helping writers in prison, to now needing help as a writer in prison himself—the irony escaped no one.

A PUBLIC SPACE

It's safe to say that without the web, there would have been no PEN, and Liu would not have found his voice in the new century.

He wrote extensively about his close encounters of the digital kind. On October 7, 1999, he was released from prison for the third time after a three-year stint. When he got home, there was a computer on the table. A friend had given it to Liu Xia, who was learning to type and wetting her feet in the ether. The old-fashioned tower became Liu Xiaobo's fast work and social bud, while Liu Xia started using it less and less.[8]

Friends sang its praises. At first, like many writers used to pen and paper, Liu felt "blocked" before the screen. After much wheedling and handholding, he grew more able to do things with it and more unable to live without it. As a writer, a participant in the 1989 democracy movement, and an unwavering political activist, Liu couldn't thank the digital revolution enough.

He spent a week writing his first piece on the computer. It used to take him a day on paper. He almost gave up. Friends told him to keep at it. He even felt like he was abandoning his old stock in trade, as he wrote Hu Ping: "It's been six months. I've been typing everything. Now as I'm putting pen to paper, I feel a little sad, like I'd abandoned my profession and let myself go to waste. This is real—this pen in my hand—this is what reality feels like. This is the real me. It's as if the stuff on the computer belonged to somebody else, composed by a hand that I couldn't control, that controlled me."[9] Soon he sent in his first manuscript by e-mail and got a reply within hours. He was stunned, then and there setting his heart on getting the hang of this new technology.

After Tiananmen, Liu could only publish abroad. BC—before computer—revising and mailing handwritten manuscripts were a hassle. To avoid confiscation, he had to bike from west to east Beijing, find a foreign friend with a fax machine, and ask the friend to fax the manuscripts for him. Of course, something like this would take a toll on one's efficiency in and passion for anything. One or two pieces a month in a foreign outlet were a godsend.

Then it changed. Suddenly the realm of his knowledge and reach of his senses expanded beyond belief. The computer gave him convenience in writing; cyberspace gave him convenience in communication. They boosted his input and output. The WWW super generator helped its user churn out products at unprecedented speed and volume, shattering his own mid-1980s record.

Moreover, the Internet has become impossible for the state to censor completely. It has become a precious channel of information and expression and an important platform for grassroots organization. Liu would know.

In an authoritarian state, individual and collective open letters are an important tool for the people to resist the regime and fight for freedom. The mid-1990s saw a small wave of open letters by intellectuals in and outside the system on anticorruption, pro-democracy and rule of law, repeal of reeducation through labor, workers' rights, and human rights in general.

Around the sixth anniversary of Tiananmen in 1995, a series of letters appeared, including "Welcoming the United Nations Year for Tolerance with an Appeal for Tolerance in China." The letter was started by veteran CPC moderate Xu Liangying and circulated by nuclear physicist Wang Ganchang for signature by Chinese Academy of Sciences members and other intellectuals. The same year, Tiananmen Mothers published their first letter to the NPC and would continue doing so every year after. Liu and Bao Zunxin's plea for the safeguarding of dissident Chen Ziming in seeking medical attention abroad was also met with popular support.

The time and resources needed to produce a single one of these letters must sound like a fairytale to cyber watchers today. A month's preparation was a must. Finding authors and getting people together was a headache. Debates on content, style, and timing took days. Typing, printing, and copying were often done by foreign colleagues near Jianguomen in east Beijing. Most time and energy consuming of all was actually getting the signatures. Because of tapped phones, people had to bike or bus all over town for dozens of signatures, if they were lucky.

The Internet was a game-changer.

In Liu's eyes, both quantity and quality of open letter writing soared. Overhead dropped. Drafting, discussing, revising, printing could all be done at the stroke of a key and click of a mouse. E-mail and websites made it possible to get hundreds, thousands, of signatures instantly from all over the globe. When groups tracked and reported on their own activities, a cyber watch was formed, usually with their own site. Public opinion was expressed and heard more readily and often influenced traditional media coverage and government response. A site or bulletin board system (BBS) became a forum for the exchange and debate of ideas, a new form of freedom of assembly. The Internet, of course, also has a unique star-making power: legions of new rights defenders, opinion leaders, role models, truth tellers, and folk heroes were born. Liu saw these efforts becoming less elite driven and hierarchical and more popularized and democratized. On the 2002 public petition for the release of cyberdissident "Stainless Steel Rat" Liu Di, signatures of the intellectual elite appeared side by side with those of ordinary common folk.[10]

If the Internet was a drug, then Liu was its most unabashed addict. With the rise of sites abroad devoted to Chinese politics, Liu was getting paid more for writings online than in print. He became president and editor-in-chief of Minzhuzhongguo.org, funded by the US National Endowment for Democracy, with a $23,000 annual salary. Chinese media alleged a connection between NED and the CIA and accused Liu of being an American spy. But China's Ministry of Justice and other state departments have also applied for funding from the US government for training programs and study tours. According to the CPC's own logic, wouldn't *it* be the real Yankee puppet?

Blogs came into vogue in China in 2008. Liu started one on Sohu called "The Old Warrior's Song of Everlasting Youth." A friend managed the blog and posted mostly less controversial writings, such as literary criticisms. When Liu's trial began on December 23, 2009, well-wishers flocked to the blog. It was shut down as of December 31, 2009.

Liu quotes a Chinese Christian: "The Chinese aren't religious. Most of them don't believe in a God. But God won't abandon them. The Internet is God's gift to China. He gave us the tool to cast off our bondage and fight for our freedom."

The regime, however, is still trying to turn back the tide. In July 2002, the General Administration of Press and Publication and the Ministry of Information Industry released a set of "Temporary Regulations on Internet Publishing." Popular protests against the measures lasted two months, and on July 27 seventeen writers and scholars, including Liu, issued an "Internet Civil Rights Declaration," to little avail.

In the coming years, online censoring, filtering, and blocking would be as common as a drink of water. Liu: "I feel like I'm standing over an ever-expanding graveyard for websites. More and more headstones crowd the edges each day. Yesterday it's 'Cultural Vanguard' and 'Critical Constitutionalism'; today it's 'A Big Mess' and 'Yannan Community'; tomorrow it's 'Aegean Sea' and 'Democracy and Freedom.'"[11] As with the Hydra, when a head is cut off, two more take its place, though the bureaucracy grows, too. The 50 Cent Party, or Internet commentators paid fifty cents of renminbi by the government per pro-government post on every message board, has set up nests as well.

Liu encouraged, supported, and counseled many a young online activist, site master, board moderator, and blog author. Freelance journalist and webmaster Yang Zili was arrested in 2001 for "subverting state authority." Liu visited his site *Yang Zi's Garden of Ideas*: "I'm touched by Zili's words. Zili graduated from Beijing University in 1998. He studied mechanics, but his thought pivoted on freedom, on Tiananmen, on the suppression of Falun Gong and other marginalized members of society, and on the disintegration of intellectual communities in the 1990s."[12]

That same year when Wang Yi asked Liu to preface his essays *The Beauty That Stunned the Party*, Liu wrote: "Wang Yi and others rose through the digital ranks, and after Tiananmen, they realized they, too, had been systematically duped. Through resistance and vigilance they became brave and enlightened."[13] *Beauty* was printed and distributed underground but was eventually confiscated by the Cultural Market Inspection Brigade. Liu appealed for help. He had a particular yen for Wang's independent-writing, independent-printing, independent-marketing model, which he himself had been pushing since two decades ago.

A later PEN webmaster, Ye Du, was undaunted by shutdowns of his *Democracy and Freedom*. Liu spoke of the site: "It's one of the most important and fearless strongholds of information and discussion of current controversial political news by current controversial political figures. As a hub of online petition signing it's a force to be reckoned with."[14]

TWO FREEDOMS

PEN's biggest claim to fame to date is that it is the only popular organization in China that has broken through the country's restrictions on freedom of assembly and freedom of association. Make no mistake: the Chinese Constitution provides for the two freedoms—but reality is another matter. Nongovernment organizations have to be "supervised" by government agencies and should be called QGOs—quasi-government organizations. The China Writers Association is such a state-funded, partisan, vice-ministerial agency.

How does PEN maintain its independence?

First, it's registered in New York and off-limits to Beijing. It doesn't need to register "at home"—truth be told, given its nature, it couldn't even if it wanted to. Of course, not all PEN members are dissidents, but a majority are, and the center has never hidden the fact. In China, "independence" is synonymous with "dissidence."

Second, Independent Chinese PEN is part of PEN International, which holds special consultative status with the United Nations. China Writers Association itself has been a member since the 1980s under the names of the Chinese Center in Beijing, the Shanghai Center, and the Guangzhou Chinese Center—and still officially is today. The government, therefore, cannot give the center a hard time, either under a tax pretext or by outright declaring it illegal, like it has done with the Weiquan or "rights protection" lawyers. If it did, it would effectively declare the China Writers Association, PEN International, and the UN illegal as well.

PEN has come up through the cracks like a weed. It was not openly recognized, Liu thought, but it could no longer remain underground, either. For 2004 and 2005, the center successfully held two Freedom to Write Award ceremonies in Beijing.

On October 30, 2004, the Second Independent Chinese PEN Freedom to Write Award ceremony took place on the outskirts of the city. It was carefully planned, bureaucratic probes and blank walls notwithstanding. Sixty-two arrived, by charter bus or personal car, at Koulou Painters' Village in the Changping District.

The banquet hall was a painting studio/farm-to-table tourist restaurant. The host had built a number of cottages on the grounds, surrounded by mountains, on which dozed ruins of the Great Wall. Executive committee member, co-organizer, and writer Yu Shicun and others hung a scroll—"The Second Independent Chinese PEN Freedom to Write Award Ceremony"—white on red, the colors blending into the clamor of the guests, turning the quiet farmhouse into a bash. The host had prepared food, which the guests scarfed down and which, over the course of a half hour, due to overattendance, was gone. [15]

After lunch, people chatted and stood for pictures, especially with Liu. Member, BNU graduate, and Japan expert Liu Ning handed books

Liu Xiaobo and Liu Xia.

Liu Xiaobo, Jiang Peikun, Tiananmen victim family member Mr. Wang, and Yu Jie.

Liu Xiaobo and Yu Jie.

Sichuan writer Ran Yunfei and Liu Xiaobo in a Sichuan village.

The 2005 Freedom to Write and Lin Zhao Memorial Awards ceremony. Liu Xiaobo with Weiquan Lawyers.

Awards ceremony banquet.

Liu Xiaobo places Bao Zunxin's ashes to be interred.

Liu Xiaobo's brothers and Liu Xia dine on the way to visit Liu Xiaobo in prison.

Liu Xia, *Dead Trees 2.* **Oil on canvas.**

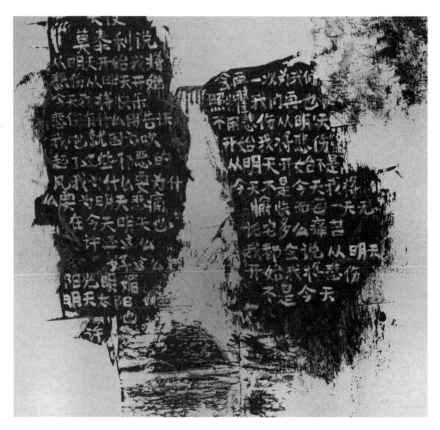

Liu Xia, *Tianshi / Motaili, Shuo / Cong mingtian kaishi wo jiang / Beishang . . .* 天使 / 莫泰利说 / 从明天开始我将 / 悲伤 . . . [The angel / Motele, Says / From tomorrow on I shall / Be sad . . .]. Oil on canvas.

Liu Xia, *Tianshi / Motaili, Shuo / Yige xiao huayuan* . . . 天使/莫泰尔/说/一个小花园 . . .
[The angel / Motele, Says / A little garden . . .]. Oil on canvas.

he had kept over fifteen years, including *Who Is Liu Xiaobo?*, to Liu to sign. They had never met. Liu signed in three places: "Fifteen years," "Thanks for remembering," and "The long-haired days are gone."

The meeting convened at 1:30 p.m. First up was Liu. The president thanked the attendees for coming. To honor the awardee, *The Past Is Not Past* author Zhang Yihe, whose father, Zhang Bojun, was named China's "Number One Rightist" in the CPC's late-1950s Anti-"Rightist" Movement witch hunt, the subject of her book, Liu said, "'Five hundred thousand rightists' is not just a problem. Five hundred thousand intellectuals losing their freedom, their creative independence, is a tragedy." He also stressed that the Freedom to Write Award was independent of the state and given only to those deemed to have a sense of responsibility to the history and reality of China.

Deputy secretary-general Wang Yi jumped in: Xiaobo had an entire generation of students under his spell. For fifteen years he had not been able to speak in front of a group of more than thirty people. Many of them had witnessed firsthand his spirit and style. At this point, people were clamoring: let him at it!

After fifteen years, former students and current friends heard Xiaobo's stuttering, cadenced voice again. Liu was fueled, talking over ten minutes, unscripted, about PEN's history and mission, setting the audience astir. Finally, he announced in all due seriousness: The Second Independent Chinese PEN Freedom to Write Award goes to *The Past Is Not Past* author Ms. Zhang Yihe.

Executive committee member Yu Jie presented the award: "With words forged from thirty years of blood, sweat, and tears, Zhang Yihe gave new substance to Chinese letters swamped by money and power. They are not only an indictment of these dark times—they are an affirmation of the human spirit, and a negation of all that seeks to destroy it." Zhang thanked the committee and stressed the necessity of truth and experience in personal and social justice. First award winner Wang Lixiong, Bao Zunxin, and others spoke. Liao Yiwu read poetry and played the flute.

In addition to some twenty PEN members, also present were writers, scholars, and artists from Sichuan, Shandong, Hubei, Hebei, and Beijing. Reuters veteran reporter and Liu's old friend Lin Guangyao covered the event and held an exclusive interview with him. The secret police "talked to" a number of attendees the next day; Liu himself "had tea" with them for several hours. Nothing came of it.

Another ceremony naturally followed a little more than a year later. On January 2, 2006, the 2005 Freedom to Write and Lin Zhao Memorial Awards were given at a smaller get-together in a private room at Jinshancheng Restaurant near Liu's house.

Beijing's Ministry of State Security leaned on Liu to cancel the event. He said no. They wanted to scout the attendees and limit the size. "What's wrong with a couple of friends getting together around New Year's?" Liu shot back. He made some concessions—no banner, no formal presentation, just friends chatting over food and drinks. The bureau approved their right to eat.

The forty-odd "diners" were made up of PEN administrators and members, Weiquan lawyers, and the Beijing intelligentsia. Previous winners Wang Lixiong and Zhang Yihe spoke first. Zhang said that though they were few, the people sitting around these tables made all the difference in the country.

Historian Wu Si won the Freedom to Write Award this year. The Lin Zhao Award winner was young college lecturer Lu Xuesong, who was awaiting trial for discussing midcentury dissident Lin Zhao in class and couldn't attend. Zhao Dagong read her speech.

Liu was walking on air that day and decided to down a tall glass of beer. His face turned flush. His chatter and laughter lingered among the tables.

The success of such a gathering is a barometer of the state of human rights in China. A ceremony was planned for December 2007 for subsequent winners Liao Yiwu and Li Jianhong (a.k.a. Xiao Qiao). The Olympics, however, made officials especially nervous. On December 22, Liu told the Associated Press the ceremony was slated for that evening, but the winners were detained by police. Li was under house arrest, and Liao, as soon as he stepped off the train from Sichuan, was held and sent home. Most of some forty attendees were harassed and threatened. Escorts stood outside Liu's house for twenty-four hours. The ceremony had to be canceled.

Conferences were another way for PEN to skirt assembly and association restrictions. On January 12, 2006, PEN and Citizen Semimonthly put on a "Literature and Memory" conference at Beijing's Sanwei Bookstore. The topic was the meaning and value of literature of personal and historical memory in contemporary China. Proceedings were published underground in 2007 as *Citizen Semimonthly*.

To avoid police harassment, Liu only made the after party. He did send along a speech. As it was read: "China today has a case of amnesia. As long as history and facts aren't given their due, as long as reality and truth remain gaffed, any speculation about and plan for China's future are dim, empty, and useless."[16] Liu practices what he preaches. He has researched and written extensively on everything from land reform, the Three-anti and Five-anti Campaigns, and the Anti-Rightist Movement to the Great Famine, Cultural Revolution, and Tiananmen. "Live, and remember" is not only the motto but also the mission of all Chinese today.

"Independence in character, freedom of thought" is the motto and mission of PEN. Next to its luminous members and friends, those weathercocks and bootlickers of writers simply pale. Liao Yiwu, Zhang Yihe, Ye Fu, Yang Xianhui, and others are influential at home and abroad and are the best Chinese literature has to offer today. Liu's role in bringing them to light cannot be stressed enough.

GET OUT INTO PRISON

Throughout the nineties for Liu, harassment and house arrests were a matter of course. The government would send him "traveling" out of Beijing on special occasions and important dates. He was also jailed for two longer periods of time—the first in 1995 for a "Proposal against Corruption" and "June 4 Sixth Anniversary Plea" for an official reassessment of the massacre, when he was simply taken from home and held in an undisclosed location outside Beijing for six months; and the second in 1996 for the "Double Tenth Declaration," when he was reeducated at a labor camp for three years.

Early morning on October 8, 1996, a loud series of knocks jolted him out of sleep. He got up to go to the door. Outside two policemen stood; Liu knew one of them, Ju Xiaofei, from the local station. Ju often dressed in plainclothes, but he was in uniform that morning. From Ju's expression, Liu knew something was up. This would not be a routine "checkup" or "bell call." Since Tiananmen, Liu had been in frequent contact with the police, including Ju. Ju was a standup and nice enough guy, always with a smile on his face.

Liu Xia was now also awake. "It's nothing, just Ju," Liu tried reassuring his wife. Liu Xia thought it was a routine visit.

At first Liu Xiaobo had hoped his wife would come with him so that in case anything happened, there would be a witness. However, he couldn't bear letting her see him being taken away. He couldn't bear to hear her gut-wrenching cries, to see the tears in her eyes. He pretended everything was fine, got dressed, and went out the door. He walked down the stairs and, a few feet from the building, looked back at the window to their apartment. It was still slightly open.

The police took him to the station on Wanshou Road, straight to the second-floor meeting room. Seven or eight other officers, some in uniform, some in plainclothes, were waiting; three sat at a long table. Liu was no stranger to the table and the room.

He sat across from the three officers. He noticed a man in the southeast corner pointing a video camera right at him. The officer directly across started questioning him. Name, age, place of birth, ethnicity—questions that, as usual, they already knew the answers to. Then they took out copies of two foreign newspaper articles, a Taiwanese *United Daily News* piece titled "Death, Defiled and Forgotten," commemorating the Tiananmen fifth anniversary, and a public appeal. They asked whether he had written them. He said yes. Finally they announced a "Ruling of the Reeducation through Labor Committee of the People's Government of Beijing Municipality," convicting him of libel and disturbing the peace and sentencing him to three years of reeducation through labor.

He was as calm as a clam. He'd been through it twice before, though this time would be even longer than Qincheng. When they asked him to sign, without even thinking about it, he said no—not in anger, but with resolve. At the same time, he said he disagreed with the ruling and would like to appeal.

The police hectored: "Think it over. It's in your best interest. If you don't, it'll be worse." They might as well have been trying to squeeze blood from a stone. At last, they had no choice but to let him write "I refuse to sign" on the document.

With the formalities now out of the way, he lit a cigarette, and the police escorted him out of the station. He said he wanted to see his wife. "We'll let her know," one of the officers replied.

Three police cars pulled up to the station. They didn't cuff him, politely ushering him into the middle car. He was sandwiched between Ju and another officer.

Sirens came on when they turned onto the main road, heading east on Chang'an Avenue, turning right on the Gongzhufen flyover onto West Third Ring Road, then onto South Second Ring. Half an hour later they entered an alley, and out the other end arrived at the Beijing Municipal Public Security Bureau at 44 Banbuqiao.

Waiting out front for intake, Ju stashed a pack of Marlboros on Liu. As he puffed in the car, a plainclothes officer passed him a couple of crullers. He ate two. He was surprised at his own appetite.

A female officer took him in and asked some questions. He asked for pen and paper for his power of attorney and appeal letter. The officer left, leaving him, Ju, and the young officer who came with them in the room. Ju asked whether there was anything he wanted to tell Liu Xia. He pulled out everything from his pockets, wallet, keys, the pack of Marlboros, and handed them to Ju to give to Liu Xia. He wanted to tell Ju something, too, to say to her, but he was at a momentary loss for words. The officer came back.

The whole thing, from when he stepped out the front door to the transfer, took about ten minutes. No due process, no Miranda. In China, a man could lose three years of his life in ten minutes.[17]

Liu was sent to Dalian at the end of January 1997. According to the labor camp deputy director Zhang, Liu wasn't sent there by accident. His birth registry was there, and so was his father. Authorities hoped father would show son the light. Plus, foreign reporters and embassies were few and far between, and Dalian had a much lower profile than Beijing. Compare this to Liu's 2009 incarceration when he was sent to remote Jinzhou Prison for eleven years. The Chinese judicial system has not progressed. If anything it is even more backward today.

As Zhang told it, Liu loved chatting about politics. An inmate informed on him once, saying he was bad-mouthing some guards. As he was talking, Zhang gestured as if he were grabbing Liu by the shoulders and said: "I warned him, if you keep it up, you're gonna get the stick." Guards carried rubber stun batons. Administrators also had a practically illiterate juvenile tail him all day. "He's got a PhD, don't he? That must be torture for him, talking to a wall dumb as the day's long," an officer gloated.[18]

To Liu, prison came with the territory. As a dissident, he was practical about it, treating it like a job, shaved head and all. It was normal "going to work"; when he was lucky he'd have "time off." Without this attitude, he might as well give up. You don't plant a few trees without getting your hands dirty. In the foreword to the memoir of writer Qin Geng, jailed for his Tiananmen involvement, Liu wrote: "Political prisoners are not super heroes. We don't go to prison for bragging rights. A calm and steady mind can look at a steel gate and see a road to freedom. We put up a fight outside, we hold our ground inside—it's the same." How did he keep from going crazy? "In a tough environment, you have to stay calm and hopeful. Don't let a moment's despair be your hemlock. Don't turn suffering into self-pity, into 'Why me?' Get out of your head. Get over yourself. Only then will you have the strength to get back up, not feeling like the world owes you, not unloading your negativity on people and things around you."[19]

He especially liked Qin's idea of "loving your cell as you love your home." It's a rare trait and "professionalism" all dissidents should have. You choose to resist, to rebel. You can stay quiet, like everyone else. But you don't. So you have to accept everything your choices might bring. Even when you don't get the reputation and respect you think you deserve. You can't complain. You can't think society owes you, that you're going to wrest from it what you're convinced is rightfully yours. In fact, the brighter the halo around your head, the clearer your mind has to be. A plain view of the world and modest look at yourself are the antidote to the intoxicating effects of fame and glorification. This is the mark Liu holds himself to. He gives up freedom of flesh for freedom of spirit. To him China is a big prison; he's merely been back and forth between the big prison and small prisons all this time. But instead of breaking down, he remembers his humility and humanity.

DAYS OF GLASS

Among Chinese dissidents, Liu by no means has the corner on most time spent in prison. Even if he serves his current term in full, all four of his arrests together would amount to "only" about seventeen years. Some "disobeyers" in China have been sentenced to twenty, even life. No one has maintained the dissident status longer than he, however. Even his life out of prison was unfree, abnormal to say the least. When the police become your "extended family," how normal can a trip to the grocery store be?

Remember the 2007 Oscar-winning German movie *The Lives of Others*, about an East German secret police officer who looked after and protected a writer he was supposed to surveil? Supposedly the filmmakers wanted to shoot on location at the original Hohen-schönhausen Prison, now a memorial for victims of the Stasi. The director refused, saying no Stasi ever protected his victims. Reality was crueler than fiction. No Public Security Bureau (PSB) ever cared for or looked after Liu, either—with one exception, a Beijing PSB commissioner Gao in the early 1990s, who showed him some kindness. Gao was later accused of being a "rightist" sympathizer and resigned.

Friends were used to the scene: whenever they met Liu, the police were always trailing him like flies. College classmate Wen Yujie remembers throwing a party for him in Changchun when he got out of jail the first time. Liu sent his younger brother to relay the stipulations: guests had to be handpicked by Liu; only 555-brand cigarettes were allowed; and Liu must bring his handler, a Changchun PSB commissioner. Wen met the conditions. At the party, Liu was excited to catch up on old times; there was no talk of politics.

Wen moved to Zhuhai in Guangdong in 1992. In 1996 Liu paid him a visit out of the blue. Wen put him and his half-dozen friends up for supper, surprised at how many people he knew locally. Afterward they played mahjong until dawn. Liu left. Five days later, someone knocked on his door at 1 a.m. It was the police. They asked him a couple of questions offhand: "Why are you in Zhuhai? Where do you work?" Wen knew this was about Liu; they said nothing. He thought that was it and forgot about it over time. Three years later, when Macau was transferred from Portugal to China, Wen suddenly got a call from local police telling him to stay home, and he could only watch the festivities on TV. *What the f—?* was his first thought.[20]

Across the whole of China, wherever Liu was, there the police would be. At the end of March 2003, Liu and his wife visited Jiang Peikun and Ding Zilin at their old home in Wuxi, and they went to Three Hill

Island in Lake Tai. Getting there involved a train from Wuxi to Suzhou, a two-hour bus ride to Dongshan, a shuttle to the wharf, and a once-a-day ferry to the island, yet when they arrived a bunch of plainclothes had already been waiting for them for a day. The dozen or so police were stationed at a hotel next to them, windows facing theirs. According to locals, the island's only yacht was docked on twenty-four-hour stand-by, as if these four "most wanteds" posed immediate flight risks.

Literary critic Wu Liang recalls another episode. In 2006 a group of writers and critics got together in Suzhou. Liu happened to be vacationing there, and Wu texted him to invite him to the hotel, saying many friends wanted to see him. The text turned into a bombshell. Police probably thought he was going to speak at the conference. "Hotel workers later said seven policemen shadowed Liu and ordered them to turn over the conference guest list. Scared the shit out of the manager. You always hold onto these things, any way you slice them."

❖ ❖ ❖

Different places had different levels of surveillance. A cosmopolis like Shanghai can actually be extremely conservative, and Liu's "body-guards" there didn't disappoint with their high level of "service." Shanghai playwright Sha Yexin writes: "Liu, my friends, and I ran into 'company' in a Hunan restaurant once. There were nine of us in a room. There were three of them, two men and a woman, right at a table outside. Through the glass door and windows, we could see each other, clear as day." Once or twice might be interesting, but every day for twenty years? Who can endure a transparent life, days lived behind glass?

Liu's student Wang Xiaoshan's story has an even better twist. A few years ago, they were dining, and of course police hovered. In the middle of the meal, Liu turned and said to Wang, "That man with me outside was your classmate." Wang went to talk to him—sure enough, they were BNU class of 1990, but with different majors. The officer turned beet-red. "I'm embarrassed," he squeezed out the words, "spying on my own teacher. I've got no choice, it's my job." Wang feigned understanding: "I get it, it's not so bad," even asking him for the number of a long-lost mutual friend.

Wang later explained:

What I "get" is what this country, and a not-too-bad gig like this, mean to a family. Being PSB falls in this category. "Not so bad" refers to the pay. There are no fringe benefits to speak of, and they have to put up with jeers and sneers from people like me. It's not that great if you look at it this way. So what I don't get is why some people still choose to do it, and why, save a little blush on the cheeks, spying on one's own teacher leaves hardly a scuff on one's conscience.[21]

On sensitive dates and anniversaries and during important government events and foreign dignitary visits, policemen and cars showed up on Liu's front stoop and stood guard. Guests were interrogated. At times they'd let him out and keep tabs on his moves; at times they'd simply put him under house arrest, without a legal reason.

For instance, since February 24, 2004, prior to the National People's Congress and Chinese People's Political Consultative Conference annual meeting, surveillance on Liu had increased. In the beginning they merely followed him and guarded his house. Foreign reporters were barred. There weren't any problems with his phone or Internet. From March 3 through March 16 during the meeting, he could still go out but not talk to any reporters. All visitors were cased. The phone would go out of service, longer and more frequently. He got into arguments with the guards over it. Conditions continued after the meeting.

Beginning May 24, except to go to his in-laws' house, he was forbidden from setting foot outside the house. His phone would cut out if he was talking with reporters or other "sensitive" figures. Internet would also go out after minutes. He bumped heads with the guards again and even complained to China Telecom.

The next day, phone and Internet were pretty much completely down. On June 1 his phone was cut completely, and he could no longer see his in-laws. There were constant visits by the local PSB, friendly on the surface but an intimidation tactic in reality. The "Tiananmen watch" wasn't relaxed until June 11.

Liu sighed: "This night isn't the night of nature's day and night. It's the permanent darkness under a dictatorship. . . . They've blinded, deafened, and muted me from the world."[22] In total he was under surveillance for four months, a third of the year.

Things got worse in 2005. The Hu-Wen administration turned out to be even more paranoid than the Jiang-Zhu administration. Liu could vouch for this personally.

It was New Year's Eve, and the guards were on duty:

> It's New Year's Eve, and they're here. At my, Zhang Zuhua's, and Jiang Qisheng's houses, at the same time. They're still letting us out. On duty on New Year's—that's a first. Maybe this year's cutting too close to the meeting. I went down to protest. They said this one's coming straight from on top. Those of us being watched can at least spend tonight with our families. The police have it worse: they don't have anything to do, anyone to talk to. Making the police stand guard on New Year's Eve—it's not just a violation of human rights: it's an affront to human decency. I'm letting my protest be heard![23]

The meeting took place over two weeks. Zhao Ziyang's death spurred another two weeks of raised alert, from January 17 to January 31. Tiananmen anniversary, two weeks. Liu's house was searched, his property seized, on December 13; court summons and proceedings took two more weeks. During this time the police often sat in the stairwell, prohibiting Liu from leaving, even following Liu Xia to the grocery store.

For Condoleezza Rice's visit on May 20, 2005, Liu was put under house arrest. He later criticized these practices in writing, calling out the government's hypocrisy in its stance on human rights and illegal use of force to curb personal freedom.[24]

On August 29, UN High Commissioner for Human Rights Louise Arbour came to Beijing. Arbour wanted to not only meet with Hu Jintao but also sign an agreement to facilitate China's ratification of the International Covenant on Civil and Political Rights. You'd think for a meeting on human rights the Chinese government would try to improve its track, if only for the five days the commissioner for said rights was in town.

What followed instead was a theater of the absurd. Inside the Great Hall of the People, Hu and Arbour chatted about human rights; outside the hall, dissidents were on full lockdown. Liu challenged:

> Five, six policemen and cars are downstairs again. . . . If we are living in a "harmonious society" that puts "people first," then why are my

rights and the rights of those like me not worth a bucket of warm piss? Why does a "harmonious society" have to be founded by policemen on sentry duty? How do we with our asses plopped at home reading and writing all day long pose a threat to the chitchat, handshakes, and photo-ops in the Great Hall—unless you think we have superpowers?[25]

At 8:00 p.m. on November 21, 2005, Liu was taken from home by Beijing police for a little "heart-to-heart." They sat at a teahouse almost an hour. It turned out that President Bush was visiting, and authorities were trying to soft-pedal their house arrest "policy."

Watched, harassed, cut off, locked up—this was Liu's life. But his attitude toward the police was:

A policeman without a uniform is just a human being. He knows right from wrong like everybody else. If he tries to rile you up, you have to not let him. Counter barbarity with civility. Reach out to the human being. If he calls you a dog, and you call him a dog back, you're not only adding fuel to the fire, you're handing him an excuse to cast off his humanity. He'll think, you think I'm a dog, I'll show you what a dog is, and right and wrong won't work on him anymore.

He tried to turn the other cheek for the most part. He was at a friend's once with a couple of guards downstairs. An hour later he got a call: "Professor Liu, I've been holding it in, I can't spot a john anywhere. Can I come up?" His friend okayed it, and they let the guard in.

Another time, Liu Xia and he went out, trailed by some bobbies. The Lius missed the taxi and took a bus instead. Suddenly they noticed a Volkswagen Santana in front, an Audi behind, a motorbike alongside—nothing but the royal treatment. In time the bus driver took note, too, mumbling: "What are they doing? There's road enough for everybody. Are they nuts?" Beijing bus drivers are known to be fearless. In 1989 many took their "livelihoods" to the streets to block the tanks. At the next stop, the driver couldn't take it anymore, got off the bus himself while passengers were coming on and off, walked to the Audi, and banged on the window. The secret police, secret as they were, couldn't roll down the window and crouched low inside. At the next stop, the driver saw that the Audi was still tailing him, got off, and banged on its window again. This continued until the Lius got off. Liu laughed and later told friends it was free comedy.

❉ ❉ ❉

Not everything was funny. The worst were the summonses.

On December 13, 2004, when Liu, Yu Jie, and Zhang Zuhua were drafting a human rights report, they were summoned by the police. Liu was released at 2:30 a.m. the next day:

> A dozen people rammed into my house around six last night, notice in hand, turned everything upside down, took pictures, made videos, swiped my computer. They took me down to the station and asked me about my writings, laying out a half dozen of my pieces on a table in front of me. . . . It happens from time to time, for the past fifteen years. The search and seizure was new, in fact the first since I got out in 1999. Caught me off guard.

Liu happened to be on the phone with friend Xu Youyu when the police burst in. He didn't hang up; the police didn't notice. Xu heard everything and quickly spread the information. Otherwise, with Liu's phone cut and Liu Xia being under house arrest later, no one would have known.

The phone was ringing off the hook when Liu got home. Friends, acquaintances, and strangers offered consolations. Foreign media, too. In the dead of winter, such kindling stoked his heart. "On December 21, a number of people called to tell me I won the Fondation de France Prize. The news filled the bare prison of my room with warmth and encouragement."

This showed that the Hu-Wen "New Administration" was the same old dog. Legal scholar Wang Yi protested that very night, pointing out this was another round of the regime's tricks, "a bald-faced, cutthroat threat" to "weiquan," to political expression, to public intellectual life.

> They [Liu and Yu] have always pushed for gradual reform. Violence-based revolution and radicalism are anathema to them. Mr. Liu said not without sadness fifteen years ago it would take three hundred years of being colonized for China to have a true revolution. I can't help being reminded of that today. Where is our promised land? If

we can't even have that in our own, private apartments, if we can't stop the secret police from kicking down our doors, what's the difference between home and prison? We're nothing but the communist party's half-prisoners and half-hostages.

On the afternoon of June 4, 2008, the PSB wanted to have another "chat" with Liu. "Today of all days, I don't feel like talking to you. Go away," he said. Downstairs, they wouldn't leave him alone. Finally, he went back up and shut himself in. At six, Liu Xia and he were heading out to dinner at her parents' house when they were stopped and physically assaulted by a gang of police. The station chief and others beat Liu. They dragged him into a traffic box–looking dark shack built to spy on him. Liu Xia cried and yelled for help. A crowd gathered. Some scolded the officers. A middle-aged man claiming to be a Beijing Municipal People's Congress rep tried to stop the police and called the Beijing PSB. Some official showed up, trying to smooth things over: "This is a misunderstanding." The police apologized to Liu. The Lius were finally able to return home at around 7:30 p.m. In this ugly instance, not only were the stupidity and brutality of law enforcement shown but also the fear of the regime toward Liu.[26]

To protest, many human rights activists put out an open letter that day: "For nineteen years Mr. Liu has upheld the principle of peaceful and rational resistance, tirelessly calling for others to break the cycle of violence, to counter hatred with tolerance and dialogue. Yet the government sees fit to brutalize this advocate for freedom. Again, though the government has amended its constitution in 2004, saying 'the State respects and protects human rights,' we have yet to see it in practice. The Chinese people's rights still lack basic protection."[27]

Six months before his last arrest, Liu's life had become a living hell. One reason was the Olympics. All the world wanted to do business with the "Great Power" and were more than happy to turn a blind eye to its offenses. Another reason was the general backsliding of human rights under the Hu-Wen reign and increasing pressures on political dissidents like Liu.

The Transition Institute, a grassroots think tank started by Beijing scholars Guo Yushan and Zhang Dajun that put on talks every Saturday at 3:00 p.m., invited Liu to speak on November 29. With his status in mind, they wanted to test the bureaucratic waters: if Liu could show his face in a popular forum like this, no matter what he talked about, it would still be a step forward. So they chose a perfectly placid topic, "Tragedy in Literature." On November 28, Liu got a call out of the blue from the police, asking him not to attend, which he refused.

At 2:00 p.m. the next day, he left to keep his appointment. On the way out he was stopped by three policemen. Liu argued, intent on keeping his promise, walking toward the yard gate. Five more officers surrounded him. He asked for their documents. "It's an order from the top" was the response. Liu couldn't leave that day. He told the media later: "For many years after Tiananmen, after I was fired from BNU, I've been unable to teach or speak in public. For the lecture's sake, I wasn't going to touch politics." Still, they wouldn't let him go.

Afterward, someone by the handle of "Balls under the Red Flag" posted a diary entry on a blog:

> The "Tragedy in Literature" Did Not Take Place
> Went to TI weekend talk. "Tragedy in Literature." LXB billed. Gonna start @ 3. Arrived 10 m early. Dozen seats left (50–60 total). No big turnout—considering.
> @ 3, TI said LXB accosted by police, still working it out.
> @ 3:30, LXB trapped at home, def not coming, sorry yadda yadda.
> Everyl left.[28]

In these times, "LXB" remains the center wheel of a continuing movement in China toward peace, nonviolence, reason, reconciliation, and rule of law. The mud kicked up around him is not slowing him down.

And there's no turning back.

6

FINAL WARNING: CHARTER 08

77 AND 08

Liu's fourth arrest was because of Charter 08.

He didn't start it, but he had an important part in editing and putting it together. It was the collection of some thirty open letters and statements, the culmination of twenty years of reflection since Tiananmen by Liu and friends, a memorandum from three generations of politically independent intellectuals and socially conscious citizens for the times.

It was a dangerous task.

Liu's old friend Jiang Qisheng sought advice and support on the charter from his mentor, scientist and human rights advocate Xu Liangying. "You can't use the word 'Charter' lightly," he warned. "If you do, you better be prepared for cops on your doorstep."[1]

The Sakharov Physics Prize winner was right. But what he didn't foresee was how a single charter grew, because of Liu's arrest, imprisonment, and receipt of the Nobel Prize, into something much greater, an epoch-making event.

Ding Zilin had encouraged Liu before his second arrest to write under his own name and auspices of "personal opinion" rather than risk more public petitions. His three priors were all for the latter; ironically, his own pieces were much more polemical. And ironically, the state could tolerate individual thought but not collective action—but isn't that what communism is supposed to be all about?

During the charter's drafting, Liu Xia sensed intuitively and from the experience of living with Liu Xiaobo the great danger inherent. Over drinks at a restaurant with friends, wife said to husband, "If you do this, I have a feeling I'm going to be traveling a lot, again."

Liu tried cheering her up. "I'm only gonna sign. I won't get in too deep. Promise."

The first rough draft and thirty-odd signatures came in—the emphasis was on "rough," and there weren't nearly enough signatures, nor signatures from enough important people. Liu was very dissatisfied. The charter should be something that stood the test of time. "If we're gonna do it, let's do it right."

The charter became the center of Liu's work and life in the fall months of 2008. He sought signatures and opinions from friends in all places. He knew it would not enlighten the whole of China right away, but at least it would be a crack in the darkness. With the Olympics just finished, the government was busy patting itself on the back. The atmosphere in Beijing was more relaxed, and Liu and company were able to slip under the radar at first.

Charter 08, published on December 10, 2008, didn't just pop out of nowhere. December 10 was the sixtieth anniversary of the United Nations General Assembly's Universal Declaration of Human Rights. The charter itself was a tribute to the anti-Soviet Charter 77 declared by Czechoslovakian dissidents in January 1977.

Charter 77 architect Václav Havel said:

> More than three decades later, in December 2008, a group of Chinese citizens has taken our modest effort as their model. They have made a similar call—for human rights, good governance and respect for the responsibility of citizens to keep watch over their government—to ensure that their state plays by the rules of a modern open society. The document they have issued is an impressive one. In it, the authors of Charter 08 call for protection of basic rights, increased judicial independence, and legislative democracy.[2]

Of course, Havel saw, Charter 08 wasn't a copy of Charter 77. The problems facing China today are very different from those facing Czechoslovakia in the 1970s. The latter had been a Soviet satellite with hard-core Marxist-Leninist political and economic policies, almost completely isolated from the West. Plus, its government was installed by the

Soviet army rather than elected and fell relatively quickly. The Czech and Slovak Republics have a comparatively long democratic tradition, fueled in part by their religious freedom and tolerance. In contrast, the CPC founded itself. It is self-righteous. From Mao to Deng to Jiang and Hu, China has become a land of "noism-ism," a bastard of crony capitalism and decentralized authoritarianism. The secret to China's economic development lies in its sliding itself into the world-system with a low "human rights" overhead, creating a kind of Frankenstein's monster of economic wealth and political poverty that thrives on conflict and contradiction. This makes a democratic transition more complex and difficult, which Charter 08 signers knew well.

Havel: "With the passage of time, we have come to realize that a free and open society means more than the protection of basic rights. To that end, the signatories of Charter 08 also wisely call for better environmental protection, a bridging of the rural-urban divide, better provision of social security, and a serious effort to reconcile with human-rights abuses committed in decades past."[3]

Charter 08 signers reaped the benefits of the experience of their Eastern European forerunners. From Havel's "power of the powerless" to Leszek Kołakowski's "living in dignity," from Hungarian writer and sociologist György Konrád's "antipolitics" to Adam Michnik's "new evolutionism," the opposition came up with a series of new ideas, attitudes, and values that shook up traditional political culture.[4] A group of independent intellectuals, including Liu Xiaobo, is doing just that in China today, Charter 08 being a fruit of their labor.

Havel and others were sent to prison after publishing Charter 77. They were victims of violence and corruption. Sympathetic to his plight, when Liu was arrested, Havel was one of his and the charter's loudest supporters. Braving illness and the cold, Havel tried to personally deliver a protest letter to the Chinese embassy in Prague. Bureaucrats would not open the door.

Three weeks before the 2010 Nobel announcement, Charter 77 spokespersons Havel, Dana Němcová, and Václav Malý called in the *New York Times* for the Nobel committee to award Liu. It was a shot of adrenaline to the 1.3 billion people of China:

> Despite Liu's imprisonment, his ideas cannot be shackled. . . . Liu may be isolated, but he is not forgotten. . . . We ask the Nobel

Committee to honor Liu Xiaobo's more than two decades of un-flinching and peaceful advocacy for reform, and to make him the first Chinese recipient of that prestigious award. In doing so, the Nobel Committee would signal both to Liu and to the Chinese government that many inside China and around the world stand in solidarity with him, and his unwavering vision of freedom and human rights for the 1.3 billion people of China.

Malý, in particular, a Catholic human rights activist who had been banned from priesthood for his involvement with Charter 77 and reinstated after the Velvet Revolution as an executive committee member of Pax Christi International and later as the auxiliary bishop of Prague, visited China at the end of August 2005 on a tourist visa and met with some independent intellectuals and religious figures. Watched as soon as he stepped onto Chinese soil, he was asked to switch rooms after he checked in at the hotel. That afternoon he invited Liu to the bar. Due to the time constraint and language barrier, they couldn't discuss issues at length yet immediately felt like old friends. Malý was probably the only Charter 77 signer Liu had ever met.

After Malý got back to Prague, he said that of everyone he had met, Liu made the deepest impression on him. He talked to Havel about Liu and the rise of a public intellectual collective in China, but little did they know that three years later, Liu and others would create their own tribute to the Czechoslovakian charter and Liu would be sentenced to eleven years because of it, a sentence longer than that of any of Charter 77's signatories. As soon as they heard the news, Charter 08 in hand, Havel, Malý, and others called for Liu's release. But most surprising of all to Malý was perhaps Liu being awarded the Nobel, echoing Havel's career.

Half a decade after their first meeting, Bishop Malý said a prayer for an old friend.

BIG DEMOCRAT IN LITTLE CHINA

Havel had said, "Charter 77 belongs to all the Chartists, and it's immaterial which one of them happened to have a hand in preparing the founding document." The same applies to Charter 08. Charter 77 was a team effort, and Havel was the team leader. Charter 08 was also born out of an esprit de corps, and Liu was the spirit.

Though not its founder, Liu had the biggest hand in its editing and collected the most signatures for it. Authorities later laid all 303 signatures on him, but he'd gotten only about seventy. Still, it was a quarter, and a significant quarter at that. It would not be an exaggeration to say that without Liu Xiaobo, there would be no Charter 08.

In fall and winter 2008, every meal with Liu and friends turned into a charter powwow. Once they were trying to come up with a title at a restaurant.

The working title had been "Collected Political Writings." They kicked around "Declaration of Human Rights," "Human Rights Charter," "2008 Charter of Human Rights." Finally they chose to name it after Charter 77, and "Charter 08" was clear and to the point. Liu slapped his thighs. "Then it's settled!"

Many signers' faith in Liu went beyond their faith in the document per se. Famed contemporary art critic and curator Li Xianting said, "To tell you the truth, I didn't read Charter 08 that closely, but I signed it, anyway, because I had complete faith in Liu Xiaobo as a person and in what he represented." Tibetan writer Woeser: "I remember in the middle of the night Liu's stutter trickling through Skype inviting me to sign. Out of trust and respect for him, out of gratitude for his longstanding concern about the Tibetan people, I put my signature down without a second's hesitation." Wang Xiaoshan: "As one of the first signers, I did it because I believed in my teacher. I didn't read it, really, and never thought it'd blow up like this. I did read it later and basically (ninety-nine-percent) agreed with it. I chose to sign it; no one made me. I'd sign it again. I admire my teacher. I love truth even more. Turned out they weren't far apart at all."

Like many signers, Liu didn't see eye to eye with all of the charter. He leaned more toward the Anglo-American model of small government and free market than the continental European socialist model of big welfare states with high tax burdens. From a Western view he might seem libertarian or even conservative. This marked an important departure point for him from most signers, even Chinese intellectuals in general, but was not reflected in the charter. Millennia of Confucianism have made the Chinese more afraid of inequality than poverty. Scholar Qin Hui was one who refused to sign because he thought the charter didn't speak enough to social welfare. On the contrary, for Liu, it already sounded like too much.

He knew, though, the charter wasn't about his or anyone's say-so in particular. To quote Havel: "[W]hatever came out of this would be pluralistic in nature. Everyone would be equal, and no group, regardless of how powerful it might be, would play a leading role or impress its own 'handwriting' on the Charter."[5] Or in American philosopher John Rawls's words, they needed to reach "overlapping consensus" with the greatest common denominator in mind, while respecting differences as the "cement" of civic society.[6] Liu listened to and took in differing opinions with patience, the end product being the culmination of a collective wisdom. Scholar Xu Youyu recalls being not too gung-ho about the project, thinking the timing was off, until Liu convinced him otherwise: "What he said made a lot of sense and gelled with my own ideas, so I signed. I made some suggestions for improvement, which he told me later he incorporated into the document."[7]

Liu had long prepared to land in prison for this, like Havel for Charter 77. The latter describes how he felt just before publishing it: "If my intuition told me that I was headed for prison . . . it was not merely a premonition of something unknown, but a clear awareness of what it would mean: quiet perseverance and its unavoidable outcome." Those who hear the call of history must carry out its mission of failing and failing again, turning truth into reality with honesty and humility. Havel says:

> I was calm and reconciled to what would follow, and I was certain within myself. None of us know in advance how we will behave in an extreme and unfamiliar situation (I don't know, for example, what I would do if I were physically tortured), but if we are certain at least about how we will respond to situations that are more or less familiar, or at least roughly imaginable, our life is wonderfully simplified. The almost four years in prison that followed my arrest in May 1979 constituted a new and separate stage of my life.[8]

For Liu, this stage would last eleven years.

Compared to their 1977 predecessors, the 2008 chartists grossly underestimated the extent of the government's response and the ruthlessness of its retaliation. Unlike their forebears, they didn't manage to get their ducks in a row by setting up a series of spokespersons first.

The 1977 chartists elected three spokesmen first—ex-communist official Jiří Hájek, philosopher Jan Patočka, and Havel. Then they elected a second and a third round of spokespersons. As soon as one batch was arrested, the next would take its place, ensuring the movement's sustainability.

The 2008 chartists had no such long-range plans. Almost everything stopped with Liu's arrest, and there were no more spokespersons. In fact, some people tried to put one over on the public, for instance, by setting up a Charter 08 discussion forum online on their own and publishing under the charter's name, mostly complimentary of Premier Wen. Yet nothing could be done about it because no policy was in place.

The state wants to stamp out civil society, compress public space, and atomize its subjects. Divide and conquer. Democrats feel segregated, isolated, and powerless. Liu is the mediator and glue that holds three generations of dissidents together.

He got the signatures because of his connections. Not to cast aspersions on the charter, but in a society where who you know matters more than what you know, people back such things mainly because they trust whoever is behind them, and no one more than Liu wields such pull. Most people belong to certain cliques and circles, and Liu is one of the few line-crossers. Friend Chen Jun says, "I know Xiaobo's a good man. His words may come out wrong, and he may make mistakes, but his passion for going after his ideals and bettering himself makes me feel that he has a higher spirit and broader view than most freedom fighters and activists, and that he can do something truly great. He really plays a unique and hard role."

Tiananmen bound Liu and Zhao Ziyang together by fate, their footsteps, though down different paths, echoing each other's. Zhao was placed under house arrest for sixteen years until his death on January 17, 2005. He couldn't even see his secretary and confidant Bao Tong, never mind Liu. He was able to read some of Liu's writings family and friends brought from Hong Kong and was extremely complimentary.

Bao, former director of the Office of Political Reform of the CPC Central Committee, was the highest-ranked official convicted for the Tiananmen protests. Zhao thought Bao went to jail for him and felt guilty. The Lius tried to visit Bao in 1996 when he got out, but he was under surveillance, and the PSB had local police escort the Lius home.

They gave it the old college try and were finally able to get together for tea. Bao and the Lius hit it off and ended up eating, drinking, talking, and commiserating regularly. After Liu's arrest, Bao put out an open letter, "Charter 08: What Is the Offense? Things That Need to Be Said."

In the couple of years that followed, Bao Tong took the place of Bao Zunxin, who had passed, and became something of a father to Liu Xia. They would meet weekly at a set time at Yuyuantan Park or a teahouse nearby until her husband's Nobel award and her own subsequent house arrest. Liu Xia said, "I'm so lucky, old Bao's gone, another old Bao's here, they're both such adorable old men!"

Bao Zunxin was a flag bearer for 1980s intellectual and political movements. After 1989 he was jailed and became jobless and homeless. Liu felt the most for him, almost mollycoddling him like a child. Once at a restaurant, a couple of friends had just sat down to order when Bao, offended by a server, simply got up and left. Liu ran after him, waved down a taxi, and helped him get in.

Meals with friends more often than not turned rowdy. Bao was no longer an intellectual mover and shaker, and Liu was no more a literary dark horse. Now they were both just butts of Liu Xia's jokes. Liu Xia called Bao "Bao-bao" ("purse") and—on Mrs. Bao's order—would snatch the cigarette from his fingers anytime she saw one.

In 2006 Bao suffered a cerebral hemorrhage and was rushed to the hospital. Without insurance, his family couldn't pay the astronomical bill, so Liu started a drive. On an icy afternoon, as Liu delivered the donations to Mrs. Bao, a miracle happened: Bao woke up. Nonetheless, his health had gone downhill. He had throat surgery and couldn't help hacking when he talked, unable to eat and drink like he used to. Liu sat next to him at meals, filling his bowl for him.

Bao died on October 28, 2007. Liu ran himself ragged putting together the memorial. He said that Bao was born an orphan and had a hard-knock life, so he deserved at least a nice send-off. Despite political red tape and police nuisance, the service was held successfully. Historian Yu Ying-shih called Liu from the States and asked him to buy a wreath for the deceased on his behalf, saying he'd mail him a check for it. "The money's nothing," Liu replied. "No need to mail it. Please let me pay for it."

At the service, a friend said to Liu, "You look sloppy as usual and even took your dirty old backpack on stage when you gave your eulogy. You're killing the mood." Liu explained: "I had so many things on my plate, how I was dressed completely slipped my mind. In the backpack were tens of thousands cash for the funeral home. It's everybody's money. I didn't want to lose it, so I kept it on me. The dozen cops outside looked all green-eyed. I couldn't let my guard down."

On the anniversary of Bao's death, Liu and some thirty others held an interment ceremony for his ashes on the outskirts west of Beijing. Liu picked the site, a hill looking out over a vast countryside. They spread out on the grounds, and Liu jumped into the pit, dirt on his skin and clothes and all, looking for the best spot for the ashes. Bao's children handed them to him, and he bowed and laid them down. He climbed out and, tears running down his face, shoveled in the first heap of dirt. Cemetery workers thought he was the deceased's son and looked to him for decisions, and he did not say anything to correct them.

Democrats inside and outside the system are for the most part fire and water, which is more than anything a hindrance to their goals. As an outsider, Liu does not feel superior to those on the inside. He even thinks some of the work they do is more meaningful. As long as both recognize values in common and decry one-party dictatorship, they should learn to coexist and cooperate. Liu sang pioneer party moderate Li Rui's praises for pushing for open political discussions; he railed against the shutdown of China Youth Daily's "Freezing Point" weekly supplement; and he had nothing but good words for the historical research of China through the Ages editor Wu Si, who received PEN's 2005 Freedom to Write Award.

As a result, he made more and more friends inside and out, from scholars to businessmen, from artists to political petitioners to even low-level bureaucrats. Liao Yiwu remembers Liu staying with him often in Chengdu. People would knock on the door in the middle of the night to take Liu out to drink or eat, many of them former Tiananmen protesters who'd gone into civil service or business. They weren't afraid to hang around the controversial figure. Wang Xiaoshan: "Earlier on, folks would say, 'These people are crazy!' and steer clear. You couldn't even get them on the ringer. But people are less afraid now. . . . Brave or not, we're all in the same boat. They'll come for each of us eventually. We knew it before Charter 08. Change is already on the way. Leaders like Liu didn't appear out of thin air. The clouds of revolution have long been gathering."

In the 1980s, Liu ate at fancy restaurants with foreign diplomats, journalists, and scholars. Since the 1990s, entrepreneurs and mercenaries by and large have been taking him to such places. They went to a private club once, tailed by a PSB officer. The manager bounced the officer and wouldn't let him in, even with his badge. The policeman had to stand out in the cold, shivering. Another time the PSBs couldn't afford to order from the expensive menu on their per diem, so they each got a drink and watched Liu and friends eat steak.

Liu's circle got bigger and bigger. A friend invited him to a wedding and introduced him first onstage, with the police right behind him. He went to see some friends in Shanghai; they were trailed by police cars, but the young people weren't afraid and even took pictures of the cars. "People's fear is disappearing, and that's worth noting." A dictatorship is built on fear. Once people stop being afraid, it starts to crumble.

Liu was in his hale fifties and became pivotal for democrats in and out of the system partly because of his age. The other part was his bright personality, energy, and sociability. He clocked in for and put muscle into public works from which he gained little personally—helping political prisoners, collecting donations, writing open letters. By talent and experience, Liu has proved, at least so far, irreplaceable.

SUBVERTING STATE POWER

On December 8, 2008, around 9:00 p.m., police swarmed the downstairs floor of Liu's building. At about 11:00 p.m., a dozen or so charged into his place with a warrant for his arrest on "suspicion of inciting subversion of state power," and took him away.

Right after, they started confiscating things. Eleven officers worked until nine in the morning, taking the Lius' three computers, all mail, and books.

Liu Xia and her lawyer knocked on doors at the Beijing PSB, state council, and NPC. No answer. No one had heard from him. Liu Xiaobo had vanished.

Four months later, the state finally arranged a meeting between Liu Xia and her husband at Xiaotangshan Conference Center north of town. Under the gaze of the police, the couple shared a meal. They met once more. Liu said he had been kept at a secret location in a ten-by-ten windowless room, unable to go out, with nothing to do except answer interrogations. He hadn't read a book or seen the sun in four months.

After being illegally detained for more than half a year, according to Xinhua News Agency, on June 24, 2009, Liu was formally charged for "spreading rumors, slandering and in other ways inciting subversion of the government and overturning the socialist system," violating article 105 of the PRC's penal code.

Liu Xia was also notified that morning her husband had been held at the Beijing No. 1 Detention Center since 11:00 a.m. on June 23.

Only then could Liu Xiaobo speak to a lawyer. First, he asked whether anyone else was arrested for the charter. He was relieved to hear no. But the reason the government didn't go after the first 303 or the tens of thousands of eventual signers wasn't mercy. Society had changed; there were practical limitations. It wasn't that the government wouldn't, only that it couldn't.

When Liu saw his wife, he specifically requested Mo Shaoping, who defended Shi Tao in the Yahoo case, as counsel. The state wasn't happy. On June 25 Mo and two colleagues paid the PSB a visit. The police told them: "Mr. Mo, your name came up in Liu Xiaobo's files. You may be implicated in the case, so you can't represent him." Mo replied: "The issue of who has the right to approve or deny an accused's attorney, if it's the police, procurator, or judge, is unclear under current Chinese law, but in principle it should be the judge, not the police. To be sure, if you still think I'm unfit to be Mr. Liu's lawyer, then I'll need an official writ, clearly stating why." The police were up a tree; they didn't have anything. Mo kept at it: "Until the procurator or judge implicates me, I have the right to defend the accused."

But to get Liu on board as soon as possible, Mo handed the case to two associates, Shang Baojun and Ding Xikui, who registered June 25 and saw Liu June 26. Shang told the media: "Liu Xiaobo appeared to be in good physical and mental health. We asked whether he had been interrogated or tortured. He said things were more civilized now than in 1996. The longest interrogation lasted just four hours."

Liu also had something to say about the charges. Shang explained:

He does not contest the facts of the case, that is, his involvement with Charter 08 and the twenty-some articles he published online between 2001 and 2008. However, he maintains these acts are constitutional under the Constitution of the People's Republic of China, which gives Chinese citizens freedom of speech, and he also maintains he does so as a patriot without subversive intent. If there is disagreement about the content of these writings, Mr. Liu remains open to discussion and debate. Disagreement is not a crime.

After being held up another six months, Liu was tried on the deadline of December 23, 2009, in Beijing's First Intermediate People's Court at 16 Shijingshan Road, Shijingshan District, escorted by eight police cars.

On the stand Liu offered the following defense: "I am opposing dictatorship and monopoly. I am not 'inciting subversion of state power.' Opposition is not subversion." He underscored the importance of freedom of speech: "A state cannot establish legitimacy by suppressing dissenting opinions. It cannot ensure peace and longevity by censorship." He called for China to end censorship: "Only when we root out censorship systematically will the phrase 'freedom of speech' in the Constitution have any meaning for the people, and only when the people's freedom of speech is systematically protected will censorship be a relic of the past."

Liu Xia and many of Liu's friends were under house arrest that day. Only Liu Xia's younger brother and Liu Xiaobo's younger brother, Liu Xiaohui, were in the gallery. The state had tricked Liu Xia a few months before: police invited her to tea, asked her seemingly harmless questions, and had her sign something. Liu Xia later found out it was her husband's interrogation proceedings, so she became a "witness" under police "protection" and couldn't attend trial.

Representatives from American, Canadian, Australian, and fifteen EU embassies rushed to the courthouse but were all turned away. Ambassadors stood outside reading their own countries' statements.

Journalist Du Bin described the scene: police tape cordoned off the courthouse surrounded by stationary guards, with patrols on transceivers nabbing anyone who looked like a petitioner and hauling them off to Majialou jail. Foreign reporters were rounded up inside the tape.

Still, everyday citizens showed up for support. Lei, forty-eight, was a signer and took the train 1,200 miles from Jiangxi to Beijing. "I'm a card-carrying member of PEN just like Liu Xiaobo. Was in the barracks. Decorated. Switched tracks. Laid off. Quit the CPC. Pink-slipped the red party. Charter 08 promotes democracy and rule of law. It doesn't subvert state power. Are ordinary folks making suggestions overthrowing the government?"

Song, another signer and a Christian from Beijing's Pinggu District, snuck past his guard and took a taxi there at 5:00 a.m. Clothes covered in slogans, he was helping get the word out on jailed petitioners. In front of three policemen watching him like hawks on the other side of the steel fence, he yelled: "No to tyranny! Long live democracy! Long live freedom! Long live Liu Xiaobo!" He made an obscene gesture at the judge, who didn't dare arrest him on camera. A marshal charged out, camera in hand, taking his picture. The man fixed his hair, straightened his collar, and smiled at the photographer: "Ay-ay-ay, thank you for all the trouble you've taken, brother. Please take a few more. That way I'll have a place to eat and sleep for good. Thanks for all your hard work, brother!" The marshal clicked the shutter a few times and then went back in.

University students turned up bearing yellow ribbons for supporters and calling for Liu's acquittal. Shanghai forced eviction petitioner and charter signer, forty-six-year-old Tong Guojing, wore a ribbon on his chest, threw his arms up, and shouted: "Long live democracy! Long live freedom! Long live Liu Xiaobo! Let Liu Xiaobo go!"

Reporters and diplomats waited outside for the verdict with bated breath. At 12:30 p.m., a judge came out. Smiling at the reporters, he said, "The trial has ended. Liu's family and attorneys have left through the back door." "When's the verdict?" The judge smiled. "To be determined." Someone asked: "What's your name?" The judge grinned, turned, and left without saying another word.

On Christmas 2009, the court handed down its decision. Liu Xia was allowed at the hearing at counsel's insistence.

"Beijing Municipal No. 1 Intermediate People's Court Criminal Verdict: (2009) First Intermediate Court—Criminal Case—First Instance—No 3901" states:

> Beijing Municipal People's Procuratorate Branch No. 1 charges the defendant, Liu Xiaobo, with the crime of inciting subversion of state power; on December 10, 2009, the indictment was tendered to this court for prosecution. This court assembled a collegiate bench of

judges in accordance with the law, and heard the case in open court. Beijing Municipal People's Procuratorate Branch No. 1 assigned procurator Zhang Rongge and deputy procurator Pan Xueqing to appear in court to support the public prosecution. The defendant, Liu Xiaobo, and his counsel, Ding Xikui and Shang Baojun, appeared in court to participate in the proceedings. The trial has concluded.

[T]his court hereby sentences him according to stipulations of the Criminal Law of the People's Republic of China, Article 105 (2); Article 55 (1); Article 56 (1); and Article 64, as follows:

1. Defendant Liu Xiaobo has committed the crime of inciting subversion of state power. He is sentenced to a fixed-term imprisonment of eleven years and to two years' deprivation of political rights.

2. All items used by Liu Xiaobo to commit the crime, which had been delivered with this case, shall be confiscated.

Presiding Judge: Jia Lianchun
Deputy Judge: Zheng Wenwei
Deputy Judge: Zhai Changxi

Charter 08 clocks in at a mere 4,024 words—divided by eleven, 365. In other words, a day per word.

It was a case of classic absurd trampling of due process by the Chinese government. Judge Jia limited the defense duration to that of the prosecution. The prosecution read for fourteen minutes, so the defense had fourteen minutes to rebut. Liu couldn't read all of his prepared statement. The defense attorney objected that the time limit was without precedent or merit. Jia responded, "It's my court. Whatever I say goes."

December 28 was Liu's birthday. He met with the two lawyers at 2:00 p.m. They read him a poem Liu Xia wrote, "Untitled." It was the best birthday present he received. The detention center head came to see him as well, with a pot of braised pork.

At first Liu asked: "If I don't appeal, does this mean I don't recognize the legitimacy of the verdict?" In the lawyers' view, even if it offered little hope, they should follow the process through, if only as a testament to history and the Chinese legal system. Liu changed his mind and chose to file.

On February 9, 2010, Beijing Municipal High People's Court rejected the appeal:

The People's Court of First Instance made its judgment according to the facts, nature, and circumstances of Liu Xiaobo's crime as well as the extent of its harm to society. The conviction and application of the law are correct; the penalty and disposal of the items related to the case are appropriate; the trial procedure is lawful; and they should be upheld. On these grounds, in accordance with the stipulations of Article 189 (1) of the *Criminal Procedure Law of the People's Republic of China*, this court rules as follows:

Liu Xiaobo's appeal is overruled and the original judgment is affirmed.

This ruling is the final verdict.

Presiding Judge: Zhao Junhuai

Deputy Judge: Lin Bingbing

Deputy Judge: Liu Donghui

The hearing was even shorter this time—ten minutes. No one spoke except the judge reading the decision and Liu Xiaobo, who said, loudly, just three words: "I am innocent."

The room was small. According to Xinhua News, the Liu family and other public figures were present. Liu's lawyers pointed out that the near thirty in the gallery, other than Liu Xia and Liu Xiaohui, were all strangers, extras planted for show. A dozen diplomats were also barred from entry.

As the verdict said, it was final. The lawyers did everything they could to defend their client.

Liu told them, "I believe what I do is just. China will be a democracy. It will be free one day. Everyone will be able to live under the sun without fear. For this I'll pay. But it's worth it. In a dictatorship, prison is the first door to freedom. My foot has already crossed the threshold. Freedom can't be far off."

✿ ✿ ✿

On this side of the threshold, the police, prosecutors, and judges remain shackled. Next to Liu, they're unfree. Liu might have been judged in a court of law, but they will be judged in the court of history.

Patočka believed totalitarianism produces devolved human beings who voluntarily or involuntarily give up their conscience. A person is reduced to a role, an individual cog in the machine. He is dehumanized.

Milan Šimečka in *The Restoration of Order* wrote about friend and writer Ladislav K's trial: "I was fascinated by the judge. As soon as I set eyes on him, I recognized with despair the features of a person just doing their job, one for whom the idea of justice had no wider significance."

Does "I have no choice" excuse these running dogs? How are they responsible? Zhenmingwang BBS owner and literary critic Wu Hongsen thinks: "A man is sent to jail for eleven years for speaking his mind, and all I hear are abstract complaints. Not a word has been said about the actual culprits, judges Jia Lianchun, Zheng Wenwei, Zhai Changxi (and of course Zhao Junhuai, Lin Bingbing, Liu Donghui). That's not right."

In a system without separation of powers and checks and balances, the ultimate decider in Liu's case was not the judges but the Central Politburo, that is, the top dogs. Something this big had to pass through the Standing Committee's hands, under Hu Jintao's own eyes. From Liu's 2008 detention to June 2009 arrest, to the December 2009 verdict and 2010 appeal overturn, the calvary and debacle lasted well over a year.

Just after the verdict, Liu Xia saw her husband in a chamber off the courtroom. Despite it all, he seemed to be in good spirits. They talked and laughed for twenty minutes, mostly about home matters, nothing in particular. "In the room, there's a large table between us. I asked if I could give him a hug. I embraced him deeply. He'd lost a lot of weight." The embrace was the beginning of a separation. "A hug—who could ask for anything more? Down the line, the only thing we can hold is a phone across a glass partition, unable to touch each other, for the next eleven years."

On May 24, 2010, Liu was finally transferred from the detention center in Beijing to Jinzhou Prison in Liaoning. The decision took longer than usual; the state was scratching its head about where to send him. Beijing was ground zero for embassies and media, with all eyes on Liu. Dalian was no better. So the state broke its own laws and sent him out of jurisdiction to Jinzhou, where it had also sent Tiananmen student leader Wang Dan in 1996.

Jinzhou Prison at 86 Nanshan Road, Taihe District, Jinzhou, is the provincial prison of and one of the biggest in Liaoning Province. It had been used to house Japanese POWs after World War II. The facilities are nothing to write home about but not terrible, either. It is now primarily for those sentenced to ten years or more. It also runs two factories, Jinzhou Jinkai Electrical Group and Jinzhou Switch Factory, and is in the charge of Ma Zhenfeng.

The administration didn't tell Liu Xia about the transfer until May 30. Three days later she got her first right of visit, bringing food, clothes, and books. In a reception room, they had thirty minutes and did not have to talk through glass. Liu said he had an hour of yard time every morning. A political prisoner, he didn't have to labor. He got along with his five cellmates. Life was routine. He felt fine.

Liu's arrest and incarceration drew heavy popular fire. Hundreds of Charter 08 signers scored a letter, "We Cannot Be Separated from Liu Xiaobo," stating: "We share ideas and ideals. The bond between Liu Xiaobo and us cannot be broken. The Charter is our soul. We are its flesh. We are a whole. You hurt one of us, you hurt all of us. If one of us isn't free, none of us are."

Even veteran party moderates, including *People's Daily* editor Hu Jiwei, former Xinhua deputy director Li Pu, senior Xinhua reporter Dai Huang, NPC delegate Chang Wanli's former secretary Wu Xiang, and honorary CASS member He Fang, wrote a series of open letters. They might not see eye to eye with Liu but questioned how his case was handled and asked that it be reopened.

Liu's fate didn't scare off his supporters. Instead, a whole country is now waking up. More people know about Liu Xiaobo and his cause than ever. Tens of thousands voted for him online as one of the 2010 *TIME* 100. During the trial, the Chinese blogosphere started a yellow ribbon campaign. Statements like "Please sign and support Liu Xiaobo: *He and I, we all stand together*" abounded.

Twitter was littered with yellow ribbons and head shots of Liu. Thanks to young people, democracy was no longer just a political phenomenon but a cultural and artistic one as well. Sixteen- and seventeen-year-old high schoolers, college students, and young urban professionals googled "Liu Xiaobo," "Tiananmen," and "Charter 08" as never before.

Reactions rippled across the pond as well. Amnesty International, Human Rights Watch, Reporters Without Borders, and PEN International clamored for Liu's release.

Protesters in Hong Kong surrounded the Liaison Office of the Central People's Government, burst through the police into the courtyard, and hung yellow ribbons on the front façade. Former bishop of Hong Kong Cardinal Joseph Zen said Liu "spoke the truth with peace and conscience." Dozens of Hong Kong youths and twentysomethings who signed the charter "turned themselves in" in Shenzhen, wanting to do time with him. The HK Alliance, Professional Teachers' Union, Journalists Association, and China Human Rights Lawyers Concern Group distributed sixty thousand postcards for residents to write on and sign and mailed them to Liu in prison.

In Taiwan, Academia Sinica professor Sechin YS Chien, filmmaker Hou Hsiao-hsien, writers Chu Tien-wen and Chu Tien-hsin, and thirty-seven others asked jointly: Do Chinese citizens have the right to express difference of opinion with regard to form of government? Do they have the right to criticize the method of governance by those in power? National Tsing Hua University sociology professor Ding-Tzann Lii pointed out this was not just for Liu; it would also bridge two peoples and extend support on the mainland for Taiwan.

The European Association for Chinese Studies, made up of more than eight hundred researchers from thirty-six countries, also sent a letter to Hu Jintao: "If the problems and suggestions for their solution as they are outlined in Charter 08 are criminalized instead of discussed, they could in the long run impede the healthy development of the country. . . . We urge you, your Excellency, to reconsider the official position of the highest leadership of the People's Republic of China in this matter, and to use all your authority to ensure that Liu Xiaobo's case will be reconsidered and he will be released."

On March 10, 2010, more than 150 scholars, writers, lawyers, and advocates from around the world wrote a letter to NPC chairman Wu Bangguo: "We believe that Dr. Liu was arrested solely for exercising his right to freedom of expression, as guaranteed under China's constitution and by international law. We believe further that the crime of incitement to subvert state power as currently defined in Chinese law violates international human rights standards." Calling on the Congress as the highest organ of state power in China, the undersigned urged Liu's immediate and unconditional release and included Salman Rushdie, fellow Nobel laureate Nadine Gordimer, and others.

"I HAVE NO ENEMIES"

Liu's last words in court were: "I say again today what I said in the 'June 2 Hunger Strike Declaration' twenty years ago: I have no hatred, I have no enemies."

This created backlash at home and abroad.

Those brutalized in prison couldn't abide by descriptions of some of his more positive experiences there. It was inappropriate, they said, to laud the Chinese court and prison system for its antlike steps forward while advocates and activists were still being tortured. Wasn't puckering up when he should be speaking out proof that Liu was thinking of nothing but saving his own skin?

Liu's statement needs to be put in context.

He was describing only what he personally went through and saw. The place where he was detained in Beijing was a model center open to the United Nations and foreign legal delegates. It was hardly the norm. Liu simply testified to what he witnessed. He never lied or sugarcoated anything.

There was another reason not to be harsh. Liu had hoped some goodwill would persuade administrators to let him serve in Beijing, closer to his wife. Eleven years of long-distance travel would be too much for frail Liu Xia. The man was not made of stone. It was certainly understandable. Beijing turned him down, of course.

In addition, he never denied others were maltreated, even tortured. A friend asked why he didn't write a prison memoir, common for political prisoners of some notoriety. "Because I'm kind of an outlier," he responded plainly. He wrote Liao Yiwu:

> My three stints pale next to your four years. I had a room to myself in Qincheng; other than the dead silence and solitude at times, I had it much better than you. My treatment in the compound at the foot of Xiangshan hill was even more swell; besides freedom, I had pretty much everything. I was housed alone again in the Dalian camp. Having undergone the "royal treatment," I wouldn't be able to live through what you lived through. I'm embarrassed to even say I went to prison three times.

He added: "I know many Tiananmeners got longer, harsher sentences than me, and their lives under lock and key are mostly unimagin-

able. . . . Words can't describe my shame. For the dead, for those
suffering and unnamed, I live. Everything passes, but the blood and
tears of the innocent will forever be a rock in my heart. Heavy, cold,
and sharp."

When news of Gao Zhisheng, Teng Biao, and Li Heping being beat-
en and tortured broke, Liu immediately wrote in support of these Weiquan Lawyers. Whenever Falun Gong and underground "home
church" members were abused and arrested, Liu was without exception
one of the first to speak out against the perpetrators.

The most common question people, from exile Cao Changqing to
artist Ai Weiwei, ask him is: you're in jail, you're obviously an enemy to
them, but you say you have no enemies. Aren't you just lying to yourself?

Writer Yi Ping has this to say:

> To understand what Liu Xiaobo means by "I have no enemies," you
> have to understand his non-violent, non-antagonistic, non-hateful
> stance. It's an epigram of principles he's long put into practice. . . . In
> face of a savage, vicious regime, he's pushed for peaceful transforma-
> tion headed by reason. He at once puts his faith in the people and
> warns the resistance they'll need extraordinary courage through
> these trials and tribulations to hold on to their compassion, dignity,
> and generosity. In a moment of terror and despair, "I have no ene-
> mies" simply states again the belief Liu Xiaobo's held for twenty
> years.[9]

Already on "Our Demand: Free Speech in Classrooms," the first
poster he tacked on the bulletin boards in 1989, he wrote: "The first
step toward democracy in China is getting rid of 'enemy-think.' There
are no enemies in a democracy, only a balance of interests. . . . Democracy fighters, don't let hatred poison your wisdom." Further, from the
June 2 declaration: "We're striking and calling for the Chinese people
over time to give up anti-this-anti-that and eye-for-an-eye ways of thinking. No more politics based on class struggles. Hate only begets hate;
tyranny only engenders tyranny. The new China will be founded on the
tolerant and cooperative spirit of democracy." The statement truly
transcends history and in fact rings truer today.

"I have no enemies" is a profoundly religious, especially Christian,
sentiment. The teachings of Christianity have had a deep impact on Liu

since the mid-1980s. It was just the shot in the arm a corrupt and decaying society needed. "The tragedy of China is the tragedy of being without a God."[10] Time and again he found Christ's footprints across the history of Western thought. "In faith is transcendence, in repentance loyalty. Heaven reveals people's weaknesses to them. Selflessness and self-correction are Christianity's gift to the world. . . . Modern Westerners' desire to do their duty, to rise above their lot, to constantly reevaluate themselves all flows from their Christian bloodline."[11] The last book Liu wrote in 1989 was called *Walking Naked toward God*. Copies were confiscated and destroyed before ever seeing the light of day.

In 1989, Liu said a number of times he was hunger-striking "for God." "St Augustine's *Confessions* was one of my favorites. I read and reread it. My impulse to follow in the footsteps of saints became a conscious yearning for faith."[12] But he was still a way from the cross. Barmé notes many Chinese cultural martyrs "were men and women who were willing to be crucified only if they could survive the process and eventually alight from the cross of persecution to enjoy the benefits of those who had played brinkmanship with the devil."

For Liu, an awareness of a higher power stems man's bent toward self-aggrandizement and denial of his own limits. "I believe when people are contrite and want to atone for the wrongs they have inflicted on others, they are at their most sincere, pure, passionate, and alive." The Chinese, on the other hand, find contentment mostly in what is, not what may come. They are happy with a roof over their head, clothes on their back, and food in their bowl. They have no need for God, forgiveness, or salvation.[13]

On February 26, 2010, Liu met with lawyer Shang Baojun at the detention center, during which he explained his no-enemies stance more. First, it's not that *he* has no enemies. The emphasis is not on him as an individual. All of humanity should have no enemies. Only then can hate be eradicated, the cycle of violence broken, and history pushed forward. Second, in his experience, particularly from 1989 to 1991 and 1996 to 1999, courts and prisons have treated their charges better and become better managed. Again, he is speaking from only his own experience and not claiming to speak for others. Finally, no matter the judgment, he maintains his innocence, from beginning to end.

One more thing, he said. He would like to thank Romanian-born German writer and 2009 Nobel Literature Prize winner Herta Müller if he could. He'd happened to read about Müller in *Beijing Daily* at the detention center one day and felt an immediate kinship with her.

What he didn't know was that Müller was a staunch supporter for his Nobel Peace Prize nomination. Under the Ceaușescu regime, she knew perhaps more than anyone the kinds of difficulties and suffering Liu was going through and the conviction it took to come out of them with one's head high. On March 26, 2011, Müller published "Solidarity with Nobel Prize Laureate Liu Xiaobo: When the Other Shoe Dropped" in the *Frankfurter Allgemeine Zeitung*. The reference was to Liu Xia's description of husband and wife's life together. Liu Xia hadn't slept well in a long time. She was always waiting for the other shoe to drop. With Liu Xiaobo's arrest, the second shoe hit the floor. She could at last close her eyes in peace.

Müller believes there are two kinds of freedom fighters—those suffering from an overinflated ego, and those plagued by self-doubt— which are mutually exclusive, for the most part. But Liu is both. A human being, flesh and blood, full of contradictions. "I try to imagine: Xiaobo so lonely and anxious, pacing barefoot in his head thousands of times, from one temple to the other."

"How far is 'I have no enemies' from 'three hundred years of being colonized,' and how do we measure it?" scholar Su Xiaokang asks. "It's the distance between culture and politics; between Nietzsche and Gandhi; between rebelliousness, hubris, and Narcissus' scorn, and reflection, humility, and Orpheus' sacrifice."[14] The world is learning only when we turn the other cheek can justice and reconciliation prevail. "I have no enemies" may still be only an echo in China's vast, empty valley, but like Tang poet Du Fu says, spring rain always follows the wind secretly into the night, and moistens all things, softly, without sound.

7

LIU XIA

EAT DRINK MAN WOMAN

Liu Xiaobo and Liu Xia met in the mid-1980s.

They had their own families. It was a love of poetry and literature, particularly Kafka and Dostoyevsky, that brought them closer as friends. They ran into each other often in the same circles.

Xia worked at the State Administration of Taxation (SAT), a plush job. She was given a two-bedroom house near Shuangyushu in Haidian, then a rare commodity for young people. Even as a lecturer, Xiaobo had to resort to sponge-style living. Xia's tiny abode became a popular salon in Beijing at the time.

She remembers: "We all ate at the Bank of China cafeteria. I met a friend of his from college, Zou Jin, first. He wrote poetry, too. Friends were made in that cafeteria. Wang Xiaoni was one. Xiaobo as well. I was the only one with a house, so they all liked to hang out, eating, drinking, shooting the breeze. He really, really liked my poems, and my food." Connected at the bank, she often smuggled people into the cafeteria. Intellectuals lived on pocketfuls of change, and freeloading off your rich friends was pro forma—not just accepted, but encouraged. It was the Last Supper of a planned economy.

Poets were the public's darlings. Liao Yiwu recalls liking Xia's work in *Star Poetry Monthly* and writing her. They got to know each other, and through Xia, Liao met other writers and critics. Everyone agreed Xia wrote the best poetry. Xiaobo joined in the fun, too, sometimes, but people made fun of his poems for being too crude. Ever the contrarian, Xiaobo shot back.

Xia was married to writer and editor Wu Bin. Once they fought, and she set off for Tibet by herself. Passing by Liao's in Fuling, Sichuan, she crashed a few days with him and his wife. Xia drank and smoked. A half-liter of liquor a sitting was nothing; neither was eating Sichuan hotpots every day. It was as if she came straight out of the American Beats. In mid-eighties small-town China, that was something to behold.

After the 1989 movement, she and her husband toured Sichuan again. Their marriage was on the rocks. Liao was writing "Massacre" and planning a film, *Requiem*, to commemorate Tiananmen. On intuition, Xia warned him: "Hey, Beard (Liao had a beard then), you're in deep. Better get outta Dodge, quick." She even helped him map out an escape, introducing him to people in Shenzhen so that he could hop over to Hong Kong. Before the plan could materialize, however, Liao was arrested.

During the planning phase, they brought up a mutual friend, Xiaobo, who was in prison. Xia said the square was helter-skelter before June 4 and she couldn't get near Xiaobo. She stuck her neck out like a giraffe; amid throngs of bodies, a tiny, blurry figure came into view. She later wrote: "I didn't get a chance to say a word to you / You turned into pages of newspaper and television screens lining the side of the street / Looking up at you with everyone else / I felt tired / So I pulled out of the crowd / Lit a cigarette and / Looked at the sky."[1]

❁ ❁ ❁

With fame came fans, and pretty young girls swarmed Xiaobo like bees to honey at the end of the 1980s. And far be it from him to say no. Student movement leader Zhang Boli remembers the first time he saw Liu: May 3, 1989, BU Dorm 28. They were talking about the May Fourth Declaration. Liu wanted to meet all the student leaders. That was the first time. On his heels was a woman dressed to the nines.[2] Xiaobo later admitted to fooling around with foreign reporters and other women at the square.

He wasn't the only one. Imagine: in eighties China, poetry and literature were an aphrodisiac. Xiaobo loved talking about sex and women. It was a way to challenge tradition and seek freedom. Old friend Meng

Taoer knew this. She writes: "In New York, in Hawaii, in Europe, the philandering rumors spread. He had a thing for white women. . . . I saw someone yearning for a greater civilization, whose soul wanted to break free of its body. It's a pain only the Chinese, and peoples long cut off from the rest of the world, could understand."[3] Against the sexually repressive Mao regime, Chinese dissidents believed that to liberate the soul, one had to liberate the body first.

Meanwhile, a pair of eyes quietly fixed their gaze on his back. He said, "Before, I had an urge. I wanted to uncover, unearth all kinds of beauty, from hundreds, thousands of women." His appetite was insatiable, his thirst quenchless. Then he met Xia. He continued: "Now I have all the beauty I need in one woman." Eighties Xiaobo was "afraid to burden lovely girls with his affection" (a line by May Fourth poet Yu Dafu), whereas Xiaobo from the nineties on was more like C. S. Lewis in *Lenten Lands*, who "had built happiness from the ashes of a promise."

When they met again in the early nineties, Xiaobo's marriage was over, and he'd just gotten out of prison without a dime to his name. Xia had divorced as well. Democracy movement backer, Stone CEO Wan Runnan: "When Liu Xiaobo and Tao Li broke up, I blamed him at first. I'd subconsciously come to see Tao as family. Then I read some of his poems to Liu Xia and began to change my mind. Who knows? With these things it's always hard to say."[4]

Xia has a story: "In 1996, when I came back from the States after a month, he picked me up at the airport. He had a bundle of flowers in his hand. My flight must have been late, and he must have stood there for a long time, because the flower stems were all wilted from his grip. I still remember how they felt. When we got home, there were flowers everywhere. I thought I'd stumbled into a flower market."

Xia is a blue blood. Her father is a Bank of China (BOC) proxy and was party secretary of the Central University of Finance and Economics. Both her parents, like Xiaobo's, had been diehard Maoists. Once when she was little, her father brought back a flowered skirt from an assignment in Hong Kong. But her mother stowed it away in a box. Young Xia cried all night.

She told Xiaobo stories about her grandfather. Grandpa read at BNU (then known as Beijing Advanced Normal School), took part in May Fourth, and was one of the students arrested. During the republic, he was a county head and started farms and schools. After 1949, he was branded a counterrevolutionary and died in prison in the early 1950s. He had four daughters and a son who almost never talked to their father or to their kids about their grandfather.

Xia was extremely smart but hated school and gained admission to a junior college. On graduation, she worked at the SAT and China Financial Publishing House, though she wasn't cut out for civil servant desk jobs others would kill for, and so she quit. Money can buy freedom, but without freedom, money is worthless. Nothing scares Xia more than money and numbers. With Xiaobo around, she always leaves her wallet at home.

Her parents supported their relationship. Moderates now, they took an immediate liking to the frank and sincere young fellow, treating him like a son. Xiaobo hung out with and was closer to Xia's little brother Hui than his own brothers. They were the family he never had.

Xia's parents joked, "All our kids hated school, but our daughter managed to bring home a PhD—and the most famous literary PhD in China at that. We couldn't be prouder."

In winter 2008, Xia's family moved to the suburbs and let their daughter and son-in-law move into their two-thousand-square-foot house. The apartment is on prime real estate, north of the Central Military Commission, on the fifth floor of a small high-rise with a penthouse overlooking Yuyuantan Park. On a clear spring day you can see falling cherry blossoms and ripples in Yuyuan Lake.

At last, Xiaobo had a study big enough for all his books. But he never lived or worked a day in this house.

He was in prison when renovations began. Xia took the project on. Before, she would've left it to Xiaobo.

Now she had to do it all.

❀ ❀ ❀

Xiaobo is definitely enamored with Xia's talent in the kitchen. Her specialty is Western cooking, and Xiaobo happens to be one of the rare Easterners who truly prefer fare from the other hemisphere. From cioppino to foie gras, he gobbled it all up; from Ukrainian borscht to London broil, he wolfed it all down. Even for McDonald's and the

Colonel, "I get a craving at least once a week." Talk about complete Westernization.

Xia's pantry is chock full of rare and exotic ingredients—at least to the average Chinese palate. To stock up, she travels halfway around Beijing, her head a veritable map of international grocers in the city. She can rattle off an encyclopedia about each unique, treasured component of her concoctions.

Xia cooked a lot, putting on spread after spread, night after night, making use of wines, cheeses, salamis, pâtés, and other booties comrades pillaged for them abroad. Xiaobo almost never set foot in the kitchen, his specialty being mostly "stews" of his own creation.

Under a dictatorship, life was loving, cozy, grounded.

Xiaobo's mantra is: the love of food is the love of life. He ate with friends. Eats were more important than eateries, and he was as much at home at lavish banquets as at no-frills holes in the wall. There is a rundown greased-out mom-and-pop shop, Chongqing Chicken, about three hundred square feet, near Jiangzhaikou, serving up the best shredded chicken over cold noodles, tripe salad, and braised rooster in town. Xiaobo was a regular there, and he never left without the leftovers.

Their favorite was friend Zhou Zhongling's Sichuan spot Shizhongtang in southeast Haidian, backed by Bao Zunxin and the Lius themselves, specializing in hotpots—chicken, tripe, frog—a destination for the city's heat seekers, Xiaobo included. Bao wrote most of the calligraphy on the walls. The twice-cooked pork and Mapo tofu at Jinshancheng by Xiaobo's were standbys.

Liu is also a fan of fine Huaiyang cuisine. The Lius often took Ding Zilin and Jiang Peikun to West Lake for liver stir-fry, braised duck, and kalimeris with dried tofu. The well-known Xinkaiyuan on West Fourth Ring and Zhangshengji on North Third were old haunts. You can write a foodie's guide to Beijing with the Lius' dining tabs. It's a miracle, probably because he drank so much tea, that he didn't fall prey to high blood pressure, high cholesterol, or diabetes.

Reporter Gao Yu remembers a friend from Hong Kong taking them out once, and Gao was in charge of the menu. She was trying to tally the tab in her head while ordering; everyone was chatting, and no one paid her any attention, except Xiaobo, who kept shouting: "Crabs! Crabs!" at her, beseeching her with longing eyes. Gao thought: "A crab per head, they'll probably be washing dishes a while after the check comes," so she ordered a stir-fry and told the server to throw in a couple of crabs. Xiaobo didn't drink. Either words were coming out of his mouth or food was going in. "Once the chow-down began he wasn't picky—claws or flippers, it didn't matter. A pair of turnip oyster buns went right down the gullet. If he could eat it, he ate it, no ifs, ands, or buts. He had a thing for seafood, a true coast-born and bred 'erster,' as we call it. A real ladies' man—if you catch my drift."[5]

Xiaobo and Xia could be seen together at most tables around town. Xiaobo's table manners were nonexistent. If he were a raptor, Xia, by contrast, nibbled like a graceful swan. Xiaobo downed his meals with soda, and it had to be Coca-Cola. Xia was an oenophile, especially of reds.

He only ever ate out without her when she was sick. If he came across something good, he'd whip out his phone: "This is really good! I'm gonna have them wrap it up for you." Then he'd turn to the host, point to the dish, and say, "One more round, okay? I'm going to take it home to Xia." What he wanted, he asked for. He never put on airs.

Xia is proud of her culinary skills. She says her poems are better than her stories, her paintings are better than her poems, her photos are better than her paintings, and her food is better than her photos. After her husband's arrest, she said, "What I miss most every day is going to the grocery store and asking what he liked to eat." His reply, of course: meat, meat, meat. In prison, meat is scarce. Xia said quietly, "When he's gone, my career as a chef is over as well."

"I WANT TO MARRY THAT ENEMY OF THE STATE!"

When Xia chose Xiaobo, she also gave up a normal life.

On May 18, 1995, Xiaobo was arrested and held by the Beijing PSB at a secret location in the city's Western Hills for eight months because of an open letter he cowrote on the sixth anniversary of Tiananmen. Xia was allowed to visit twice a month with food and books. They weren't married then.

Xiaobo was taken from home the morning of October 8, 1996. Three years of reeducation through labor followed. He wrote her:

The sun was so bright that morning. It seemed so strange, eerie, to someone like me used to staying up all night and getting out of bed past noon. In this unexpected blankness, a hand at the door knocked us out of our dreams. Two familiar policemen stood at the threshold. You knew the moment would come. You thought about it, went over it back and forth, whirled it around in your mind like a marble. But it still shattered your day to bits. The pain prevented me from lifting my arm and waving goodbye to you. And so I can only wait, numbed by time.[6]

He was sent to the Dalian labor camp. Because they weren't married, the administration prevented Xiaobo and Xia from seeing each other. For the first half of the three years, she could only take food, books, and sundries to him through guards.

Not only did administrators fail to break them up, they helped cement the lovers' decision to get married. Xia filed an application. "I want to marry that enemy of the state!" she said.

Marriage is a human right, and the right to marry is in the Chinese Constitution and guaranteed by law. Still, hurdles remained for someone like Xiaobo. A friend introduced them to Tao Siliang, who was finally able to help them cut through the red tape. Tao's father, Tao Zhu, was number four after Mao, Lin, and Zhou, but she herself was progressive, sympathized with student protesters in 1989, and was relieved of her position as deputy head of the Sixth Work Session of the National United Front. Tao has deep roots in the system and is currently vice president of the China Association of Mayors.

They got their marriage certificate at the camp. A photographer had been arranged; the ceremony was under way—except that the shutter stopped working. "This has never happened before," the photographer kept pressing and pressing it, beads of sweat running down his forehead. Fortunately, Xia had brought their individual photos and decided at the last minute to paste them together on the certificate for the state's stamp. Lucky or not, they were now husband and wife, with probably the only "collage" marriage certificate in the history of matrimony.

Time for a celebratory lunch—a couple of dishes from the cafeteria. It was the best meal they ever had. It was the only meal they ever had together in three years. Watching her husband scarf down the food, Xia felt sad. She tried to smile.

Afterwards, she went home, and he went back to his cell. Later they would tell the story of their "wedding" calmly and with humor, like they were talking about someone else. Xia smiled: "Once we were married, I could see him legally."

She'd also gotten into the habit during that time of writing and putting up a postcard on her walls every day. In three years, her house was plastered with more than a thousand postcards, each a missive of her love for Xiaobo.

She wanted to renovate the house before he came home, but she'd just quit her job and didn't have any savings, and she didn't want to ask her family for money. So she went to Zhou Zhongling, who lent her the money for the work.

Xiaobo never took her for granted. Since the 1990s, responsibility and family have been front and center in his thought and action. He regretted: "In the past I rarely cared about concrete, living human beings around me. My head was in the clouds, searching for justice, human rights, freedom. I looked down on my family's fear for my safety as mundane and cowardly." He asked himself: How was he any different from the communists?

He found the answer the hard way when his first marriage broke up and when he talked with Tiananmen victims' families. Ding Zilin remembers the first time she saw Xia. It was New Year's Eve 1999. Xiaobo had just been released. Ding and Jiang recall a simple, slight wisp of a figure, "sitting next to Xiaobo, listening to us talk, smiling, laughing softly at times. Her hair was then down to her ears. Not yet forty. But with a few twinklings of gray already." They hit it off, and Ding and Jiang treated her like a daughter. "We thought, a single, vulnerable woman, trekking from Beijing to Dalian and back, month after month, year after year—it must've taken a superhuman will and strength. Our hearts went out to her. Fate brought us together."[7]

From Xiaobo's side: "Before I left, Professor Ding kept saying to me, take good care of Xia, don't be thoughtless and abandon her in an invisible prison. That hit home with me. They really care about us. Being family to a political prisoner is harder than being a political prisoner. I think Professor Ding worries about Xia more than me because she knows what it's like to lose someone you love. In a society without conscience run by a government without limit, it's the families of those who fight that suffer—the possibility of being separated at any moment, the surveillance and lack of privacy, the pressure all around you to become indifferent, to forget."[8]

What Xiaobo wants most in life is not a prize. It's not even democracy. It's time, to spend with his wife, Xia.

A DANGEROUS GAME

Wrapped in a shawl, her head shaven, she shocks people when they first meet her. No wonder Xiaobo studies aesthetics, they say—his wife is practically a work of art!

There's a bohemian air about Xia—impoverished, vagrant, rebellious, creative—she wants to cut all ties and is not even that attached to her husband's ideal of democracy. She's not holding out for humanity and politically is an anarchist more than anything. Economist and philosopher Guy Sorman goes so far as to call her a "Chinese Jew," comparing her and those like her in China to the historically oppressed and marginalized minority. The Eikhah verse, "[t]heir visage is blacker than a coal, they are not known in the streets, their skin cleaveth to their bones, it is withered, it is become like a stick," seems to describe her appearance.

These are the two faces of Liu Xia. She writes: "I see myself and I / Playing a dangerous game in life."[9]

Xia loves photography, painting, poetry, traveling, smoking, fine food, fine wine, fine living. She doesn't set foot in politics and rarely speaks in public, but because she married "that enemy of the state," politics and the public began following her, chasing her in a never-ending nightmare. "I'm not really interested in politics. I don't have high hopes for social change. I rarely read what Xiaobo writes. But when you live with someone like that, even if you don't care about politics, politics cares about you."

Still, she has her own political views. She was one of the first at the Democracy Wall. Xiaobo recalls: "Young people in Beijing were lucky: they could go see the Wall whenever they wanted. Xia was one of its most avid readers." At eighteen, she walked to Xidan Street every day and tried to push her way, her small stature notwithstanding, to the front of the crowd and copy the writings.

She has at once compassion and an unwavering sense of right and wrong. Li Guiren, a publisher purged after 1989, recounts meeting Xia, an editor then, at a media and publishing conference in the mid-1980s. The Anti-Spiritual Pollution crusade was at a height; a General Administration of Press and Publication deputy asked editors to vet manuscripts carefully, to which Li objected. At lunch, Xia sat next to him to show support. Afterwards, at the airport, she strode past the guardrail, squeezed his hand, and said, "You're a big man!" Li was thrown in jail after Tiananmen. One day, he got a letter. It was from Xia. "She didn't mention politics or even my arrest. She just asked: 'How's the weather over there?' and ended with 'Tomorrow, the sun will rise as always, and your sister Xia will be young forever!'" [10]

If she didn't agree with Xiaobo's politics, she wouldn't have married him and shouldered all that entailed. To friends, she's a big sister. After Xiaobo was gone, she continued to invite families of political prisoners for meals.

When you first meet her, she comes off as being in left field, cold. To Xiaobo, she's ice. "My love, you sit bathed in the midsummer sunset, but I see the ice in you. You've always been cold, born with frost on your fingertips." Ice is also transparent; nothing can hide under the clarity of her gaze. She's a better judge of people than her husband. Razor-tongued, Xiaobo is warm and trusting on the inside, defenseless against users and schemers. Xia was his advisor, and as far as people went, nine times out of ten she was right.

Under Big Brother's gaze, Xia walks on eggshells. Hormone imbalance, skin rashes, chronic insomnia are just a few side effects of this "life." She needs pills—else a full bottle of wine—to get through the night. Friends suggest one remedy after another, even getting her pricey foam pillows—nothing helps. In times like these, sleeplessness is a price you have to pay for being a dissident's wife.

Yet after Xiaobo's arrest, friends ask how she is; she says better, actually. "A shoe hit the floor above long ago. All these years I've been waiting for the other shoe to drop. Now it has. I can lay my mind to rest."

She smiles: "This is the life we've chosen."

☼ ☼ ☼

Laughter is Xia's trademark expression.

She seems to laugh for no reason. Strangers are often taken aback by the bold laugh. In that laugh are a faith in freedom, a longing for love, a contempt for corruption. Xia is Xiaobo's rock. They share happiness and sadness, joy and pain, all of which are condensed into this singular expression. Liao Yiwu writes: "That's what I remember, her constant laugh, to the point of idiocy. . . . Like me, she doesn't have a degree pedigree and mostly dabbles and dallies; unlike me, while I'm a glutton, she's a lush. I wonder if a woman like her can still laugh herself silly after marrying Liu Xiaobo."[11]

The laughing woman, wife to China's public enemy number one, to communism's universal foe, was finally forced to tears. After Xiaobo was taken in 1996, his whereabouts were unknown. Xia told friend Zhou Zhongling, who volunteered to look for him with her. He might be at the PSB compound by the Beijing Botanical Garden, she said. He'd been held there before. They split up to look and actually found the compound, but no one answered. Walking the periphery they called for Xiaobo over the walls until they went hoarse, losing their voices. Xia hoped Xiaobo could at least hear her voice. Nothing, no response. Later they found he was never there.

Liao called when she got home. As soon as she said, "They won't let me see . . ." she burst into sobs. She cried for twenty minutes. Liao couldn't find anything to say and just listened. "Her husband's gone, taking her laugh along with him. Only the mask remains."

In 2009, after Xiaobo received an eleven-year sentence, Woeser wrote:

> I texted Xia when I found out. It was almost midnight before she replied: "I'm fine. Xiaobo and I talked and laughed for ten minutes." . . . She sent another text shortly, saying she didn't break down until she got home—"'break down' is too strong." . . . She texted again immediately: "I even went out to eat and drink." I think she doesn't want people to worry and tries to laugh it off, be cavalier. But I heard she was crying on the phone one night to Wang Lixiong, about how exhausting it was to pretend, to laugh, every day.[12]

They say you can't keep a good woman down. "Xiaobo's been in jail more times than I can count. Even at home he's not free. As his wife I have no choice but to cast my lot with him." She treats the chicanery and buffoonery of a malevolent power like water off a duck's back. "I always think the worst. Before I lived to laugh; now I laugh to live. People say I tend to repress. I'm too glass-is-half-empty, and I don't really want anything to do with society. I'm hardest on myself. When things hit the fan, I find, through my black-tinted lenses, they're never so appalling as I imagined."

When Xiaobo was arrested in 2008, friends were optimistic about a speedy release. Ten years, Xia reckoned, however. When the sentence was handed down, people couldn't believe their ears. It was a year more than she saw coming. Xia laughed: "It's only a year longer than I thought. Why don't we make it easy and just call it a twelve-month sentence?"

Can there be democracy without love? Xiaobo says no. Xia says no, too. Xiaobo ended his trial with: "Liu Xia's the best thing that's happened to me in the last twenty years. She can't be here today, but I want to say to you: my love, I believe in your belief in us."

The room, the people, the law fell away, as if he were proclaiming, speaking, whispering to her alone. It was the last piece of evidence. Xiaobo never shied from showing emotion in public. In a land without love, as a writer once described China, what Xiaobo and Xia have is a miracle.

ART AND FREEDOM

Xia has a love of photography, painting, and poetry. At gatherings, while Xiaobo ran on about current events with his friends, Xia delved into photos, paintings, and poems with hers. "I'm not Xiaobo's flunky," she says. "I'm passionate about poetry and painting."

She is yin to his yang. She's pessimistic but not nihilistic, saved by her passions. Graham Greene once said, "[S]ometimes I wonder how all those who do not write, compose or paint can manage to escape the madness, the melancholia, the panic fear which is inherent in the human condition." For Xia, art is therapy.

She takes pictures because "it's fun." An amateur in the literal sense, she loves what she does and has never thought about going pro. For her, once something becomes a career, it loses its appeal. How she thinks, how she lives is in this regard very "unprofessional." Many artists are like this; she's just more up front about it. It's this "unprofessional-ism," not doing it for the bang or the buck, that makes her work always bright and fresh, that makes it spark and glow.

Even her camera is nothing special. She is, she says, an "idiot" when it comes to the nuts and bolts of photography. Imagine her husband's shock when he found one stunning photograph after another from someone who he thought didn't even know how to point and shoot. From portraits of him to shots of places and things on the fly, it's nearly impossible to mistake her work for someone else's.

Friend and scholar Perry Link notes that her photos are all black-and-white squares. "In ancient China, the walls around cities formed squares. The Forbidden City is square. Tiananmen Square is square. Square in China means order, regularity, solemnity, confinement." In addition, "[t]raditional Chinese painting sometimes includes color, but the purest art, calligraphy, is always in black and white. If we read Liu Xia's photos as commenting on China in recent decades, and clearly we must, their use of black and white also seems to be making a certain documentary claim, as if saying: *Look, here is history.*"[13]

Most powerful are her "ugly babies." Old, broken, deformed dolls are her subjects. Dolls are elegant or garish, princesses or harlequins. Xia's dolls are grotesque, disfigured, bound, tortured—more Chucky than Barbie. She asks friends to fetch dolls for her on trips; they bring back ornate, handmade, rare collectibles to find they're not what she's looking for.

Link says, "They are odd creatures, the size of infants but with adult faces—faces that show pain or terror, frozen cries, a hint of biliousness. They are unpleasant to look at, but we look at them anyway—in part from a sense of duty to the real human beings whom we know lie beyond. If the dolls are infants, their faces have already been imprinted with the grisly futures of adults. If they are adults, they somehow never grew. Genderless, they are everybody."[14]

Xia gave an "ugly baby" photo to Ding Zilin, who said it was the best gift she'd ever gotten: "They brought us a huge black-and-white photo-graph. In it a pair of dolls face an altar of lit candles. One doll's head is lowered; the other has its eyes and mouth wide open, as if screaming or crying. That twisted face drives a stake through my heart. This is Tia-nanmen. Xiaobo said Xia took this when he was in prison." It was an unflinching indictment out of the mouths of babes.

In 2000 Xiaobo put on an exhibit for his wife. An older American lady saw a large print of the photo and started to cry, and eventually she bought it. Ding and Jiang have hung the photo by their son's. It's a tie binding the souls of the living and the dead, friends and strangers. "We're grateful to Liu Xia, who took this picture, and to the American lady, who understood it."[15]

Xiaobo unravels his wife into sentences, words, letters: "No matter how you trim your hair, you can't trim the pain away. No matter how gray you become, you will never grow old. You have a tongue of fish and skin of rain, savoring the sun's azure rays in the sea's splendid depths— how strange they taste." In return, Xia freezes her husband frame by frame. Before his arrest she had him model, snapping a series of him with the dolls. No photos have captured Liu Xiaobo's restless spirit and inner tumult like these.

Xia taught herself painting, too, having never been to art school or under anyone's tutelage. She picked up a brush one day, and it came to her like drinking water. In the 1980s her stories and poems were well regarded in literary circles. Since the 1990s she has all but given up on fiction, with the occasional poem and painting as her outlet. Xiaobo was her biggest cheerleader. As soon as he discovered her gift, he went out and bought the best easel, canvases, paints, and brushes. He was her first fan and critic.

Over the years she's made hundreds of paintings, none of which have been exhibited or put up for sale. They're simply a part of her life. In rare instances she has given them to close friends, or shown them when they come over. Xiaobo would get unusually excited, set up the paintings himself in their small studio, and play docent. Xia would chime in: "Stop it, you're embarrassing me."

Their two-bedroom home in Qixian Village, Haidian, was about one thousand square feet. The living room doubled as the study. Xiaobo wrote in the corner on a small computer desk next to a bookcase covering the whole wall. He left the other bedroom as a studio for Xia, a room of her own. Still he felt bad. He was able to provide food and clothing with his writing but couldn't afford a bigger shelter for them in Beijing's bull market.

Most of Xia's pieces were made in this room. Painting is manual labor. The frail Xia worked slowly and would be exhausted each time, bouncing back after days. Her palette is cold and somber; even her flowers are mostly black and blue with sharp, steel-hard lines. She does primarily abstract landscapes—trees, flowers, grass fields. A wilderness lives in her.

Some compare her to Munch. Chilling, floating, eerie, nervous. A brittleness spreads across her canvases, but light seeps in through the hairline cracks. Closer than those considered contemporary Chinese art representatives, she gets to the country's heart of darkness. Yet human beings survive there, like trees and flowers and fields of grass, season after season, age after age.

After Xiaobo's trial, she went back to life—painting, taking pictures, reading, writing—with exhibits, finally, planned in Paris and Prague, two of her favorite places. She was champing at the bit; Havel was even slated to open in Prague—but news of Xiaobo's Nobel laurels broke, and she could no longer leave the country. The artist is once again burned by the politician, art the sacrifice of a "harmonious society."

Still, it's the dream of this Munch's heir to set foot on his soil someday.

❊ ❊ ❊

Xia has been a poet longer than a photographer or painter. She has been published in *Poetry, People's Literature, China*, and others. (Her work and Xiaobo's critique were published one after the other in issues of *China*.) Against the nationalistic 1980s, she abandoned grand narratives for individual observations and reflections. She looks despots and patriarchs in the eye and asks what it means to be a woman and free: "An onlooker like me / Hides in a corner outside the story's plot / In the shadow of the curtains / Mending a bed sheet / With clumsy fingers / As if my whole stage / My whole life / Consisted of this one prop / Cocooning me / And no one can hear / A soul / Crying in stitches."[16] Liao Yiwu says, "Outside twentieth-century China's literary brothel, Liu Xia is the lone surviving poetess."

As protest after Tiananmen, she stopped submitting to publications in China. She writes for herself, for Xiaobo. Vice versa. Link says:

> In art, in life, she nourishes, stimulates, and inspires him, and he her. When they say two hearts as one, it sounds cliché, I know, but it's true for Xiaobo and Xia. . . . Xiaobo titled many poems "Xia," "For Little Xia," "To My Wife" when she was often not the subject, which

could range from Tiananmen or Kant to Galileo or a stray dog. But you can still say they're written "for Xia" because she's his life partner, his soul mate. They stand shoulder to shoulder, looking together, feeling together, worrying together.[17]

Her favorite poet is Sylvia Plath. In the early 1980s, she put pictures of Plath above her bed and under the glass top of her desk. Xia found lasting love. Plath wasn't so lucky.

Xia has never published a poetry book on her own. Shortly after Xiaobo's third release, he put together a collection of poems by him and Xia as a gift to her. Something like this couldn't be printed in China, so he had to look elsewhere. Poetry books don't sell, and it was hard finding a backer. Hong Kong *Frontline* magazine editor and So Far publisher Liu Dawen decided to take it on. "A couple of friends asked if I'd do it. Xiaobo saw it as a celebration and a demonstration. The Greenfield Bookstore owner had helped him out, but he was too embarrassed to ask, so I chose to accept my 'political' mission. *Selected Poems of Liu Xiaobo and Liu Xia* was born in 2000."[18]

The book hasn't gotten much attention in the past decade or so. People think it's neither literary enough nor political enough. What it is, in fact, is a chronicle of Xiaobo and Xia's relationship. Xiaobo says: "My wife's been through hell and back for me in the last three years. I want to dedicate this book to our marriage, to our love, to what we went through together."[19] Many of the hundreds of poems were written when they were apart, two prisoners, one in a visible cell, the other in an invisible one. Poetry was the lifeline between them.

Still, Xia likes comparing herself to a little bird in her poems, like the trademark doves in John Woo movies. "I want to set you free / Under the cover of the dark sky and rain / Fly now / Go back to your darkened field of rye / And never wake up." Liao Yiwu remembers: "There was a story she wrote. A little girl is walking along the shops down the street, her hand brushing past the windows. The sun is trailing her."

And when the light hits, the handprints, one by one, turn into little sparrows.[20]

THE END?

It's got something to do with time.

Anyone can be a dissident for a day, like a meteor, fast rising and even faster falling, burning up without a trace. Xiaobo, on the other hand, has been a hardheaded, unbending needle in the Chinese government's eye for twenty years. How many people can you say that about?

Same with love and marriage. It's easy to fall in love for a day. What newlyweds aren't on cloud nine, starry eyed? But being married twenty years takes something else, especially considering what the Lius have to deal with. You just don't see that much anymore.

When Xiaobo met Xia, the dark horse found its way and hit its stride, like in his poem to her, "One Letter Is Enough": "Two tracks suddenly overlay / Like a moth to the light / In flight eternal / Tracing your shadow."[21]

He was the prodigal son. She liked making fun of him, calling him "Doctor Dumb," and he'd chuckle. Meng Taoer says, "He was a ladies' man; now he's a woman's man. He fought for himself; now he fights for others. . . . Once he became true to himself, he became free. Now he can do. Now he can love."[22]

Xiaobo and Xia do not have children. Xia: "We talked about it a long time ago. We're not going to have kids. Having a father in prison is a cruel thing to make a child go through. So, we're still dinks." There's another reason. Xia never felt loved as a child by her mother. She doesn't want history repeating.

Without children, they find love in each other. Home is wherever the heart is. They would come back from dinner around ten, bedtime for most—but not for the Lius. Their day was just getting started.

He liked to brew a cup of tea so dark you couldn't tell the color and write on the computer or chat with friends on the phone in the study/living room. Meanwhile she would paint, write, read, or take photos in the studio. They were separate yet together. They worked until four or five in the morning before settling down to sleep and didn't get up until one in the afternoon. Try calling them in the morning, and you might as well be ringing Fred Noonan and Amelia Earhart on Howard Island.

The living room television was décor more than anything unless there was a game on. Former PEN secretary Zhao Dagong recalls Xiaobo watching the game and being on the phone with him at the same time, talking him through it play by play. Just as he doesn't read contemporary Chinese literature, he doesn't watch Chinese soccer. To him, sports are sports. They're about beauty and strength, not national pride.

He watched most of the 2010 World Cup in Jinzhou Prison with his cellmates.

He's worldlier than she is in some ways. To use an old psychology word, Xia is "maladjusted." Helpless with Xiaobo around, she was too scared to even cross the road by herself and had to hang onto his hand like a child. For the longest time she didn't know how to use a computer or cell phone; Xiaobo or others had to dial for her and hand her the phone.

Getting in on the night of December 8, 2008, she saw her husband typing away at Charter e-mails. At around eleven came a series of knocks on the door. It could only be the police. Xiaobo yelled to her: "Get on the cell phone!" She froze. She had no idea how to use it. When they dragged him away, she hadn't made a single call and just waved: "Too late."

"I feel like Kafka was writing about us," she says. "Through reading, we can experience other people's lives, however extreme. Like the Holocaust. I've seen others worry, suffer, or simply disappear. When it happened to me, I felt like I was reading just another book."

After Xiaobo was gone, she had to learn to use a cell phone and can now even text, without punctuation—she hasn't figured that out. Like ancient written Chinese. She also learned to use a computer, typing, e-mailing, skyping.

Unlike her social, outgoing husband, Xia is shy and guarded. Used to living in her head, she doesn't like to engage strangers, especially reporters and bureaucrats. She hates the limelight; her life is not public property. Yet she has no choice but to open herself up, talking to foreign media and diplomats to help Xiaobo. Photography, painting, and poetry are a cakewalk next to this.

She's pessimistic but not despairing. She's compassionate toward life, toward those around her, even ones who hurt her. She smiles at the guards who call her "Sister Xia," without contempt or resentment.

She's spent her life on the way to and from jail since she married Xiaobo. He recounted the third time he was in jail: "In three years she visited me thirty-eight times, going back and forth between Beijing and Dalian. Eighteen of those times she couldn't even see me and had to leave things with the guards." He continued: "I remember seeing her once, and suddenly realizing her hair had turned white."[23]

A round trip between Beijing and Dalian is about 1,200 miles. She traveled by herself, lugging around bags of food and books on filthy, crowded trains. No one wanted to get mixed up with her troubles. Worse, Xiaobo's parents didn't accept her and wouldn't see her. She even got into a fight with her mother-in-law.

In May 2010, Xiaobo was moved to Jinzhou Prison; in June, Xia got permission to visit monthly. Normally, family could visit weekly. If Liu serves out his sentence, Xia will have visited him more than a hundred times. Jinzhou is six hours, or three hundred miles, from Beijing, which over eleven years would amount to 1,600 hours or 80,000 miles.

Déjà vu. Xia knows the visits give him something to look forward to. He wrote the last time he was in prison: "The tougher the going gets, the harder we got to keep the faith. The darker it is out, the brighter it is in. Like your smile—it's a red umbrella amidst the dreary gray."

Eleven years doesn't feel like time; it feels more spacious, like a thing, a mountain, before you:

> First, I want him to know: I'll be there every month. I'll write. I'll bring books. As long as I can walk. Then, I have to adjust. I have to live my life. I can't just be the wife who visits her husband in jail. I have to have my own things, be as normal as possible under abnormal circumstances . . . read when I'm supposed to read, paint when I'm supposed to paint, take pictures when I'm supposed to take pictures, write when I'm supposed to write. I can't just sit on my ass and bitch all day, like I have nothing to do or say without him. If I spend eleven years like that, he'll be sad when he gets out.

Her health is failing, but more and more friends are pitching in. They have even set up a schedule to have a couple of people go to Jinzhou with her, helping her carry all the food, books, and other things. A year's slots quickly filled up.

She had visited him three times already before the Nobel. The last time the gang split up: a friend and she took the train; a couple of others hauled the cargo by car. They were meeting up in Jinzhou with Xiaobo's brothers Xiaoguang and Xiaoxuan, who stopped off to see their father in Dalian first. Dalian police were going to escort them to Jinzhou, but the Northeast was hit by a flood; sixty-four thousand people were evacuated. The brothers ended up on a last-minute train with no seats. They stood in the aisles all night.

In Beijing, Xia and a friend got on the 1:00 a.m. train. As soon as they sat down in the sleeper, a police came over, asking for identification. He looked only at Xia's. Afterward, Xia and the friend chatted, downed some wine, and caught some winks at around 3:00 a.m. The train reached Jinzhou at 7:00 a.m.

Visiting hours were in the afternoon. Having settled into a hotel and eaten, everyone piled into a cab for the prison. It was raining. They sat in twenty minutes of traffic. Only family could visit. Xia and Xiaobo's brothers went in; others waited in the car.

The visit lasted longer than the previous time, about two hours. Xia came back out, beaming ear to ear. She said they met in a room, no glass, and they each got to hug Xiaobo. Emotions ran high; everyone cried saying goodbye. They'd brought him butter, braised pork, fruits, and books, including books by friends Xu Shicun and Liu Ning. He was happy.

The gang took a taxi to the train station, where Xiaoguang and Xiaoxuan said good-bye to Xia, who went back to Beijing that night. On the train, she said Xiaobo was moved. He didn't have much of a relationship with Xiaoguang, his big brother, and never thought he'd come.

Prison food is also the worst, she said. You have to have a diamond stomach to grind the steel shavings passing for rice every morning. Xiaobo has stomach problems and had asked for porridge. It got pushed to the warden's back burner.

The day after the Nobel news broke, Xia was taken to see Xiaobo. She was originally going to see him the next week. Administrators didn't censor their conversation this time. He said if she could go accept the award on his behalf, she must use his final statement to her in the trial as the speech. "I said okay," she said, "but it'll be hard for me." The end of the two-thousand-odd-word statement is as follows:

> I still want to say to you, my dear, that I firmly believe your love for me will remain the same as it has always been. Throughout all these years that I have lived without freedom, our love was full of bitterness imposed by outside circumstances, but as I savor its aftertaste, it remains boundless. I am serving my sentence in a tangible prison, while you wait in the intangible prison of the heart. Your love is the sunlight that leaps over high walls and penetrates the iron bars of my prison window, stroking every inch of my skin, warming every cell of my body, allowing me to always keep peace, openness, and bright-

ness in my heart, and filling every minute of my time in prison with meaning. My love for you, on the other hand, is so full of remorse and regret that it at times makes me stagger under its weight. I am an insensate stone in the wilderness, whipped by fierce wind and torrential rain, so cold that no one dares touch me. But my love is solid and sharp, capable of piercing through any obstacle. Even if I were crushed into powder, I would still use my ashes to embrace you.

My dear, with your love I can calmly face my impending trial, having no regrets about the choices I've made and optimistically awaiting tomorrow.

His health is good, Xia later reported. He gets an hour in the yard every morning and afternoon. There's a TV in the cell, and he can catch CCTV-1 and Liaoning's LRTV. No papers, though. Xiaobo rarely watched TV at home and thinks the shows are "weird, not like real life at all!"

It is six to a cell. His mates are criminals and don't know much about his background, though according to him, they get along. As far as the guards go, Xia says they're "polite." Xiaobo also doesn't have to do hard labor as a political prisoner.

The visit was on Sunday. Prison authorities were reluctant, but Beijing insisted. They didn't want anyone else around. Workers were tired; the atmosphere was tense. "The locals looked like they were about to rebel," Xia says.

She asked her husband how he was doing. Stomach's been hurting, he pointed down. Right away the prison captain standing next to them said they'd make over the menu that afternoon. They'd even give him his own hotplate. He would also get box lunches—more meat-and-three than Michelin, but better than the boiled cabbage most inmates got.

Authorities confiscated their letters. Xiaobo had written Xia a poem last time he was inside: "The ice in you / Melts into a myth of fire / In the executioner's gaze / Fury turns into stone."[24] The poem was called "One Letter Is Enough." Did administrators take that literally? "Since he started serving we haven't stopped writing. We get a letter every five to eight days, ten if the censors are working especially hard. I have twenty letters to date." The couple checked and realized they're both missing one—the love poems they wrote each other. *Why?* was the question. Were the officials green with envy or simply dead on the inside? Xia laughed: "Maybe they felt the contents were too arousing, and would get him too fired up!"

She brought him a dozen books, including *Lolita* and Salinger's *Nine Stories*. All Western literature. "We only read Western writers," she says. "We don't read Chinese ones." His favorite is Celan, whose poetry and biography he pored over again and again and said he wanted to write something about.

Aftershocks of the award rippled. Xia was placed under house arrest. Whether she was still allowed to see Xiaobo was unknown. Two months before the ceremony, she got permission to grocery shop. "They drove around and around, dropped me off at some store God-knows-where, and tracked my every move. They carried my baskets for me, even helped me pick produce." They didn't make her cover up; no one knew her, anyway. There weren't many shoppers; even then, no one noticed a woman with four bodyguards. Ultimately she ran into someone she knew, and her supermarket privileges were revoked.

The simple life became even simpler. Get up, toast and milk, a meal a day. "I hardly smoke. Two packs. Esse slims. Got a stash. They don't need to get them for me." Currently, no one can see her besides her parents and brother. Her mother lets her withdraw a couple thousand yuan a month from the nest egg. Xia and Xiaobo have writing money, but he has told her to save it. "We'll need it when we're older, when I get out."

On October 20, 2010, Xia posted "An Open Invitation to Xiaobo's Friends" online:

> I regret to say that since October 8, I have been under house arrest and am no longer free to leave my home, making it very difficult to communicate with the outside world. I don't know how long this situation will last. I want to express my strong protest towards this limitation on my freedom. I call on the authorities to abide by the law, stop obstructing my daily routine, and respect the requests from both inside and outside the country to release Xiaobo and allow us to once again live a normal life.

She knew Xiaobo's and her chances of going to Oslo were next to none and so invited about a hundred friends and peers from around the country to attend the ceremony.

Before the ceremony, the government put all the invitees on the no-fly list. No one from China was present at the event. After the ceremony, Xia was banned from setting foot out of the house altogether. Phone lines were cut. Internet was out. Liu Xia effectively vanished.

On the night of the 2011 Lantern Festival, she managed to get on a neighbor's wifi and sent a friend a message: "I'm going crazy. The government is holding our whole family hostage." With firecrackers outside, she switched to voice and sent a few more garbled messages. They were her first SOS in months.

In March 2011, the UN Working Group on Arbitrary Detention issued Opinions Nos. 15/2011 and 16/2011 regarding Liu Xiaobo's and Liu Xia's cases, concluded they had been arbitrarily deprived of liberty, and asked the Chinese government to release Liu Xiaobo, to end Liu Xia's house arrest, and to provide compensation to both.

The Chinese government responded about Liu Xia on March 29, stating that after careful investigation, it found no legal measure had been enforced against her. It responded about Liu Xiaobo on April 13, claiming that the PRC respected rule of law and its people enjoyed freedom of speech, including freedom to criticize the government, and that Liu was convicted of inciting subversion of state power. It also asked the replies to be in all UN relevant files.

Today Liu lives on one island; Xia lives on another. With power, he likes to say, it's always a game of patience. Whoever blinks or looks away first loses. Like Sisyphus and his stone, Quixote and his windmills, Connors and his groundhog, there's only one way to "keep on keepin' on."

Xiaobo and Xia have already found it in each other.

8

NOBEL: A CROWN OF THORNS

TWENTY-ONE YEARS LATE

On October 8, 2010, the Norwegian Nobel Committee announced Liu Xiaobo as the winner of the 2010 Nobel Peace Prize "for his long and nonviolent struggle for fundamental human rights in China."

The committee further affirmed Liu's work and achievement: "For over two decades, Liu Xiaobo has been a strong spokesman for the application of fundamental human rights also in China. . . . The campaign to establish universal human rights also in China is being waged by many Chinese, both in China itself and abroad. Through the severe punishment meted out to him, Liu has become the foremost symbol of this wide-ranging struggle for human rights in China."

Response to the news was almost unanimously positive.

According to the *New York Times*, "[t]he prize is an enormous psychological boost for China's beleaguered reform movement and an affirmation of the two decades Mr. Liu has spent advocating peaceful political change in the face of unremitting hostility from the ruling Chinese Communist Party."

The *Washington Post* wrote: "Liu's award could resonate more deeply within China than any similar act in years."

Die Presse in Austria had this to say: "[T]he jurors hit the mark. . . . For years he has fought for democracy and paid for it with his own freedom."

Polish *Gazeta Wyborcza* stated: "This is a great day for China, as it was for Russia when Solzhenitsyn and Sakharov were awarded the prize, as it was for Poland when Wałęsa got it. It is a great day for people of all continents who love freedom and are willing to defend it. It is also a great day for all political prisoners in the world."

Reactions from world leaders and representatives were equally impassioned.

UN secretary-general Ban Ki-moon: "The award of the Nobel Peace Prize to Liu Xiaobo of China is a recognition of the growing international consensus for improving human rights practices and culture around the world."

European Commission president José Barroso: "The decision of the Nobel Peace Prize Committee is a strong message of support to all those around the world who, sometimes with great personal sacrifice, are struggling for freedom and human rights. These values are at the core of the European Union."

PEN International president John Ralston Saul: "Awarding Liu Xiaobo the Nobel Peace Prize is an affirmation of the central importance to everyone of freedom of expression, of which he is a courageous exponent."

Former German president Christian Wulff sent Liu a personal letter: "Your courage to work peacefully for human rights in your country has my utmost respect."

Norwegian prime minister Jens Stoltenberg: "Liu Xiaobo has been awarded the prize for defending freedom of expression and democracy in a way that deserves attention and respect."

US president Barack Obama: "I welcome the Nobel Committee's decision to award the Nobel Peace Prize to Mr. Liu Xiaobo. . . . The Nobel Committee has chosen someone who has been an eloquent and courageous spokesman for the advance of universal values through peaceful and nonviolent means."

On October 25, fifteen Nobel Peace laureates publicly petitioned Ban Ki-moon and G20 heads in Seoul to demand Hu Jintao free the Lius: "We strongly urge you to impress upon Chinese president Hu Jintao that the release of Dr. Liu would not only be welcome, but is necessary." Signers included Desmond Tutu, F. W. de Klerk, the Dalai Lama, and Lech Wałęsa.

The prize was long overdue for China and for Liu. After Tiananmen, protest leaders should have been recognized, but Zhao Ziyang's silence, Fang Lizhi's bomb-sheltering in the US embassy, the breakup of intellectuals, and the fickleness of students left a glaring void. Zhao was no Gorbachev, Fang was not on the same level as Sakharov, and no Wałęsa stood out from the workers. Tiananmen Mothers didn't exist. The 1989 Peace Prize was given to the Dalai Lama. Twenty-one years later, the laurels fell on Liu.

Liu never sought the award, which he thought should be "for the lost souls of June 4," though the prize is not given posthumously. He believed the candidate in China most qualified was Ding Zilin's Tiananmen Mothers. On January 10, 2002, urged by supporters, the Independent Federation of Chinese Students and Scholars nominated the Mothers.

The next day, Liu published an endorsement:

> I humbly, respectfully, and wholeheartedly support the Tiananmen Mothers for the 2002 Nobel Peace Prize. . . . They have the courage and wisdom, patience and faith, to keep fighting while being threatened, monitored, followed, detained, even robbed. They talk to survivors and families, gathering every shred of evidence, turning blood-soaked facts into living truth, and truth into memory. They bear witness to the 1989 movement, to the massacre, to society's conscience. They see and remember each and every perversity perpetrated by the Chinese regime for the past twelve years. Since Tiananmen, the Mothers' humanitarian efforts have been the most influential and effective grassroots work for human rights in China, gaining widespread support and accolades from the international community at large.[1]

He believes progress on human rights and a course change toward democracy in China pivot on Tiananmen. "Giving the Mothers the prize is the biggest hand the international community can lend to the Chinese's fight for rights, freedom, and democracy." He even invited eight scholars in China to write in support of the nomination.

Tiananmen will always be a bloody wound in Liu's mind. He poured his heart into helping the Mothers. At his suggestion, in 2006, the PEN executive committee voted to give Ding Zilin the Freedom to Write Award.

On the afternoon of December 7, 2008, a gravely ill Jiang Peikun was taken to the Beijing University Third Hospital. He had difficulty moving and talking. Ding didn't want visitors; the Lius insisted, as if they knew it would be their last chance. They sat by Jiang's bed for half an hour. The next day, Liu was arrested.

Before he left the hospital, Liu turned to Ding, saying the Charter was coming to a close and he was getting overseas scholars on board the Mothers' Nobel nomination. He thought that was the most important thing to do for the Tiananmen twentieth anniversary next year.[2]

Hu Ping in New York vouched for his efforts: "We skyped just a couple days before his arrest. He told me to tell Human Rights in China to keep fighting for the prize for the Mothers."[3]

Liu could no longer join in the efforts himself. Meng Taoer says prison changes you, either turning you into a loser, a failure, or making you tougher, stronger. There's a third possibility: you become a Nobel Peace laureate—a year and ten months later. They that sow in tears shall reap in joy.

The Chinese are hardy and adaptable, even in reigns of terror. It's our strength and, in a way, weakness: we're survivors at almost all costs. Liu wrote Liao Yiwu in 2000: "We're wimps next to revolutionaries in Russia, Poland, Czechoslovakia. How tragic. We have no heroes, no Havel."

How long is twenty-one years? A child can grow up in twenty-one years. A man can grow old in twenty-one years. When people saw the familiar name online or heard it over the phone, many broke down in tears. They were scholars, businessmen, freelancers, even public servants. They had said goodbye to their youth at the square. They would disappear into the crowd without a word.

But their blood still seethes.

❋ ❋ ❋

Firecracker noises popped open the stitches of the night sky over BNU and Shandong University. Some students clinked a small toast for an alum winning an award. At BNU, someone told a foreign reporter they were going to build a memorial to an old grad. Central Academy of Fine Arts student Wei Qiang put up a banner saying a Nobel Peace Prize winner was in jail. Weiquan lawyer Xu Zhiyong and others tried hanging a "Congratulations to Liu Xiaobo for Winning the Nobel Peace Prize" banner in the park and were shooed by police on the spot.

Authorities broke up many a party. A meme was born—*fanzui*, "wine and dine," sounding like "break the law." Finance writer and poet Su Xiaohe wrote a poem, "Night of October 8, We Were So Happy We Cried": "Drunk before midnight / Fucked 'til dawn / Day for night / Straight to sunrise / On the way a brother gave the night the one-finger salute / A brother was taken downtown / The sumbitch was without doubt sauced / He said, am I breaking the law simply by being happy?"

None should sleep that night, knights and knaves alike. Old media were on lockdown; the evangel spread in the ether. A bloodless "war in heaven" had begun. Whole buildings in Zhongguancun, China's Silicon Valley, stayed lit. Websites such as Sina, Sohu, and 163 were ordered to remove any content concerning the prize.

An inside source described a dozen censors burning the midnight oil, doing battle with Weibo users: "Our entire unit, fifty of us, was on it, checking and deleting posts until three, four in the morning. And came back at seven and did it all over again." Missives were being fired faster than they could be quashed.

9 Yuyuantan South Road was cordoned off. Police stood between hundreds of foreign reporters and the Lius' house. Video and audio equipment was in place; cameras and mics all pointed at building 17. Since that afternoon, Liu Xia had been under house arrest, her phones and Internet cut.

It was not usually a busy road, next to the Central Military Commission. Passersby asked: "What's going on?" "Who is Liu Xiaobo?" "What did he do?" A young man told a reporter five people had already come up to him, and he taught them how to circumvent censors to get the news online.

For Hu Jintao, Wen Jiabao, and their ilk, this was a disaster worse than the 2008 Great Sichuan Earthquake, because it was in part thanks to them Liu got the attention he deserved.

They must really be kicking themselves.

WHY LIU?

Alfred Nobel, chemist and inventor of dynamite, born in 1833 in Stockholm, was a rich and brilliant businessman. He didn't have children, and he left his fortune to create a series of prizes for those who "shall have conferred the greatest benefit to mankind" in physics, chemistry, physiology or medicine, and literature; a peace prize was also established. This was the beginning of the Nobel Prize.

The Nobel Foundation awards a gold medal, diploma, and prize money to recipients. The amount of money depends on the foundation's income each year and has steadily increased since the 1980s. In 2010 it was 10 million kronor, or about $1.4 million.

The Nobel has long been viewed as the *ne plus ultra* of recognition, with the Peace Prize carrying the highest esteem. Unlike the other prizes, which are awarded in Stockholm, the Peace Prize is given in Oslo. Five Norwegian Nobel Committee members, appointed by the Norwegian parliament but not formally responsible to it, select the Peace laureate. The committee emphasizes its independence from any government, corporation, or organization.

The ceremony typically lasts ninety-five minutes, including fifteen to twenty minutes—often more—of the winner's speech. These lectures have become an important document and testament to the vicissitudes of the times and the constancy of the human spirit.

Liu's award shows again that peace and human rights are two sides of the same coin. According to the committee, it "has long believed that there is a close connection between human rights and peace. Such rights are a prerequisite for the 'fraternity between nations' of which Alfred Nobel wrote in his will." It makes clear further: "China is in breach of several international agreements to which it is a signatory, as well as of its own provisions concerning political rights."

After two world wars, beyond peace negotiations, a more fundamental set of problems emerged—human rights. Since the second half of the twentieth century, more and more Peace Prize winners have been human rights advocates and activists—Martin Luther King, Jr. (1964), Andrei Sakharov (1975), Lech Wałęsa (1983), Desmond Tutu (1984), Elie Wiesel (1986), the Fourteenth Dalai Lama (1989), Aung San Suu Kyi (1991), Nelson Mandela (1993), Kim Dae-jung (2000), Shirin Ebadi (2003), Wangari Muta Maathai (2004)—to name a few. The prize itself has become synonymous with and a force in the advancement of human rights around the world.

Former committee chair Francis Sejersted commented: "[A] lasting peace must be based on respect for the human rights of the individual. . . . [T]he concept of peace on which both Nobel's will and the Nobel Committee's practice are founded is a moral concept. . . . Laureates must be more than skilled diplomats; it is important for them also to be able to stand out as symbols of good will." The *Universal Declaration of Human Rights* of 1948 even more points to human rights as an international issue.

The committee usually doesn't respond to objections but made an exception here to China's attacks. China claimed the Peace Prize had become politicized. Committee secretary Geir Lundestad responded on *Deutsche Welle*: "Peace has certainly something to do with politics. It is a very political question. How do you achieve peace? What we have focused on this year is the connection between human rights, democracy and peace. And the Nobel Committee has argued for many years that there is such a connection." And:

> This is what many governments say—that the Nobel Committee is disturbing peace. This is what Hitler said when we gave the prize to Carl von Ossietzky. This is what the Kremlin said when we gave the peace prize to Andrei Sakharov and Lech Wałęsa. This is what they said in South Africa, in Burma and this is what they say in Iran. They all say that this is disturbing the peace. In the long run, there is this connection between human rights, democracy and peace. You cannot have a more permanent peace if we have governments that more or less systematically suppress their population.

The closer the ceremony got, the faster and more furious China's onslaughts came. Committee chair Thorbjørn Jagland replied in the *New York Times* in an article, "Why We Gave Liu Xiaobo a Nobel":

> The authorities assert that no one has the right to interfere in China's internal affairs. But they are wrong: international human rights law and standards are above the nation-state, and the world community has a duty to ensure they are respected. . . . The United Nations, founded in the wake of two disastrous world wars, committed member states to resolve disputes by peaceful means and defined the fundamental rights of all people in the Universal Declaration of Hu-

man Rights. The nation-state, the declaration said, would no longer
have ultimate, unlimited power.

In other words, "[China's] condemnation of the Nobel committee's se-
lection . . . inadvertently illustrates why human rights are worth defending."

Jagland also indicated that although China wasn't a constitutional
democracy, it was still a UN member and shared the responsibility of
defending freedom of expression—even if it disapproved of what was
said. This is what the committee stands for. A man jailed eleven years
for expressing his beliefs is a tragedy. "If we are to move toward the
fraternity of nations of which Alfred Nobel spoke, then universal human
rights must be our touchstone."

A question remained for the committee—why Liu and not other
Chinese? There were activists who had been doing it longer, who had
done more time and been punished worse, who were more vocal and
radical in their anticommunism. It certainly wasn't for a want of recent
nominees—Wei Jingsheng, Harry Wu, the Tiananmen Mothers, Hu Jia,
Gao Zhisheng, Chen Guangcheng, and more. So why Liu?

Since 1989, this member of the Four Noblemen has been gaining
international recognition but is still less known in the West than Mandela, Sakharov, Kim Dae-jung, and others. Hu Ping calls attention to
the fact that, as a writer, Liu is little translated in the West, though he
knows many Western scholars and journalists and is friends with a number of dissidents in exile.

Nominators included previous winners, but Liu had never actively
sought their support before his imprisonment. He'd spoken out about
Tibet and thus gained the Dalai Lama's respect. He'd admired Gorbachev for giving up his power in face of the Soviet Union's dissolution
and received a personally signed copy of his autobiography. Still, he was
a relative outsider to the illustrious circle.

The award, however, was no accident. The committee did its homework gathering every bit of information over the years, evaluating every
aspect of its significance. On the eve of the banquet, the Norwegian
Conservative Party held a press conference during which Jagland and
Lundestad explained the committee's choice. According to them, the
committee had for years considered awarding a Chinese dissident, but
there were problems.[4]

First, should it award a Chinese dissident? China's situation is complex and ever-changing, but just as the committee had awarded dissidents in Burma and other places, it could do the same to send China a message about its abuses. The answer to the question was a resounding "Yes."

Then, whom should it award? Liu's influence as an activist had broadened in recent years. His words and actions carried import and impact in the committee's eyes. The Chinese government also in a way helped seal the deal. Given an unusually cruel punishment, Liu was no longer just one activist in China but became a symbol for all activists around the world. The committee knew how divided Chinese dissidents were and was glad to note Liu's wide circle of support.

Finally, would awarding Liu stir the pot more? The committee knew—everyone knew—what would happen in the short term. We see it: his wife and hundreds of friends have been placed under house arrest, even tortured.

There were more reasons for the award.

One. The committee typically chooses activists who have stayed in their country, close to their people in their hour of need, who have their finger on the pulse and ear to the ground. They often have a more direct impact than their peers who have either chosen or been forced into exile.

Two. Time is a factor for the committee. From Tiananmen to Charter 08, Liu has been in the ring more than twenty years. He has weathered the ups and downs of China's democracy movement, often right in the teeth of the storm. While many of his friends have switched lanes or come to a stop altogether, Liu has been unwavering in his course down a road less traveled.

Three. The committee likes generalists, those able to cross boundaries and play many roles with wide appeal. Neither just a writer nor just an activist, Liu has contributed to the efforts and commands the respect of other independent writers, human rights lawyers, and grassroots organizers. A thinker and a doer, he's a link *sine qua non* among disparate dissident circles.

Four. Candidates should hold human rights universal. Liu cares about not only Chinese democratization but also the welfare of Tibetan, Uyghur, Inner Mongol, and other minorities. A champion of local autonomy, he supports the Hong Kong people's demand for democracy and remains liberal toward Taiwan's independence. This sets him apart from many of his peers and has won him the esteem of various groups at home and abroad.

Five. In addition to recognizing achievement, the Nobel is a spirit award. For instance, "Sakharov's love of truth and strong belief in the inviolability of the human being, his fight against violence and brutality, his courageous defense of the freedom of the spirit, his unselfishness and strong humanitarian convictions have turned him into the spokesman for the conscience of mankind, which the world so sorely needs today." Kim Dae-jung stated in court after he was sentenced to death in a South Korean military tribunal in 1980: "There shall be restoration of democracy in our country in the eighties. At this time and from this place, I ask you, as my last will before my death, not to ever resort to political reprisal when our democratic government is reestablished." Liu's principle of no violence, no hate, and no enemies is essential to China's peaceful transformation.

Six. The committee singles out those presently victimized by their government in hopes of pressuring for early release or bettering prison conditions. Other laureates jailed or having their freedom otherwise curtailed at the time of the award included Sakharov, Wałęsa, and Aung San Suu Kyi, and among laureates, Liu will have spent less time in prison than only Mandela and Suu Kyi.

Seven. Nominators are important. The 2010 nominee list was said to have reached a record of some two hundred, but few had "references" like Liu did—Desmond Tutu, the Dalai Lama, Wałęsa, Havel, Herta Müller, PEN International and more than a hundred of its centers around the world, and hundreds more.

Eight. The committee wants to strive for political fairness. After years of accusations of leftism, especially after Obama's 2009 award, this was the opportunity to strike a balance as Liu could be seen as more "right" or libertarian by Western standards. Obama himself announced hours before the 2010 ceremony: "Mr. Liu Xiaobo is far more deserving of this award than I was. . . . The values he espouses are universal, his struggle is peaceful, and he should be released as soon as possible."

Will China's political system change someday? Liu hopes so; 1.3 billion Chinese, with 5.7 billion others in the world, await the answer.

✿ ✿ ✿

When Liu said he had no enemies, Chinese officials declared him public enemy number one. The title was previously held by the Dalai Lama.
In 1989, when the Dalai Lama was awarded the prize, Chinese authorities were busy cleaning the blood off their hands. This time, the
claws came out in full force. Hot on the Olympics' and World Expo's
tails in a roaring economy, the regime went after Norway with a ven-
geance, boycotting Norwegian salmon, even burning Haruki Muraka-
mi's *Norwegian Wood*.

To authorities, Liu's award was the shame of the nation, a flashback
to the world's condemnation of Tiananmen. After a few days of silence,
the motors started running; the gears began grinding; the old communist propaganda machine was cranking up again.

On October 9, a *Global Times* editorial read: "The [Nobel] committee disgraced itself." "By making paranoid choices, the committee con-
tinues to deny China's development. In 1989, the Dalai Lama, a separ-
atist, won the prize. Liu Xiaobo, the new winner, wants to copy Western
political systems in China. . . . The controversy in the West over Liu
Xiaobo's sentence is not based on legal concerns. It is based on a desire
to impose Western values on China. Obviously, the Nobel Peace Prize
this year is meant to irritate China." The truth is that the administration
likes to pick and choose what "Western values" to adopt, even extol, in
an about-face to suit its rhetoric—communism, but not democracy, for
example. It itches and chafes at the Nobel's standing as it writes off
what it stands for in one fell swoop.

On October 18, *China Youth Daily* published "What Tune Is the
Nobel Singing Now? Beijing Students Cast Doubt on 2010 Peace
Prize." Reporters allegedly interviewed a half-dozen college students
expressing dismay at the committee for awarding "a sentenced criminal
who incited subversion of state power" and promoted the agenda of
anti-Chinese "Western forces." However, many "interviewees" immediately revealed on Weibo that they never said those things, leading a
veteran *China Youth Daily* reporter to cry out in shock and outrage at
the "blatant, shameless" news falsification.

Two days before the ceremony, in press conference, PRC Foreign
Ministry mouthpiece Jiang Yu called Liu supporters "clowns"—the
word Maoists used to refer to counterrevolutionaries during the revolu-

tion—claiming more than a hundred countries and organizations have voiced support for China: "[Liu supporters] are putting on a self-orchestrated anti-China farce. We firmly oppose anyone making an issue of Mr. Liu Xiaobo to interfere in China's internal affairs and judicial sovereignty."

German *Die Welt* responded: "Chinese communists have missed the chance in Liu Xiaobo's case to show maturity in dealing with dissenting voices. Instead they cling brutally to the illusion of a monolithic power in order to intimidate their Western neighbors."

And there were dissenting voices, as with all Peace Prize awards, and Liu was never a stranger to controversy ever since the 1980s.

Veteran Chinese civil rights activist Wei Jingsheng believes Liu's post-massacre confession and statement "No one died at the square" destroyed the student movement. To Wei, Liu was an accomplice. Liu was against violent measures enacted by some protesters, so he wasn't a "team player."[5] Wei claims the award was a result of "the communists having bought out the capitalists." Yet why would Liu's "accomplices" send him to prison—for eleven years at that? And if they wanted the award, and it were the plan all along, why would they black out the media instead of giving themselves a pat on the back?

Fellow Chinese and 2000 Nobel Literature laureate Gao Xingjian in France had "no comment" on the whole affair. Liu had previously criticized Gao's writings for being too "Western" and not original enough.

Before Havel, Tutu, and others voiced their support, more than a dozen Chinese dissidents outside China sent the committee an open letter: "[A]warding the Nobel Peace Prize to Liu Xiaobo, with his defective image and being a representative of the 'cooperative faction,' will have a negative impact on the Chinese peoples' struggle for human rights, freedom, and democracy." Following up four days before the award announcement, they wrote again: "[W]e urge the Nobel Committee to seriously consider our opinion, namely, as a highly controversial figure, Mr. Liu Xiaobo has lost the moral image fit for a Nobel Peace Prize recipient."

Liu is not unimpeachable and, as a Nobel candidate and recipient and public figure, is subject to certain scrutiny and criticism. He is okay with it and thinks it's normal, as he told his lawyers when they met after sentencing. Criticism is distinct from insult and defamation, however. The irony of those free and sheltered abroad attacking someone jailed and tormented at home should also escape no one. One thing is clear: you can say you are anticommunist and be communist in spirit through and through.

A relative bystander, Herta Müller, spoke frankly: "I supported Václav Havel's nomination of Liu Xiaobo for the Nobel Peace Prize, and as a result I received some nasty e-mails from a number of Chinese exiles. Slander, denunciation, and shameless assassination of Xiaobo were the nature of those letters. Perhaps Chinese intelligence has infiltrated the émigrés, perhaps they have gone mad themselves, playing revolutionaries on paper, viciously rampaging with words." In return, they accused her of sounding "just like . . . propaganda during the era of Nicolae Ceaușescu in Romania."[6]

The infection runs deep in the Chinese mind. Hong Kong scholar Liang Wendao: "A totalitarian state not only restricts people's rights; it also constricts their minds. It's terrifying enough by itself, but what's sad is it turns its opponents into just like itself."[7]

"AND IF YOU WAIT ON HIGH, I SHALL MEET YOU THERE"

December 10, 2010, was the 114th anniversary of Nobel's death. It was also Human Rights Day. The 2010 Nobel Peace Prize award ceremony was held in the afternoon in Oslo City Hall. The recipient's chair between Jagland and committee member Kaci Kullmann Five onstage was empty. A larger-than-life portrait of a smiling Liu Xiaobo hung to the right.

"It will be a magnificent ceremony," Lundestad told the press. "One could say that some of the most important ceremonies we have had in our 109-year history have been the ones where the laureate could not be present."

Guests were welcomed by Oslo Police Orchestra at the city hall entrance. In attendance were the Norwegian prime minister and cabinet members, parliament president and some eighty representatives, supreme court chief justice, ambassadors, and various other national and local officials. Forty-eight foreign dignitaries were present. A forty-six-strong Chinese contingency showed. The audience totaled about a thousand. Countless prodemocracy and human rights activists demonstrated in support outside.

At the gate, everyone waited for the arrival of King Harald V and Queen Sonja. They were received by Jagland and Lundestad. People entered the hall. The ceremony officially began.

Renowned Norwegian soprano Marita Solberg and pianist Håvard Gimse led the festivities with "Solveig's Song" from Ibsen's *Peer Gynt* scored by Grieg. When the words "May God protect you, wherever you go / May God comfort you, if at his footstool you stand / Here I shall wait till you come back / And if you wait on high, I shall meet you there" echoed through the hall, a palpable sadness permeated the air.

Jagland's presentation speech followed. "We regret that the laureate is not present here today. He is in isolation in a prison in northeast China. Nor can the laureate's wife Liu Xia or his closest relatives be here with us. No medal or diploma will therefore be presented here today. This fact alone shows that the award was necessary and appropriate. We congratulate Liu Xiaobo on this year's Peace Prize." A thousand attendees stood up and applauded for over a minute and a half.

After summarizing Liu's life and work, Jagland stated:

> The human rights activists in China are defenders of the international order and the main trends in the global community. Viewed in that light, they are thus not dissidents, but representatives of the main lines of development in today's world. Liu denies that criticism of the Communist Party is the same as offending China and the Chinese people. He argues that "Even if the Communist Party is the ruling party, it cannot be equated with the country, let alone with the nation and its culture."

He concluded: "Therefore: while others at this time are counting their money, focussing exclusively on their short-term national interests, or remaining indifferent, the Norwegian Nobel Committee has once again chosen to support those who fight—for us all." The speech ended to a minute-long standing ovation.

A group of Chinese attendees put out an "Oslo Declaration" afterward, describing the speech as "principled, sincere, convincing, civil, elegant, possessing the utmost integrity, a legacy."

Next was the music program. Chinese American violinist Lynn Chang played Chinese folk tunes "Jasmine Flowers" and "Colorful

Clouds Chasing the Moon" and Elgar's *Salut d'Amour*. Chang won the 1974 Paganini Competition and helped found the Boston Chamber Music Society. For him, coming here wasn't an easy decision. "I thought of my own professional and personal possible repercussions, and I asked [the organizers] for a twenty-four-hour period in which I can really think about this," fearing retaliation by the Chinese government against his relatives overseas and students applying to the US schools where he taught. He chose the first two pieces because they had a special place in the Chinese heart. The Elgar was a tribute to Liu's final words at the trial to his wife, telling her how much he loved her.

Liu probably would not have picked the Chinese tunes. Every Chinese man, woman, and child can sing "Jasmine Flowers" by heart, and the Chinese government often uses it as propaganda for "Chineseness." Zhang Yimou used it during the Olympics. The same song played differently can sound very different. On the Olympics stage it was happy, almost kitschy; at the Nobel ceremony it was filled with sorrow. Still, Liu would have preferred something else. Like music having to do with Tiananmen. Like Wang Xilin's *Symphony No. 4*, which he told friends privately he wrote to commemorate the massacre. Like Esmond Lim's *Requiem for Tiananmen Mothers*, crying out the victims' names, one by one. Like Liao Yiwu's "Massacre," recited to music at Independent Chinese PEN award ceremonies. Of course, the committee couldn't have known all that under China's lockdown.

Liv Ullmann then read in English Liu's "I Have No Enemies" trial statement, choking up, tears streaming down her face.

The Norwegian National Opera Children's Chorus, conducted by Edle Stray-Pedersen and accompanied by violinist Ragnhild Hemsing, closed with the traditional Norwegian wedding march and other songs. A Chinese American children's choir was slated, but parents worried about retaliation, so the Norwegian National Opera stepped in. In brilliant traditional garb, the children walked on stage. The ceremony ended on an upbeat and bright note.

When Liu met with his wife on October 9, he expressed his wish for a children's choir at the ceremony. He loves to hear children sing. To him they are hope, they are peace, they are the future. He had to give up his own child to be what he is today.

The king and queen were supposed to personally congratulate the recipient after the chorus, but this part had to be removed due to the winner's absence.

That evening 1,500 from Norway and elsewhere, chanting "Democracy Now" and "Free Liu Xiaobo" in English and Chinese, paraded with torchlights to the Grand Hotel, where the laureate would normally greet marchers on the balcony and spend the night. That night the balcony was closed. A giant image of Liu was projected on the hotel façade. People read a poem in Norwegian that Xiaobo had written Xia.

The Nobel Peace Prize Concert was held as usual the following evening. Hosted this year by Denzel Washington and Anne Hathaway, the event boasted six thousand attendees, including the king and queen, and was broadcast in more than one hundred countries. Among the performers were Herbie Hancock, Barry Manilow, Florence and the Machine, Jamiroquai, and Robyn.

The concert started with a chant to "free Liu Xiaobo." Footage of demonstrations in Oslo the last few days played on dual screens. Washington told the audience the laureate is not scheduled for release from prison until June 21, 2020; however, he said, "one day he will be able to watch it on the net, on television, or on DVD. Liu, tonight, we are honoring you. Artists from all over the world have come to Oslo to perform in praise of your courage, your perseverance, and your commitment to human rights. There are six thousand people in the audience here tonight. You will see admiration and respect in their faces, and hear it in their thunderous applause."

Aung San Suu Kyi sent a video greeting in which she hoped for the release of all "prisoners of conscience." The prize, she believed, was a boost to democracy in China. Everywhere, in Burma, in China, democracy is the wave of the future, and the future is now.

The Young Norwegian Strings performed the Rigaudon from the *Holberg Suite*. An hour in at halftime, footage of Liu since Tiananmen was shown. Washington and Hathaway chronicled his life's work and reread parts of "I Have No Enemies." Jamiroquai's Jay Kay told the audience after an apt and poignant rendition of "Virtual Insanity," "When you go to your bed tonight, think about that man on his own in that cell."

The Liu Xiaobo exhibit *I Have No Enemies* opened December 12 at Oslo's Nobel Peace Center. Through photos, films, and texts, visitors could learn about the Tiananmen Square protests of 1989, Charter 08, and Liu the poet and writer. The history of China's economic progress and those it has left behind was also brought into sharp relief.

THE TRUTH BEHIND THE EMPTY CHAIR

Germany, 1936. Journalist and pacifist Carl von Ossietzky, under surveillance in a Berlin hospital after three years of incarceration and torture in the Sonnenburg and Esterwegen-Papenburg concentration camps, was denied a passport to go to Oslo to receive the 1935 Nobel Peace Prize. Lawyer Kurt Wannow collected the prize on his behalf but embezzled most of the funds. Since then, the committee has delayed issuing the medal, diploma, and money until the winner or family can collect them in person.

The Soviet Union, 1975. Andrei Sakharov's award was a bombshell. The Soviet government and media launched a blitzkrieg against the laureate and forbade him from leaving the country to collect the prize. His wife, Yelena Bonner, accepted the award for him.

Poland, 1983. Lech Wałęsa was afraid his country wouldn't let him back in were he to travel to Oslo to accept the award. His wife, Danuta, went instead.

Burma, 1991. Aung San Suu Kyi incurred the junta's wrath with her award, which was given to her sons Alexander and Kim from England.

Iran, 2003. Tehran reacted strongly against the committee's decision to honor human rights attorney Shirin Ebadi for her work on women's, children's, and refugee rights. However, Ebadi was allowed to attend the ceremony along with former Iranian senior diplomat to Norway Hashem Hakimi. Yet the government boycotted the 2010 ceremony. Ebadi said, "Liu Xiaobo is an activist and I regret that he is in prison. But I am also convinced that he will be freed soon. I hope the Chinese government is going to understand that it was a mistake to jail him and to threaten countries to get them to stay away from the ceremony. I am sorry that my country, Iran, has decided not to take part in this universal tribute to a human rights activist."

With Liu in prison and his immediate family forbidden to leave the country, for the second time in its century-long history, the committee placed an empty chair on stage for the ceremony. The first was for Ossietzky.

Jagland set the medal and diploma embossed with "LXB" on the chair. "Ladies and gentlemen, it has not been possible, as you know, for Liu Xiaobo or any of his close relatives to come to Oslo to receive the Nobel medal and diploma. At this stage in the ceremony, when we normally hand over the medal and the diploma, I place them in the empty chair held by Liu Xiaobo." The applause lasted almost an entire minute.

Curiously, in August 1998, Liu Xia had written a poem "Empty Chairs," about van Gogh's chair paintings. "Empty chairs, empty chairs," she wrote, "So many empty chairs / In every corner of the world / Van Gogh's chairs are especially enticing / I take a seat in one quietly / And swing my legs back and forth a bit / A cool scent seeps through the chair / Stiffening them / They can't move / Van Gogh, brush in hand, still / Retreats, retreats, retreats / There is no funeral tonight / Van Gogh tries to hold my gaze / Forcing me to lower my lids / I'm like pottery / Sitting among flames of sunflowers."[8]

China vilified Liu and censored everything about the prize. Accounts were deleted; websites like BBC and CNN were blocked; "Liu Xiaobo," "Nobel," even "empty chair" were unsearchable. On December 12, *Nanfang City News* printed on its front page a picture of chairs and cranes (in Chinese, "crane" sounds like "congratulations").

Global Times called the award "sinister" and the ceremony a "farce." On November 5, deputy foreign minister Cui Tiankai had warned European officials not to attend: "If they make the wrong choice, they have to bear the consequences." Nineteen countries, including Russia, Sudan, Iran, Iraq, Egypt, and Afghanistan, bowed out. Four—Ukraine, the Philippines, Serbia, and Colombia—had changed their mind and showed.

About forty Chinese protesters surrounded Oslo City Hall with banners reading "Opposition to Nobel Peace Prize to Liu Xiaobo," "Peace Prize = Political Tool!" and "No Meddling in China's Internal Affairs!" A leader, Ma Lie, shouted through a megaphone: "Liu Xiaobo is a criminal!" and the award was a "wrong decision." Protesters tried to wrest a "Million Signatures to Free Liu Xiaobo" sign out of disabled Tiananmen survivor Fang Zheng's hands.

According to Amnesty International sources, Chinese diplomats had gotten in touch with a number of Chinese immigrants in Norway, pressuring them with threats to join the rally. Several Chinese in Norway told Lundestad the Chinese embassy had "encouraged" them to protest. He called China's efforts in pressuring other embassies to stay away and local expatriates to demonstrate "unprecedented" in Nobel history.

Liu's family and friends and thousands of activists and dissidents were placed under house arrest or sent "traveling." PSBs demanded restaurants and bars not accept reservations for or seat parties of six or more for three days to prevent "disturbances." Honghaoge Teahouse by Liu's house and other intellectual hangouts like the All Saints Bookstore and Transition Institute were closed that Friday due to "power and water outage."

A war raged. It was a war between Liu Xiaobo and Hu Jintao, a war between truth and power. On November 4, Hu topped *Forbes*'s annual "World's Most Powerful People." Asking "Is Hu Jintao Really the Most Powerful Person in the World?" the article answered: "The Kremlin goes by a different name in Beijing—Zhongnanhai."

Liu wrote just before his arrest: "Even being surveiled every day I remain hopeful about China's future. Being and talking with those who surveil me, I realize the regime has a guilty conscience." Historian Yu Ying-shih: "For the past two decades Liu Xiaobo has been trying to save a falling nation with a lion's roar, hoping to bring it back into the fold of civilization once again."

❀ ❀ ❀

Raymond Aron compared "the bureaucrat and the member of the Communist party" to "the local *führer* and the secretary of the *fascio*," stating in Stalinism and fascism political, personal, and intellectual freedoms, as well as freedoms of press, speech, and science, disappear.[9]

Let's go back to 1933. Ossietzky had been imprisoned for treason for exposing Germany's secret rearmament despite the Treaty of Versailles. When Hitler came into power, Ossietzky was arrested again and sent to a concentration camp. The Nazis called the Nobel committee's decision a hostile act and told Norway to mind its own business. The award divided public opinion in Norway, with papers calling Ossietzky a criminal.

Hindsight is twenty-twenty; we now know there is a difference between appeasement and peace, and conflicts between countries can't be solved without a framework of laws and rights.

Ossietzky died in 1938 in police custody from tuberculosis and the abuse he suffered in the camps. The Nazis forbade his name from being written on his grave and forced his widow to change her name. Today a statue stands in Pankow, and Ossietzkystraße runs through the heart of Stuttgart. His name appears in every textbook.

We can travel to 1975. In his Nobel lecture, Andrei Sakharov saw "[t]wo powerful socialist states, in fact, have become hostile, totalitarian empires, in which a single party and the state exercise immoderate power in all spheres of life. They possess an enormous potential for expansion, striving to increase their influence to cover large areas of the globe. One of these states—the Chinese People's Republic—has as yet reached only a relatively modest stage of economic development." The Soviet Union stood behind the Iron Curtain; China, however, has sauntered onto the global stage. UN-chartered, China today is a Western venture capitalist la-la land with cheap parts and cheaper labor. The Soviet *modus operandi* was militaristic; Chinese aggression is economic. As the 2014 Crimean crisis showed, the Cold War is not dead; it's not even past, with China and Russia swapping places.

The West sees China as a paper tiger, a phrase Mao used to describe the United States. The tiger has leapt off the screen. Skeptics claim it has no ideology to stand on, but what tears at and eats into democracy more than high-cost, low-price dictatorship in socialism-with-Chinese-characteristics' clothing? Like Jagland said, never had one "democracy" tried to bully all other democracies into silence and submission. Will our dances with the tiger go on?

Wałęsa said after hearing of Liu's award, "I am very satisfied by the decision of the Nobel committee. I consider it a challenge for China and the entire world. The world must declare whether it is ready to help China enter a zone where there is respect for the principles and values [of democracy]. China is a great state and we must respect it, but it must also observe the norms and values respected in the world at large."

2010 Nobel Literature laureate Mario Vargas Llosa stated:

[D]ictatorships must be fought without hesitation, with all the means at our disposal, including economic sanctions. It is regrettable that democratic governments, instead of setting an example by making common cause with those, like the Damas de Blanco in Cuba, the Venezuelan opposition, or Aung San Suu Kyi and Liu Xiaobo, who courageously confront the dictatorships they endure, often show themselves complaisant not with them but with their tormenters. Those valiant people, struggling for their freedom, are also struggling for ours.

Thin is the veneer of civilization. Neither the corrosiveness of power nor the fragility of freedom ought to be made light. Liu's prize is not the West's gift to China; it's the West giving itself a shot in the arm. Liu is a constant reminder that the wizard lies behind China's curtain. A step forward for democracy in China is a step forward for democracy in the world.

A NEW COURSE

The life of Liu Xiaobo echoes that of Mandela, Sakharov, and Wiesel.

"We can say Liu reminds us of Nelson Mandela," Jagland said. They were ordinary men who made great sacrifices for the society in which they lived and became symbols for peace and nonviolent struggle for rights inalienable to every human being.

From a young age, Mandela had thought of himself as a politician and activist on the frontlines against apartheid, undaunted by the prospect of imprisonment. In 1970 he wrote Winnie, then his wife: "[T]he chains of the body are often wings to the spirit."[10] Having spent twenty-seven years behind bars, he became a symbol of dignity and justice for South Africans. He threw himself into politics after regaining freedom, traveling all over South Africa and visiting dozens of countries. Receiving the Nobel at seventy-five, he soon drafted and promoted a new nonracial constitution for the country, which held its first multiracial general election in 1994. The African National Congress won by a landslide, and on May 10 Mandela was inaugurated as South Africa's first black president.

Those like Mandela play a vital role in the democratic transformation of their countries.

The media also drew parallels between Liu and Andrei Sakharov. Liu won the prize at fifty-five; Sakharov, fifty-four. The awards were thirty-five years apart. Since the 1960s the latter had been outspoken against and active in preventing nuclear proliferation. He was also co-founder of the Committee on Human Rights in the USSR among other fledgling independent legal political organizations in the country and sent to internal exile for protesting the Soviet war in Afghanistan in 1979. The KGB frequently ransacked his apartment and seized his belongings. Pivotal in the Soviet Union's growing political opposition, he placed morals and ethics above interests and politics, leading Khrushchev to call him "a crystal of morality among our scientists." In 1989, Sakharov was elected to the Soviet legislature in one of twelve seats reserved for Academy of Sciences members; he died of a heart attack in December.

Sakharov, as with many dissidents, remained more or less an outsider his entire life.

Awarded the Nobel in 1986, "as one of the most important spiritual leaders and guides in an age when violence, repression and racism continue to characterise the world," Elie Wiesel wasn't mentioned in the 2010 speeches.

Wiesel was born in 1928 in Sighet, now part of Romania. When he was fifteen, his family was sent to Auschwitz. His mother and younger sister were taken straight to the gas chamber. In January 1945 his father was sent to the Buchenwald crematorium, weeks before the US Third Army liberated the camp. After the war, Wiesel became a journalist, writing primarily in French and Yiddish, and published a memoir, *Night* (originally *And the World Remained Silent*), thirteen years later. He would chair the US Presidential Commission on the Holocaust from 1978 to 1986, erecting the United States Holocaust Memorial Museum in Washington, DC.

Wiesel has never been an activist in and of itself. At heart he is a journalist, scholar, writer, seeking after truth. He loves to teach, passing history from one generation to the next.

I think Liu is most like Wiesel. The latter said, "[H]ope without memory is like memory without hope." Like Wiesel, Liu speaks for those who cannot, lives for those who are no longer: "Everything I've said, written, or done about death is rendered weightless by a single glance from the dying. It's covered in the Tiananmen Mothers' brittle white hair. A survivor stands before judgment, astonished in realization."[11] As long as judgment is coming, he has hope, for tomorrow will be today.

Perhaps Liu will be able to build a Tiananmen Square Massacre Memorial in China one day, like he always wanted.

Perhaps he will be able to write and teach about the massacre at Beijing Normal University, where he started a family and made lifelong friends.

Perhaps he will be a history tour guide.

Perhaps he will run for Congress, or more.

Here's to memory and hope.

✿ ✿ ✿

Some say the award was unwise, that it only makes hard-liners harder, setting moderates back even farther. They say a "soft" approach is more responsible, more practical. They said it in 1975 about Sakharov and the Soviet Union, in 1980 about Esquivel and Argentina, in 1984 about Tutu and South Africa, in 1989 about the Dalai Lama and China, and in 1991 about Suu Kyi and Burma. They say it over and over.

Again and again history responds, proving naysayers wrong.

All the regimes above except Burma and China have capsized. Every country is different, but there is no doubt the Nobel can make those in power nervous and deepen trenches among ruling factions. It also reminds democracies not to veer too far off course from human rights in diplomatic waters.

Winners are symbols. They knell sea changes in the near or distant future.

Months before Sakharov's award, the Helsinki Accords were signed as a good-faith agreement to improve relations between the West and the Eastern Bloc. The award affirmed the effort as not only a militaristic or economic one but also one committed to human rights. Tutu's award was also a triple play. It condemned the South African state's use of scripture to justify racial segregation, pointed out the unsustainability of the ANC's violent stance, and warned the West not to further aid and abet the unjust system.

Jagland recalled South Africa's voyage to born freedom as he presented Liu's prize: "The Norwegian Nobel Committee has given four prizes to South Africa. All the laureates came to Oslo, but the awards to Albert Lutuli in 1960 and to Desmond Tutu in 1984 provoked great outrage in the apartheid regime in South Africa, before the applause broke out thanks to the awards to Nelson Mandela and F. W. de Klerk in 1993."

Has the ship sailed for China? How many Nobel laureates does it take to bring the bow around? If Liu is the Chinese Mandela, we need not only a Chinese Lutuli and Tutu but a de Klerk who can steer the administration in the direction the wind is blowing, too.

Though in prison, Liu is charting a new course for himself and for the people of China and the world. History has chosen one of its stewards. The longer the petty dictator and his drones and cronies wait to get onboard, the less likely they will be shown mercy at the feet of the goddess of democracy when she finally rises from the turbulence of time.

"Historical experience gives us reason to believe that continuing rapid economic growth presupposes opportunities for free research, thinking and debate. . . . China's new status entails increased responsibility. China must be prepared for criticism and regard it as positive—as an opportunity for improvement," Jagland said. With a 1.3 billion population and GDP second only to that of the United States, China can be a powerful global force for good only if it respects, protects, and promotes the rights of every human being.

In this sense, giving the 2010 Peace Prize to Liu Xiaobo is perhaps the most right, brave, and important decision the Nobel committee has made in recent years.

At the banquet after the ceremony, Kaci Kullmann Five spoke, as if directly to him:

> As a member of the Norwegian Nobel Committee, I'm not allowed to disclose the content of the discussions we have before making our decision. I think I can make one small exception. Once we had decided that you, Liu Xiaobo, deserved the prize we were left with one very important question for our own consciences: Was it fair to you and your family to bestow this added burden upon you? Would you feel that we made your situation worse, if that is possible, by giving you this Prize?
>
> Your wife's first comment to CNN was that she was overwhelmed and happy. "To receive this Prize is a great honour, but it also implies

great responsibilities," she said. When she met you two days later in your prison you wept with joy and said "I never thought they would dare to give the Prize to a criminal in prison." Reading these comments I felt a profound relief and great joy as this made it clear to me that you are definitely not an unwilling Laureate.[12]

* * *

At a distance, the faint outline of a shore appears. Liu calls out. There is no turning back the tide.

The boat is rocky, but the helm still holds.

The seas are stormy, but the sun still shines.

TIMELINE

1955 December 28. Born in Changchun, Jilin Province

Father Liu Ling taught in Northeast Normal University Chinese Language and Literature Department. Mother Zhang Suqin worked at university daycare. Lived in faculty dorm.

1956 Liu Ling transferred to Choibalsan University. Family moved to Mongolia. Enrolled in Chinese embassy kindergarten.

1959 Family returned to Changchun. Transferred to NNU kindergarten.

1961 April 1. Liu Xia born in Beijing

1962 Liu Xiaobo enrolled in NNU elementary school

1966 Cultural Revolution began

1967 Started middle school at NNU

1969 "Cadre schools" established by Mao to reeducate city cadres and intellectuals as "poor and lower-middle peasants"

Lius sent to Dashizhai village, Inner Mongolia

1973 Family returned to Changchun. Continued high school at NNU.

Began dating classmate Tao Li

1974 July. Sent to San'gang Village, Jilin, to work as
Intellectual Youth

1976 Mao died. Gang of Four arrested. Deng came into
power. Cultural Revolution ended. IYs went home.

November. Returned to Changchun, doing plasterwork
for Changchun Construction

1977 College entrance exams reestablished. Admitted to Jilin
University Chinese Department.

1978 March 13. Arrived on Jilin campus as freshman among
historic class of 1977, reporting to dorm 7, room 202

1980 Became university poetry club True Hearts' seventh
member, editing eponymous semesterly

1982 Graduated with BA in literature. Admitted to graduate
school in Beijing Normal University Department of
Chinese Literature.

Studied literary theory under writer and critic Huang
Yaomian. Began submitting to academic journals.

Married Tao

1983 Son Liu Tao was born

1984 April. First work "On Art and Intuition" published in
Journal of University of International Relations,
followed by "On Zhuangzi" in *Social Science Front*

Awarded MA in literature. Stayed on at BNU as
lecturer.

1986 Began doctoral work in Chinese Literature Department

September. Gave controversial talk "The Crisis of New
Literature" at Chinese Academy of Social Sciences
Institute of Literature "A Decade of New Literature"
conference

1987 September 3. Huang died. Tong Qingbing became
advisor.

First book *Critique of Choice: A Dialogue with Li
Zehou* published by Shanghai People's Publishing
House

1988   February. *A Hundred Schools* started "The Hundred-and-First School" column, publishing Liu's "On Solitude" and others' pieces on "Liu Xiaobo phenomenon"

June 25. Defended dissertation. Committee included Wang Yuanhua and other leading humanities scholars.

August 24. Invited as guest lecturer on modern Chinese literature at University of Oslo

November 27. Visiting scholarship in Oslo ended. Invited to University of Hawaii to lecture on and research Chinese philosophy and current politics.

Stopped and was interviewed in Hong Kong in *Jiefang*, stating: "It would take three hundred years of being colonized" for China to catch up to Hong Kong

Dissertation *Beauty and Freedom* published by BNU Press

1989   February. Scholarship in Hawaii ended. Invited to Columbia University. Introduced to democracy activists in New York. Edited *China Spring*.

April 18. Published "Proposal for Reform" with Hu Ping, Chen Jun, and others

April 22. Published "Open Letter to Chinese University Students" with Hu Ping and others, suggesting points of improvement for student movement

April 26. Ended Columbia visit early. Returned to Beijing to join student movement.

April 27. Arrived in Beijing. Delivered funds donated by overseas students and scholars to Beijing Students' Autonomous Federation.

May 13. Beijing university students began hunger strike at Tiananmen Square. Liu showed support at square next day, helping with publicizing, speaking, writing, and fund-raising. Asked to manage *Beijing Normal University Hunger Strike Group Bulletin*.

Wrote and distributed "Open Letter to Beijing Normal University Party Committee," "Notice to Overseas Chinese and All People Concerned with Issues in China," "Our Suggestions," and other handouts

June 2. Published "June 2 Hunger Strike Declaration." Began hunger strike with Hou Dejian, Zhou Duo, and Gao Xin as "the Four Noblemen."

June 3. Military surrounded square in middle of night. Noblemen attempted to persuade students to retreat.

June 4. Liu among last to leave square. Hid with Hou in diplomatic compound.

June 6. Left compound for home on bicycle. Taken en route by police. Detained at Qincheng Prison. Accused as "black hand of Tiananmen."

June 24. *Beijing Daily* published "Grabbing the Black Hand of Liu Xiaobo"

September. Chinese Youth Press published denunciatory *Who Is Liu Xiaobo?*

Fired from BNU

First nomination for Nobel Peace Prize

Books *The Fog of Metaphysics*, by Shanghai People's Publishing, and *Walking Naked toward God*, by Time Literature and Art Press, banned

1990 Solitary confinement at Qincheng Prison

August. Divorced Tao

Contemporary Politics and Intellectuals in China published by Tangshan Publishing House, Taiwan

Both volumes of *Mysteries of Thought, Dreams of Man* published by Storm and Stress Publishing Company, Taiwan

Awarded Human Rights Watch Hellman/Hammett grant

1991 January 26. Found guilty by Beijing Intermediate People's Court of "inciting counterrevolutionary propaganda" but received suspended sentence for "meritorious act" of persuading protesters to leave square. Released to parents in Dalian.

Returned to Beijing after several months. Temporarily stayed in Hou's apartment.

Began dating Liu Xia. Moved into apartment together near Shuangyushu, Haidian District.

1992 First translated work *A Critique of Contemporary Chinese Intellectuals* published by Tokuma Shoten, Japan

1993 January. Interviewed in Australia and United States. Appeared in documentary *The Gate of Heavenly Peace* (1995). Published "We Are Defeated by Our Justice" in *United Daily News*, Taiwan.

April. Interviewed by Ya Yi in *China Spring*

May. Declined applying for political asylum. Returned to China.

A Survivor's Monologue published by China Times Publishing Company, Taiwan

1994 Published "Proposal Concerning the Repeal of Reeducation through Labor" with Chen Xiaoping and others

1995 February 20. Published "Proposal against Corruption: To the Third Plenary Session of the Eighth National People's Congress" with Bao Zunxin, Wang Ruoshui, Chen Ziming, Xu Wenli, and others

May. Drafted "Lessons from the Bloodbath: The Progress of Democracy and the Rule of Law—June 4 Sixth Anniversary Plea" with Chen Xiaoping and others

May 18. Detained by Beijing Municipal Public Security Bureau in city outskirts before plea was published

1996 January. Released from detention

August. Met Wang Xizhe in Guangzhou. Co-drafted "Opinion on Some Major Issues Concerning Our Country Today," also known as "Double Tenth Declaration."

October 8. Detained by Beijing PSB before declaration was published. Sentenced for "disturbing the peace" to three years at labor camp.

Awarded Hellman/Hammett grant again

1997 January. Sent to Dalian Labor Reeducation Camp

Married Liu Xia

1999 October 7. Released from labor camp. Returned to Beijing. Wrote over a million words in notes and letters at camp.

Moved into apartment at 18 Wanshou Road

2000 July. Joined Independent Chinese PEN

Selected Poems of Liu Xiaobo and Liu Xia published by So Far International Press, Hong Kong

Published *The Beauty Slipped Me a Roofie* under pseudonym Old Xia with Wang Shuo, through Changjiang Literature and Art. Only publication in China after 1989.

2001 September 12. Published "I Want to Fight for Life, Liberty, and Peace" after September 11 attacks. Sent "Open Letter to President Bush and All Americans" with Bao Zunxin and others.

November. Moved to and lived in Bank of China residences in Qixian Village, Haidian District, until 2008

2002 January 10. Supported nomination of Tiananmen Mothers for 2002 Nobel Peace Prize

July 27. Co-issued "Internet Civil Rights Declaration"

Petitioned Chinese NPC and Supreme People's Court against Tenzing Deleg's and Lobsang Dhondup's executions

A People Who Lie to Their Conscience published by
Jieyou Press, Taiwan

2003   April. Co-published "We Support the Iraq War"

November 2. Co-published "Open Letter to Premier
Wen Jiabao Concerning Speech Crime Charges against
Internet Essayist Du Daobin"

November 20. Co-published "Open Petition to Remove
Mao Zedong's Body from the Memorial Hall"

November 21. Elected as Independent Chinese PEN's
second president. Published inaugural address in
internal forum.

Awarded Chinese Democracy Education Foundation
Seventeenth Annual Outstanding Contribution Prize
for Democracy of China

2004   February 1. Co-published "Petition for Judicial
Interpretation of 'Inciting Subversion of State Power'"

June 3. Published protests against illegal detention of
Ding Zilin and Tiananmen Mothers on eve of massacre
fifteenth anniversary

October 30. Presided over Second Independent
Chinese PEN Freedom to Write Award Ceremony

December 13. Interrogated by police for drafting
"Chinese Annual Human Rights Report." Released next
day.

December 21. Recognized as 2004 Press Freedom
Defender by Reporters Without Borders and
Fondation de France

Received Ninth Annual Hong Kong Human Rights
Press Merit for "News Corrupts in the Dark," *Open
Magazine* (January 2004)

2005   November 2. Reelected as PEN president

December 10. Awarded Tenth Annual Hong Kong
Human Rights Press Prize for "Heaven for the

Privileged, Hell for the Poor," *Open Magazine* (September 2005)

Civil Awakening: The Dawn of a Free China published by Laogai Research Foundation

2006 January 2. PEN 2005 Freedom to Write and Lin Zhao Memorial Awards Ceremony held in Beijing

January 19. Visited Zhao Ziyang's residence with Ding on anniversary of death

February 23. Appeared on Radio Taiwan International

October. Became editor of Minzhuzhongguo.org

Received Eleventh Annual Hong Kong Human Rights Press Merit for "Report on Crackdown in Shanwei," *Open Magazine* (January 2006)

Single-Edged Poison Sword: A Critique of Contemporary Chinese Nationalism published by Broad Press

2007 January 23. Discussed freedoms of speech and press in China with Reporters Without Borders at Shangri-La Hotel, Beijing

August 7. Published "One World, One Dream, One Human Rights: Our Appeal and Proposal to the Beijing Olympics" with Ding

November. Left office as PEN president. Stayed on board until October 2009.

2008 March 22. Co-published "Twelve Points by Some Chinese Intellectuals on Handling the Tibetan Situation"

March 29. Invited to Think Tank for Chinese Reconciliation "Conflict and Reconciliation" conference

May. Published "Child, Mother, Spring: For Tiananmen Mothers' Website Launch"

Awarded Modern Chinese Language Institute Outstanding Contribution Prize. Delivered acceptance speech "From Reeds to Barrens" on June 3.

June 3. Restrained and beaten by police in Beijing

October. Began renovating apartment from Liu Xia's parents by Yuyuantan Park

November 29. Invited to lecture on "Tragedy in Literature" by Transition Institute. Canceled due to police detention.

December 2. Published last article before arrest, "Breaking Administrative Monopoly Is Ending Legal Robbery: A Tribute to Cabbies on Strike," on Observechina.laogai.org

Co-drafted Charter 08, signed by more than three hundred Chinese intellectuals and activists and slated for publication on Human Rights Day and Universal Declaration of Human Rights Sixtieth Anniversary, December 10

December 8. Taken and detained by police in secret location in Beijing outskirts

2009 March. Received People in Need Homo Homini Award

April. Received PEN/Barbara Goldsmith Freedom to Write Award

June 23. Charged with "inciting subversion of state power" by Beijing Municipal People's Procuratorate and held at Beijing No. 1 Detention Center

June 25. Met with lawyers Shang Baojun and Ding Xikui

December 25. Hearing began in Beijing Municipal No. 1 Intermediate People's Court. Liu Xia and hundreds of supporters placed under house arrest next day. US and European Union embassies denied trial access.

December 26. Sentenced to eleven years in prison and two years deprivation of political rights for "spreading rumors, slandering and in other ways inciting subversion of the government and overturning the socialist system." Stated "I have no enemies" in court.

Met with Liu Xia after verdict. Motioned to appeal.

Received Independent Federation of Chinese Students and Scholars Free Spirit Award

The Fall of a Nation published by Asian Culture Press, Taiwan

From Tiananmen to Charter 08, Japanese edition, published by Fujiwara Shoten

2010 January 22. European Association for Chinese Studies called for Liu's release in open letter to Hu Jintao

February 11. Appeal overruled by Beijing Municipal High People's Court

March 10. More than 150 scholars, writers, lawyers, and advocates worldwide called for release in letter to NPC chairman Wu Bangguo

May 26. Transferred to Jinzhou Prison in Liaoning

June 2. Liu Xia permitted to visit

October 4. Received Human Rights Watch Alison Des Forges Award for Extraordinary Activism

October 7. Awarded German PEN Hermann Kesten Medal

October 8. Norwegian Nobel Committee chairman Thorbjørn Jagland announced Liu as winner of 2010 Nobel Peace Prize "for his long and nonviolent struggle for fundamental human rights in China"

Liu Xia placed under permanent house arrest

October 11. Tiananmen Mothers published "Our Declaration," stating "Mr. Liu's award gives us a great deal of encouragement"

Named one of *TIME*'s "Top Ten Political Prisoners"

October 25. Fifteen Nobel Peace laureates called on Hu to release Liu Xiaobo and end Liu Xia's arrest

December 10. Nobel Peace Prize Award Ceremony held in Oslo. Liu Xiaobo, family, and hundreds invited by Liu Xia forbidden to leave China.

Medal and diploma presented to empty chair on stage. First time in prize's 109-year history neither laureate nor representative was present to accept award.

Exhibit "I Have No Enemies" opened at Nobel Peace Center

December 11. Nobel Peace Prize Concert hosted by Denzel Washington and Anne Hathaway, with King Harald V, Queen Sonja, and six thousand attendees. Aung San Suu Kyi sent video greeting.

German, American, Portuguese, Czech, and Sydney PENs named Liu honorary member. Independent Chinese PEN named Liu honorary president.

I Have No Enemies, I Know No Hate: Selected Essays and Poems published by S. Fischer Verlag, Germany

A Collection of Essays by Liu Xiaobo published by New Century Press, Hong Kong

Pursuit of Liberty: Selected Writings published by Laogai

2011 March. United Nations Working Group on Arbitrary Detention called on administration to release Liu Xiaobo, end Liu Xia's arrest, and provide compensation to both

After the Last Judgment: Selected Writings published by Iwanami Shoten, Japan

March 24. *Philosophy of the Pig and Other Essays* published by Collection Bleu de Chine, Éditions Gallimard, France

September 22. Liu Ling died. Liu Xiaobo permitted at funeral.

October. Liu Xia photography exhibit *The Silent Strength of Liu Xia* unveiled at Musée jardin Paul Landowski, Boulogne-Billancourt, France

December 8. Five Nobel Peace laureates, including Desmond Tutu, and others formed International Committee to Support Liu Xiaobo to campaign for release

Selected writings *I Have No Enemies: Two Decades of Fighting for Democracy in China* published by Fujiwara

2012 January. *No Enemies, No Hatred: Selected Essays and Poems* published by Harvard University Press

February. *Silent Strength* opened at Columbia University

February 13. Chinese vice president Xi Jinping visited United States, remaining silent on issue of jailed Chinese dissidents

June 10. *Silent Strength* opened at City University of Hong Kong

August. *Liu Xiaobo, Charter 08 and the Challenges of Political Reform in China*, edited by Jean-Philippe Béja, Fu Hualing, and Eva Pils, published by Hong Kong University Press

December 4. Petition by Tutu and 134 other Nobel laureates for Lius' release signed by more than four hundred thousand worldwide

December 6. Associated Press Beijing correspondent Isolda Morillo accessed Liu Xia's apartment while guards were at lunch and conducted first interview with Liu Xia in more than two years. Account revealed her to be in poor physical and mental health.

2013 April 25. The *New York Times* published Didi Kirsten Tatlow's "Glimpses from the Life of China's Jailed Nobel Laureate," revealing Liu Xia was allowed half-hour monthly visits of husband in prison

May 3. PEN International published on World Press Day *The PEN Report: Creativity and Constraint in Today's China*. *The Guardian* and *The Times Literary Supplement* sent open letter signed by 150 literary and cultural figures to Chinese leaders calling for artistic freedom and release of some forty jailed writers and journalists in country.

2014   February. Liu Xia admitted to Beijing hospital after police denied request for medical care abroad

May. Chinese "princelings" urged authorities to grant Liu parole, for which he is eligible after serving half of term, to "improve country's image"

May 29. Received Democracy Award from National Endowment for Democracy

NOTES

1. THE YOUNG BOY ON THE BLACK SOIL

1. Liu Xiaobo 刘晓波, *Mori xingcunzhe de dubai* 末日幸存者的独白 [A survivor's monologue] (Taipei: China Times, 1993), 38.

2. Liu Xiaobo, "Changda bange shiji de shiyi—Xu *Cai Chu shixuan*" 长达半个世纪的诗意—序《蔡楚诗选》 [Poetic feeling across half a century—Foreword to *Selected Poems of Cai Chu*], *Minzhu Zhongguo* 民主中国, October 10, 2008, http://minzhuzhongguo.org/ArtShow.aspx?AID=6421. At the time of this book's publication in English, some websites referenced, such as *Guancha* and others, have shut down; some web pages, such as those on *Beijing Spring* and others, have been removed. Some materials are archived on *Boxun* with the original publication information indicated.

3. The Cultural Revolution brought young Liu unprecedented freedom. He had his first cigarette at age eleven. See Liu, "Wo cong shiyisue kaishi chouyan—Wei 'Wenge' sanshinian er zuo" 我从十一岁开始吸烟——为"文革"三十年而作 [I started smoking at eleven—For the thirtieth anniversary of the Cultural Revolution], *Cheng Ming Magazine*, May 1996, quoted in https://docs.google.com/document/d/1RzO00D1IG3zfBeTXROFZfogqDj5K EttZhtCQlZlI0io/preview.

4. For the incident regarding the old man Yi Hai and Liu's reflection, see Liu, "Cong wawa zhuaqi de canren—Wei Wenge sanshiwu zhounian er zuo" 從娃娃抓起的殘忍——为文革三十五周年而作 [Cruelty from the cradle—For the thirty-fifth anniversary of the Cultural Revolution], *Minzhu Zhongguo*, April 2001, quoted in http://epochtimes.com/gb/1/3/31/n71014.htm.

5. Chen Jiaying 陈嘉映, "Women zhe yidai" 我们这一代 [Our generation], *Beijing Spring*, June 2011, http://beijingspring.com/bj2/2010/240/ 2011620171819.htm.

6. Geremie Barmé, "Confession, Redemption, and Death: Liu Xiaobo and the Protest Movement of 1989," in *The Broken Mirror: China after Tiananmen*, ed. George Hicks (London: Longmans, 1990), 53–54.

7. Liu Xiaobo, "Zai diyu de rukouchu: Dui Makesizhuyi de zai jiantao" 在地狱的入口處：对马克思主义的再检讨 [At the gates of hell: Further reflections on Marxism], in *Liu Xiaobo qiren qishi* 刘晓波其人其事 [Who is Liu Xiaobo?], ed. Zheng Wang 郑旺 and Ji Kuai 季蒯 (Beijing: China Youth, 1989), 102.

8. Liu Xiaobo, "Yong zhenhua dianfu huangyan zhidu: Jieshou 'Jiechu Minzhu Renshi Jiang' de daxieci" 用真话颠覆谎言制度：接受"杰出民主人士奖"的答谢词 [Subverting a regime of lies with truth: Outstanding Contribution Prize for Democracy of China acceptance speech], *Cheng Ming Magazine*, May 2003, quoted in *Liu Xiaobo Wenji* 刘晓波文集 [Collected writings of Liu Xiaobo], ed. Liu Xia 刘霞, Hu Ping 胡平, and Tienchi Martin-Liao 廖天琪 (Hong Kong: New Century, 2010), 237.

9. Yin Hongbiao 印红标, *Shizongzhe de zuji: Wenhua Dageming qijian de qingnian sichao* 失踪者的足迹：文化大革命期间的青年思潮 [Footsteps of the missing: Trends of thought among Chinese youths during the Cultural Revolution] (Hong Kong: Chinese University Press, 2009), 216.

10. Zha Jianying 查建英, *Bashi niandai fangtan lu* 八十年代访谈录 [The 1980s: Interviews] (Hong Kong: Oxford University Press, 2006), 6.

2. BEIJING STORIES

1. Liu Xiaofeng 刘晓峰 and Bing Dao 冰岛, "'Kuangren' Liu Xiaobo" "狂人"刘晓波 [Madman Liu Xiaobo], in *Liu Xiaobo qiren qishi* 刘晓波其人其事 [Who is Liu Xiaobo?], ed. Zheng Wang 郑旺 and Ji Kuai 季蒯 (Beijing: China Youth, 1989), 71.

2. Liu Xiaobo, *Zhongguo dangdai zhengzhi yu Zhongguo zhishi fenzi* 中国当代政治与中国知识分子 [Contemporary politics and intellectuals in China] (Taipei: Tonsan, 1990), 162.

3. Liu and Bing, 80.

4. Niu Han 牛汉 and Chen Huaji 陈华积, "Zhongguo zazhi, Ding Ling yu bashi niandai wenxue" 《中国》杂志、丁玲与八十年代文学 [*China* magazine, Ding Ling, and literature in the eighties], *Shanghai wenhua* 上海文化 3 (2010), quoted in http://21ccom.net/articles/read/article_2010081816056.html.

5. Niu Han et al., "Zhongguo beiwanglu"《中国》备忘录 [A memorandum for *China*], *Zhongguo* 中国 [China] 12 (1986), quoted in Wang Zengru 王增如, *Ding Ling ban* Zhongguo 丁玲办《中国》[Ding Ling and *China*] (Beijing: People's Literature, 2011), 252.

6. Liu Xiaobo, *Xuanze de pipan: Yu Li Zehou dui hua* 选择的批判：与李泽厚对话 [Critique of choice: Conversations with Li Zehou] (Beijing: Beijing Normal University Publishing, 1988), 2.

7. Zha Jianying 查建英, *Bashi niandai fangtan lu* 八十年代访谈录 [The 1980s: Interviews] (Hong Kong: Oxford University Press, 2006), 13–14.

8. Geremie Barmé, "Confession, Redemption, and Death: Liu Xiaobo and the Protest Movement of 1989," in *The Broken Mirror: China after Tiananmen*, ed. George Hicks (London: Longmans, 1990), 53.

9. Xu Youyu 徐友渔, "Yi Liu Xiaobo jian Kuai Dafu" 忆刘晓波见蒯大富 [Remembering Liu Xiaobo's meeting with Kuai Dafu], *Open Magazine*, November 2010, http://open.com.hk/old_version/1011p20.html.

10. Liu, *Xuanze*.

11. Liu Xiaobo, *Shenmei yu ren de ziyou* 审美与人的自由 [Beauty and freedom] (Beijing: Beijing Normal University Publishing, 1988), 183.

12. Tong Qingbing 童庆炳, foreword to Liu, *Shenmei*, 2.

13. Hao Jian 郝建, "'Heima,' 'Heishou' he wenzhang haoshou Liu Xiaobo" "黑马"、"黑手"和文章好手刘晓波 [Dark horse, black hand, and virtuosic writer Liu Xiaobo], in *Ziyou jingguan* 自由荆冠 [Thorned crown of freedom], ed. Chen Kuide 陳奎德 and Xia Ming 夏明 (Hong Kong: Morning Bell, 2010), 219.

14. Wan Runnan 万润南, "Guanyu Xiaobo de diandi jiyi" 关于晓波的点滴记忆 [Some memories of Xiaobo], in *Jiedu Liu Xiaobo* 解读刘晓波 [Reading Liu Xiaobo], ed. Xinxi Ziyou Guanchashi 信息自由观察室 (Hong Kong: Suyuan, 2011), 340.

3. THE BLACK HAND OF TIANANMEN

1. Liu Xiaobo, *Mori xingcunzhe de dubai* 末日幸存者的独白 [A survivor's monologue] (Taipei: China Times, 1993), 82.

2. Geremie Barmé, "Confession, Redemption, and Death: Liu Xiaobo and the Protest Movement of 1989," in *The Broken Mirror: China after Tiananmen*, ed. George Hicks (London: Longmans, 1990), 56.

3. Jin Zhong 金钟, "Wentan 'heima' Liu Xiaobo" 文坛"黑马"刘晓波 [Literary dark horse Liu Xiaobo], in *Liu Xiaobo qiren qishi* 刘晓波其人其事 [Who is Liu Xiaobo?], ed. Zheng Wang 郑旺 and Ji Kuai 季蒯 (Beijing: China Youth, 1989), 143.

4. James Tu, "Liu Xiaobo yu quanwei zhuyi de tongluren" 刘晓波与权威主义的同路人 [Liu Xiaobo and authoritarians], *Apple Daily*, December 31, 2008.

5. Hu Ping 胡平, "Wo he Xiaobo de jiaowang" 我和晓波的交往 [My relationship with Xiaobo], *Beijing Spring*, November 2010, http://beijingspring.com/bj2/2010/120/2010111204151.htm.

6. Liu Xiaobo, "'Liuer jueshi' yanjiang" "六二绝食"演讲 [June 2 hunger strike declaration], in *Liu Xiaobo qiren qishi* 刘晓波其人其事 [Who is Liu Xiaobo?], ed. Zheng Wang 郑旺 and Ji Kuai 季蒯 (Beijing: China Youth, 1989), 138.

7. Liu, *Mori*, 76.

8. James Tu, "Manhuai yingxiong zhuyi" 满怀英雄主义 [Full of heroism], *Apple Daily*, October 9, 2010.

9. Liu, *Mori*, 67.

10. Ibid., 88.

11. Feng Congde 封从德, *Liusi riji* 六四日记 [June 4 diaries] (Hong Kong: Morning Bell, 2009), 236.

12. Liu, *Mori*, 94–98.

13. Zhou Duo 周舵, "Xiexing de liming" 血腥的黎明 [Bloody dawn], *Independent Chinese PEN Center*, March 9, 2009, http://blog.boxun.com/hero/200903/zhouduo/1_1.shtml.

14. Liu, *Mori*, 107.

15. Ibid, 113.

16. Wang Xiaoshan 王小山, "Liu Xiaobo shi wode laoshi" 刘晓波是我的老师 [Liu Xiaobo is my teacher], *Ming Pao*, January 13, 2010.

17. Liu, *Mori*, 134.

18. Chai Ling 柴玲, *Chai Ling huiyi: Yixin yiyi xiang ziyou* 柴玲回忆：一心一意向自由 [Chai Ling remembers: A heart set on freedom] (Hong Kong: Greenfield, 2011), 180.

19. Liu, *Mori*, 193.

20. Huang Shuxin 黄舒心, "Wang Juntao: Liu Xiaobo de jianchi, shuaixing yu wanshi bugong" 王军涛：刘晓波的坚持、率性与玩世不恭 [Wang Juntao: Liu Xiaobo's conviction, headstrongness, and irreverence], *Mingjing Magazine*, October 2010, quoted in http://chinesepen.org/Article/sxsy/201010/Article_20101019235329.shtml.

21. Liu, "'Liuer jueshi' yanjiang," 138–39.

22. For Liu's experience of the attention surrounding the strike, see Liu, *Mori*, 206.

23. Zhou, "Xiexing de liming."

24. Feng, *Liusi riji*, 515.

25. Cai Shufang 蔡淑芳, *Guangchang huobei: Yige Xianggang nüjizhe yanzhong de Liusi xieguang* 广场活碑：一个香港女记者眼中的六四血光 [Living monument at the Square: Bloodshed on June 4 in the eyes of a female Hong Kong reporter] (Hong Kong: Sibixiang, 2009), 201–2.

26. Liu Xiaobo, "Jiyi: 'Liusi' liu zhounian ji" 记忆："六四"六周年祭 [Memory: Elegy for the sixth anniversary of June 4], in *Niannian Liusi: Liu Xiaobo shiji* 念念六四：刘晓波诗集 [June 4 elegies: Collected poems of Liu Xiaobo] (Hong Kong: Self-published, 2009), 36.

4. START FROM ZERO

1. Harry Wu, *Qincheng Jianyu: Zhongguo de zhengzhi jianyu* 秦城监狱：中国的政治监狱 [Qincheng Prison: China's political prison] (Washington, DC: Laogai, 2012), 1.

2. Liu Xiaobo 刘晓波, *Mori xingcunzhe de dubai* 末日幸存者的独白 [A survivor's monologue] (Taipei: China Times, 1993), 41.

3. Liu Xianbin 刘贤斌, *Ruowei ziyou gu* 若为自由故 [If for freedom] (Washington, DC: Laogai, 2011), 58.

4. Chen Xiaoping 陈小平, "Laowantong Liu Xiaobo: Wo youxin chengren, jianlao nai wo he" 老顽童刘晓波：我有心成仁，监牢奈我何 [Grumpy old Liu Xiaobo: I am willing to die for a cause, so what am I afraid of about prisons?], *Independent Chinese PEN Center*, June 25, 2009, http://chinesepen.org/Article/sxsy/200906/Article_20090625102827.shtml.

5. Liu Xiaobo, "Baobao, women ai ni!" 包包，我们爱你！[Baobao, we love you!], in *Bao Zunxin jinian wenji* 包遵信纪念文集 [Anthology in memory of Bao Zunxin], ed. Liu Xiaobo et al. (Hong Kong: So Far, 2008), 51.

6. Liu, *Mori*, 38.

7. Ibid., 17.

8. Ibid., 18.

9. Liu, "Zixu: Laizi fenmu de zhenhan" 自序：来自坟墓的震撼 [Preface: A shock from the grave], in *Niannian Liusi: Liu Xiaobo shiji* 念念六四：刘晓波诗集 [June 4 elegies: Collected poems of Liu Xiaobo] (Hong Kong: Self-published, 2009), 7.

10. Su Xiaokang 苏晓康, "Ba jijin jian'ao cheng wenhe" 把激进煎熬成温和 [Forging moderate from radical], *Open Magazine*, November 2010, http://open.com.hk/old_version/1011p39.html.

11. Jianying Zha, "Servant of the State," *New Yorker*, November 8, 2010, http://newyorker.com/magazine/2010/11/08/servant-of-the-state.

12. Huang Shuxin 黄舒心, "Chen Jun: Liao Xiaobo zouguo de qilu he neixin de zhengzha" 陈军：刘晓波走过的歧路和内心的挣扎 [Chen Jun: Liu Xiao-

bo's forked paths and inner struggles], *Mingjing Magazine*, October 2010, quoted in *Ziyou jingguan* 自由荆冠 [Thorned crown of freedom], ed. Chen Kuide 陈奎德 and Xia Ming 夏明 (Hong Kong: Morning Bell, 2010), 227–28.

13. Liu, "Tiyen siwang: 'Liusi' yi zhounian ji" 体验死亡：六四—周年祭 [Experiencing death: Elegy for the first anniversary of June 4], in *Niannian Liusi*, 15.

14. For Liu's feelings on his relationship with Tao, see Liu, *Mori*, 146–47.

15. Ya Yi 亞衣, *Liuwangzhe fangtan lu* 流亡者访谈录 [Interviews with exiles] (Hong Kong: So Far, 2005), 230.

16. Ibid.

17. Liu Xiaobo to Hu Ping, May 12, 2000, *Beijing Spring*, December 2010, http://beijingspring.com/bj2/2010/240/20101130143040.htm.

18. Liu, "Zixu," *Beijing Spring*, December 2010, http://beijingspring.com/bj2/2010/240/20101130143040.htm.

19. Liu Xia 刘霞, "Meiguo Bihui banfa Ziyou Xiexuo Jiang gei Liu Xiaobo: Wo de daxieci" 美国笔会颁发自由写作奖给刘晓波：我的答谢辞 [PEN American Center giving Freedom to Write Award to Liu Xiaobo: My acceptance speech], in *Lingba Xianzhang yu Zhongguo biange* 零八宪章与中国变革 [Charter 08 and China's transformation], ed. Zhongguo Zixun Zhongxin 中国信息中心 (Washington, DC: Laogai, 2009), np.

20. Liu Xiaobo, "'Liusi,' yizuo fenmu: 'Liusi' shisan zhounian ji" "六四"，一座坟墓："六四"十三周年祭 [June 4, a grave: Elegy for the thirteenth anniversary of June 4], in *Niannian Liusi*, 80.

21. Liu, "Yikuai muban de jiyi: 'Liusi' shier zhounian ji" 一块木板的记忆："六四"十二周年祭 [Memory of a wood plank: Elegy for the twelfth anniversary of June 4], in *Niannian Liusi*, 75.

22. Cui Weiping 崔卫平, "Liu Xiaobo huoxing zhishi fenzi de kanfa" 刘晓波获刑知识分子的看法 [Intellectuals on Liu Xiaobo's sentencing], *China in Perspective*, October 20, 2010, http://chinainperspective.com/ArtShow.aspx?AID=8606.

23. Liu Xiaobo, "'Tiananmen Muqin' liying dedao de rongyu" "天安门母亲"理应得到的荣誉 [An honor Tiananmen Mothers deserve], *Beijing Spring*, March 2002, http://beijingspring.com/bj2/2002/100/200372001835.htm.

24. Liu Xiaobo, "Qingting Tiananmen Muqin de shengyin" 倾听天安门母亲的声音 [Listening to Tiananmen Mothers' voice], in *Xunfang Liusi shounanzhe* 寻访六四受难者 [Interviews with June 4 victims], ed. Ding Zilin 丁子霖 (Hong Kong: Open, 2005), 3.

25. Ding Zilin and Jiang Peikun 蒋培坤, "Women yu Xiaobo de xiangzhi, xiangshi he xiangjiao" 我们与晓波的相知、相识和相交 [How we met and got to know Xiaobo], in *Ziyou jingguan* 自由荆冠 [Thorned crown of freedom],

ed. Chen Kuide 陈奎德 and Xia Ming 夏明 (Hong Kong: Morning Bell, 2010), 42.

26. Ibid.

27. Liu Xiaobo, "Zhan zai shijian de zuzhou zhong: 'Liusi' shi zhounian ji" 站在时间的诅咒中："六四"十周年祭 [Standing in the curse of time: Elegy for the tenth anniversary of June 4], in *Niannian Liusi*, 62.

28. Su Xiaokang, "Wenming juexing" 文明觉醒 [Civilization awakes], in *Xunfang Liusi shounanzhe* 寻访六四受难者 [Interviews with June 4 victims], ed. Ding Zilin 丁子霖 (Hong Kong: Open, 2005), 36.

29. Ya, *Liuwangzhe fangtan lu*.

30. Zha, "Servant of the State."

31. Ye Fu 野夫, *Jiangshang de muqin* 江上的母亲 [A mother by the river] (Taipei: Homeward, 2009), 320–21.

32. Xinxi Ziyou Guanchashi, ed., *Liu Xiaobo dangan* 刘晓波档案 [Liu Xiaobo file] (Hong Kong: Suyuan, 2011), 328.

33. Ibid.

5. ONE MAN'S WAR

1. Liu Xiaobo, *Mori xingcunzhe de dubai* 末日幸存者的独白 [A survivor's monologue] (Taipei: China Times, 1993), 207.

2. Zhou Duo, "'Xiexing de liming' xupian: Taowang, beibu, huoshi, chuguo he guiguo" 《血腥的黎明》续篇：逃亡、被捕、获释、出国和归国 [Bloody dawn, part two: Escape, arrest, release, going abroad, and coming home], *Independent Chinese PEN Center*, May 30, 2009, http://blog.boxun.com/hero/200905/zhouduo/6_1.shtml.

3. Zhou Yicheng 周义澄, "Liu Xiaobo yu gongchandang" 刘晓波与共产党 [Liu Xiaobo and the Communist Party], in *Jiedu Liu Xiaobo* 解读刘晓波 [Reading Liu Xiaobo], ed. Xinxi Ziyou Guanchashi 信息自由观察室 (Hong Kong: Suyuan, 2011), 395.

4. Liu Xiaobo, "Beiju yingxiong de beiju: Hu Yaobang shishi xianxiang pinglun zhi yi" 悲剧英雄的悲剧：胡耀邦逝世现象评论之一 [Tragedy of tragic heroes: A comment on phenomena surrounding Hu Yaobang's passing], *Jiefang*, May 1989, quoted in *Liu Xiaobo qiren qishi* 刘晓波其人其事 [Who is Liu Xiaobo?], ed. Zheng Wang 郑旺 and Ji Kuai 季蒯 (Beijing: China Youth, 1989), 116.

5. Tienchi Martin-Liao 廖天琪, "Moran huishou, Xiaobo zheng zai denghuo lanshan chu" 蓦然回首，晓波正在灯火阑珊处 [Suddenly you turn, and Xiaobo is there by the dim light], *Guancha*观察, January 1, 2010, quoted in http://blog.boxun.com/hero/201001/liaotq/1_1.shtml.

6. Meng Taoer 孟涛儿, "Yige Zhongguoren de chengzhang" 一个中国人的成长 [A Chinese's growth], *Ziyou xiezuo* 自由写作, January 1, 2011, http://chinesepen.org/Article/wk/201101/Article_20110101011453.shtml.

7. Jing Wa 井娃, "Zhongguo yuzhong zuojia wenxuan, xianci" 中国狱中作家文选·献辞 [Selected writings and messages from imprisoned Chinese writers], in *Zhongguo yuzhong zuojia wenxuan* 中国狱中作家文选 [Selected writings from imprisoned Chinese writers], ed. Huang Heqing 黄河清 and Wang Yiliang 王一梁 (Hong Kong: Morning Bell, 2009), np.

8. Liu Xiaobo, "Wo yu hulianwang" 我与互联网 [The internet and I], *Minzhu Zhongguo*, February 14, 2006, quoted in http://blog.boxun.com/hero/liuxb/513_1.shtml.

9. Liu Xiaobo 刘晓波 to Hu Ping 胡平, May 12, 2000, *Beijing Spring*, December 2010, http://beijingspring.com/bj2/2010/240/20101130143040.htm.

10. Liu Xiaobo, "Renquan yishi de juexing yu zhengzhi gaige: Zailun weilai de ziyou Zhongguo zai minjian" 人权意识的觉醒与政治改革：再论未来的自由中国在民间 [Awakening of human rights consciousness and political transformation: More on a free China's future in the people], *Boxun* 博讯, January 4, 2003, http://blog.boxun.com/hero/liuxb/49_1.shtml.

11. Liu Xiaobo, "Wei 'Shiji Zhongguo wangzhan' songxing" 为"世纪中国网站"送行 [Seeing off the Century China website], *Guancha*, July 26, 2006, quoted in http://blog.boxun.com/hero/2006/liuxb/43_1.shtml.

12. Liu Xiaobo, "Wo renshi de Yang Zili he Lu Kun" 我认识的杨子立和路坤 [The Yang Zili and Lu Kun I know], *Epoch Times*, April 24, 2001, http://epochtimes.com/b5/1/4/26/n81002.htm.

13. Liu Xiaobo, "Wang Yi jingdong le wo: *Wang Yi wenji* xu" 王怡惊动了我：《王怡文集》序 [Wang Yi shocked me: Foreword to *Collected writings of Wang Yi*], *Minzhu Zhongguo*, November 6, 2004, quoted in http://blog.boxun.com/hero/liuxb/218_1.shtml.

14. Liu Xiaobo, "Minjian wangzhan shouwangzhe Ye Du" 民间网站守望者野渡 [Ye Du, guardian of popular websites], *Minzhu Zhongguo*, January 14, 2006, quoted in http://beijingspring.com/c7/xw/ywzs/20060115003325.htm.

15. Yu Shicun 余世存, "Erlinglingsi dierjie Ziyou Xiezuo Jiang banjiang ceji" 二零零四年第二届自由写作奖颁奖侧记 [Notes to the 2004 second annual Freedom to Write Award ceremony], *Minzhu Zhongguo*, December 30, 2004, quoted in http://blog.boxun.com/hero/yushicun/47_1.shtml.

16. Liu Xiaobo, "Meiyou jiyi, meiyou lishi, meiyou weilai: Wei Beijing 'Wenxue yu jiyi' yantaohui er zuo" 没有记忆，没有历史，没有未来：为北京"文学与记忆"研讨会而作 [No memory, no history, no future: For Beijing's "Literature and memory" conference], *Minzhu Zhongguo*, January 28, 2006, quoted in http://blog.boxun.com/hero/liuxb/503_1.shtml.

17. Liu Xiaobo, "Wo de renshen ziyou zai shiji fenzhong nei bei boduo: Gei 'Sulian de gulage he Zhongguo de laogai' guoji yantaohui" 我的人身自由在十几分钟内被剥夺：给"苏联的古拉格和中国的劳改"国际研讨会 [My person freedom was taken from me in ten minutes: For the "Soviet Gulag and Chinese labor reeducation" international conference], *Guancha*, May 1, 2006, quoted in http://epochtimes.com/gb/6/5/1/n1304190.htm.

18. Jiang Weiping 姜维平, "Wo suo zhidao de Liu Xiaobo" 我所知道的刘晓波 [The Liu Xiaobo I know], *Open Magazine*, August 2009, quoted in http://chinesepen.org/Article/hyxz/200908/Article_20090804040446.shtml.

19. Liu Xiaobo, "Ziyouren miandui tiechuang de weixiao: Wei Qin Geng *Zhongguo diyi zui: Wo zai jianyu de kuaile shenghuo jishi* zuo xu" 自由人面对铁窗的微笑：为秦耕《中国第一罪：我在监狱的快乐生活纪实》作序 [Foreword to Qin Geng's *China's first sin: A chronicle of the happy times I spent in prison*], *Guancha*, October 12, 2006, quoted in https://docs.google.com/document/d/1jJNFUY0WsvXhcQiakXKdKjcUQxLX2othIcybGJXB6co.

20. Wen Yujie 温玉杰, "Shiren de quwen yishi: Jin fei xi bi de Liu tongxue" 诗人的趣闻轶事：今非昔比的刘同学 [Anecdotes about a poet: My classmate Liu then and now], *Jilin Daxue Zhongwen Xi qiqiji boke* 吉林大学中文系七七级博客 (blog), nd, no url.

21. Wang Xiaoshan 王小山, "Liu Xiaobo shi wode laoshi" 刘晓波是我的老师 [Liu Xiaobo is my teacher], *Ming Pao*, January 13, 2010.

22. Liu Xiaobo, "'Liusi' lingchen de heian" "六四"凌晨的黑暗 [Darkness at dawn on June 4], *Epoch Times*, June 6, 2004.

23. Liu Xiaobo, "Baozhu sheng zhong jingcha shanggang, zhen xinku" 爆竹声中警察上岗，真辛苦 [Police on duty amidst sounds of firecrackers, working hard], *Guancha*, February 17, 2005, quoted in https://docs.google.com/document/d/1hHt5--jdxaVfatueHR9JAYjBW0dS67KwnTY9-ZT68qA.

24. Liu Xiaobo, "Laisi you lai le, jingcha you shanggang" 赖斯又来了，警察又上岗 [Rice returns, police on duty again], *Guancha*, March 21, 2005, quoted in http://epochtimes.com/gb/5/3/21/n859124.htm.

25. Liu Xiaobo, "Renquan gaoji guanyuan lai le, jingcha you shanggang le" 人权高级官员来了，警察又上岗了 [Human rights high officials are here, police on duty again], *Guancha*, August 29, 2005, quoted in http://epochtimes.com/gb/5/8/30/n1035067.htm.

26. Zhongguo Zixun Zhongxin, "Bie zai saorao Liu Xiaobo" 别再骚扰刘晓波 [Stop harassing Liu Xiaobo], *Guancha*, June 4, 2008, quoted in http://beijingspring.com/c7/xw/rqmy/20080604201056.htm.

27. Jiang Qisheng 江棋生 et al., "Liusi ye women kangyi jingfang dui Liu Xiaobo xiansheng shibao" 六四夜我们抗议警方对刘晓波先生施暴 [On the night of June 4 we protest police brutality against Mr. Liu Xiaobo], *Guancha*,

June 5, 2008, quoted in http://chinesepen.org/Article/sxsy/200806/Article_20080605023311.shtml.

28. Zhongguo Zixun Zhongxin, "Liu Xiaobo de beiju de wenxue jiangzuo zao jingfang pohuai" 刘晓波的悲剧的文学讲座遭警方破坏 [Liu Xiaobo's tragedy in literature lecture sabotaged by police], *Guancha*, November 30, 2008, quoted in http://weiquanwang.org/?p=12096.

6. FINAL WARNING: CHARTER 08

1. Jiang Qisheng, "Shuo liangjian wo yu Lingba Xianzhang de shi" 说两件我与零八宪章的事 [A thing or two about Charter 08 and me], in *Lingba Xianzhang* 零八宪章 [Charter 08], eds. Li Xiaorong 李晓蓉 and Zhang Zuhua 张祖桦 (Hong Kong: Open, 2009), np.

2. Václav Havel, "China's Human-Rights Activists Need Support," *Wall Street Journal*, December 19, 2008.

3. Ibid.

4. Alexandra Laignel-Lavastine, *Esprits d'Europe: Autour de Czeslaw Milosz, Jan Patočka, István Bibó* [Spirits of Europe: A study of Czeslaw Milosz, Jan Patočka, and István Bibó] (Paris: Calmann-Lévy, 2005).

5. Václav Havel, *Disturbing the Peace: A Conversation with Karel Hvížďala* (New York: Vintage, 1991), 133.

6. Chen Kuide 陈奎德, "Dang xianzheng zhongsheng xiangqi: Xinnian xianci" 当宪政钟声响起：新年献词 [When the bell tolls for constitutionalism: Messages for the new year], in *Lingba Xianzhang yu Zhongguo biange*, np.

7. Xu Youyu 徐友渔, "Yi Liu Xiaobo jian Kuai Dafu" 忆刘晓波见蒯大富 [Remembering Liu Xiaobo's meeting with Kuai Dafu], *Open Magazine*, November 2010, http://open.com.hk/old_version/1011p20.html.

8. Havel, *Disturbing the Peace*, 145.

9. Yi Ping 一平, "Fei diyi, fei chouhen, fei baoli yu Zhongguo zhi weixian: Yougan Liu Xiaobo 'Wo meiyou diren: Wo de zuihou chenshu'" 非敌意、非仇恨、非暴力与中国之危险：有感刘晓波《我没有敌人：我的最后陈述》 [No enemies, no hatred, no violence, and China's danger: Thoughts on Liu Xiaobo's "I have no enemies: My final statement"], *Minzhu Zhongguo*, March 15, 2010, quoted in http://blog.boxun.com/hero/201003/yiping/1_1.shtml.

10. Liu Xiaobo, "Kuangwang bizao tianze: Lun Zhongguo wenhua de daode zhishang de zhiming miuwu" 狂妄必遭天责：论中国文化的道德至上的致命谬误 [No pride goes unpunished: On the fatal flaw of moral absolutism in Chinese culture], *Ming Pao Monthly*, August 1989, np.

11. Liu Xiaobo, *Sixiang zhi mi yu renlei zhi meng* 思想之谜与人类之梦 [Mysteries of thought, dreams of man], vol. 1 (Taipei: Storm and Stress, 1990), 115.

12. Liu Xiaobo, "Tiechuang zhong de gandong: Yu zhong du *Lun Jidutu*" 铁窗中的感动：狱中读《论基督徒》 [Touched behind steel bars: Reading *On Being a Christian* in prison], *Boxun*, September 8, 2008, http://blog.boxun. com/hero/200809/liuxb/2_1.shtml.

13. For Liu's thoughts on Christianity, see Liu Xiaobo, *Mori xingcunzhe de dubai* 末日幸存者的独白 [A survivor's monologue] (Taipei: China Times, 1993), 54.

14. Su Xiaokang, "Ba jijin jian'ao cheng wenhe" 把激进煎熬成温和 [Forging moderate from radical], *Open Magazine*, November 2010, http://open.com. hk/old_version/1011p39.html.

7. LIU XIA

1. Liu Xia, "Yijiubajiu nian liu yue er ri: Gei Liu Xiaobo" 一九八九年六月二日：给晓波 [June 2, 1989: To Liu Xiaobo], in *Liu Xiaobo Liu Xia shiji* 刘晓波刘霞诗集 [Selected poems of Liu Xiaobo and Liu Xia], ed. Liu Xiaobo (Hong Kong: So Far, 2000), 374–75.

2. Zhang Boli 张伯笠, *Taoli Zhongguo* 逃离中国 [Escape from China] (Hong Kong: Morning Bell, 2013), 102.

3. Meng Taoer 孟涛儿, "Yige Zhongguoren de chengzhang" 一个中国人的成长 [A Chinese's growth], *Ziyou xiezuo* 自由写作, January 1, 2011, http:// chinesepen.org/Article/wk/201101/Article_20110101011453.shtml.

4. Wan Runnan 萬潤南, "Guanyu Xiaobo de diandi jiyi" 关于晓波的点滴记忆 [Some memories of Xiaobo], in *Jiedu Liu Xiaobo* 解读刘晓波 [Reading Liu Xiaobo], ed. Xinxi Ziyou Guanchashi 信息自由观察室 (Hong Kong: Suyuan, 2011), 341.

5. Gao Yu 高渝, "Gongmin Liu Xiaobo" 公民刘晓波 [Liu Xiaobo, citizen], *Dongxiang* 动向, February 2009, quoted in http://chinesepen.org/Article/hyxz/ 200902/Article_20090219014241.shtml.

6. Liu Xiaobo, "Yu zhong suibi" 狱中随笔 [Prison notes], *Independent Chinese PEN Center*, July 24, 2012, http://chinesepen.org/Article/wxdgy/ 201207/Article_20120724183749.shtml.

7. Ding Zilin 丁子霖 and Jiang Peikun 蒋培坤, "Women yu Xiaobo de xiangzhi, xiangshi he xiangjiao" 我们与晓波的相知、相识和相交 [How we met and got to know Xiaobo], in *Ziyou jingguan* 自由荆冠 [Thorned crown of freedom], ed. Chen Kuide 陈奎德 and Xia Ming 夏明 (Hong Kong: Morning Bell, 2010), 45.

8. Liu Xiaobo, "Qingting Tiananmen Muqin de shengyin" 倾听天安门母亲的声音 [Listening to Tiananmen Mothers' voice], in *Xunfang Liusi shounanzhe* 寻访六四受难者 [Interviews with June 4 victims], ed. Ding Zilin 丁子霖 (Hong Kong: Open, 2005), 7–8.

9. Liu Xia, "Youxi" 游戏 [Game], in *Liu Xiaobo Liu Xia shiji*, 308.

10. Li Guiren 李贵仁, "Xiamei, ni zai nali?" 霞妹，你在哪里？[Sister Xia, where are you?], *Independent Chinese PEN Center*, January 6, 2011, http://chinesepen.org/Article/wk/201101/Article_20110106235320.shtml.

11. Liao Yiwu 廖亦武, "Shi xu: Wei Liu Xiaobo Liu Xia shiji er zuo" 诗序：为刘晓波刘霞诗集而作 [Foreword to the selected poems of Liu Xiaobo and Liu Xia], in *Liu Xiaobo Liu Xia shiji*, ed. Liu Xiaobo (Hong Kong: So Far, 2000), 22.

12. Tsering Woeser 唯色, "'Yi tian dou guo zhong, bie shuo shiyi nian le!': Ji Liu Xia" "一天都过重，别说十一年了！"：记刘霞 ["One day is too long, let alone eleven years!": On Liu Xia], *Invisible Tibet—Woeser's Blog*, December 26, 2009, http://woeser.middle-way.net/2009/12/blog-post_26.html.

13. Perry Link, "Love and Dissidence: The Remarkable Saga of Liu Xia and Liu Xiaobo," *New Republic*, January 25, 2012, http://newrepublic.com/article/politics/magazine/100036/liu-xia-xiabao-china-dissident-photography-nobel-peace.

14. Ibid.

15. Ding and Jiang, "Women yu Xiaobo de xiangzhi, xiangshi he xiangjiao," 47.

16. Liu Xia, "Dong mian" 冬眠 [Hibernation], in *Liu Xiaobo Liu Xia shiji* 刘晓波刘霞诗集 [Selected poems of Liu Xiaobo and Liu Xia], ed. Liu Xiaobo (Hong Kong: So Far, 2000), 313.

17. Perry Link, "Chenmo de liliang—Wei Liu Xia sheying zhan suozuo xuwen" 沉默的力量——为刘霞摄影展所作序文 [Silent strength—Introduction to Liu Xia's photography exhibit], *China in Perspective*, February 11, 2012, http://chinainperspective.com/ArtShow.aspx?AID=14113.

18. Liu Dawen 刘达文, "Liu Xiaobo, shenjiao sanshi nian" 刘晓波，神交三十年 [Spiritual connection to Liu Xiaobo over three decades], *Frontline*, November 2010, quoted in http://chinainperspective.com/ArtShow.aspx?AID=8996.

19. Zhang Min 张敏, "Liu Xiaobo fangtan lu" 刘晓波访谈录 [Interview with Liu Xiaobo], *Beijing Spring*, October 2010, http://beijingspring.com/bj2/2010/120/2010103101356.htm.

20. Lu Xia, "Gei Luoer Wa Sitaiyin" 给洛尔·瓦·斯泰因 [For Lol V Stein], in *Liu Xiaobo Liu Xia shiji* 刘晓波刘霞诗集 [Selected poems of Liu Xiaobo and Liu Xia], ed. Liu Xiaobo (Hong Kong: So Far, 2000), 340.

21. Liu Xiaobo, "Yifeng xin jiu gou le" 一封信就够了 [One letter is enough], in *Liu Xiaobo Liu Xia shiji* 刘晓波刘霞诗集 [Selected poems of Liu Xiaobo and Liu Xia], ed. Liu Xiaobo (Hong Kong: So Far, 2000), 275.

22. Meng, "Yige Zhongguoren de chengzhang."

23. Liu Xiaobo, "Zixu: Laizi fenmu de zhenhan" 自序：来自坟墓的震撼 [Preface: A shock from the grave], in *Niannian Liusi: Liu Xiaobo shiji* 念念六四：刘晓波诗集 [June 4 elegies: Collected poems of Liu Xiaobo] (Hong Kong: Self-published, 2009), 8.

24. Liu, "Yifeng xin."

8. NOBEL: A CROWN OF THORNS

1. Liu Xiaobo, "'Tiananmen Muqin' liying dedao de rongyu" "天安门母亲" 理应得到的荣誉 [An honor Tiananmen Mothers deserve], *Beijing Spring*, March 2002, http://beijingspring.com/bj2/2002/100/200372001835.htm.

2. Ding Zilin 丁子霖 and Jiang Peikun 蒋培坤, "Women yu Xiaobo de xiangzhi, xiangshi he xiangjiao" 我们与晓波的相知、相识和相交 [How we met and got to know Xiaobo], in *Ziyou jingguan* 自由荆冠 [Thorned crown of freedom], ed. Chen Kuide 陈奎德 and Xia Ming 夏明 (Hong Kong: Morning Bell, 2010). 54.

3. Hu Ping 胡平, "Liu Xiaobo yu Nuobeier Heping Jiang" 刘晓波与诺贝尔和平奖 [Liu Xiaobo and the Nobel Peace Prize], in *Ziyou jingguan* 自由荆冠 [Thorned crown of freedom], ed. Chen Kuide 陈奎德 and Xia Ming 夏明 (Hong Kong: Morning Bell, 2010), 11.

4. Rui Di 瑞迪, "Nuowei Nuoweihui weisheme jiang Heping Jiang shouyu Liu Xiaobo?" 挪威诺委会为什么将和平奖授予刘晓波？ [Why did the Norwegian Nobel Committee award the Peace Prize to Liu Xiaobo?], *Radio France International Chinese*, December 10, 2010, http://chinese.rfi.fr/%E4%B8%AD%E5%9B%BD/20101210-挪威诺委会为什么将和平奖授予刘晓波？

5. Wei Jingsheng 魏京生, "Rujin de Nuobeier Heping Jiang gei renmen tigong le sheme?" 如今的诺贝尔和平奖给人们提供了什么？ [What does the Nobel Peace Prize offer people today?], in *Jiedu Liu Xiaobo* 解读刘晓波 [Reading Liu Xiaobo], ed. Xinxi Ziyou Guanchashi 信息自由观察室 (Hong Kong: Suyuan, 2011), 180.

6. Herta Müller, "Wenn der zweite Schuh herunterfällt" [When the second shoe falls], *Frankfurter Allgemeine Zeitung*, March 26, 2010.

7. Liang Wendao 梁文道, "Guangming, cibei yu heping" 光明、慈悲与和平 [Bright, compassionate, and peaceful], in *Jiedu Liu Xiaobo* 解读刘晓波

[Reading Liu Xiaobo], ed. Xinxi Ziyou Guanchashi 信息自由观察室 (Hong Kong: Suyuan, 2011), 33.

8. Liu Xia, "Kong yizi" 空椅子 [Empty chair], in *Liu Xiaobo Liu Xia shiji* 刘晓波刘霞诗集 [Selected poems of Liu Xiaobo and Liu Xia], ed. Liu Xiaobo (Hong Kong: So Far, 2000), 333–34.

9. Robert Colquhoun, *Raymond Aron*, vol 1, *The Philosopher in History, 1905–1955* (Beverly Hills: Sage, 1986), 111.

10. Nelson Mandela, *Conversations with Myself* (New York: Farrar, 2010), 45.

11. Liu Xiaobo, *Daguo chenlun* 大国沉沦 [Fall of a nation] (Taipei: Asian Culture Press, 2009), 272.

12. Kaci Kullmann Five, "Banquet Speech," *Nobel Peace Prize*, December 10, 2010, http://nobelpeaceprize.org/en_GB/laureates/laureates-2010/banquet-speech.

BIBLIOGRAPHY

WORKS BY LIU XIAOBO

"Baobao, women ai ni!" 包包，我们爱你！ [Baobao, we love you!]. In *Bao Zunxin jinian wenji* 包遵信纪念文集 [Anthology in memory of Bao Zunxin], edited by Liu Xiaobo 刘晓波, Zhang Zuhua 张祖桦, and Xu Xiao 徐晓, 44–56. Hong Kong: So Far, 2008.

"Baozhu sheng zhong jingcha shanggang, zhen xinku" 爆竹声中警察上岗，真辛苦 [Police on duty amidst sounds of firecrackers, working hard]. *Guancha* 观察, February 17, 2005. Quoted in https://docs.google.com/document/d/1hHt5--jdxaVfatueHR9JAYjBW0dS67K wnTY9-ZT68qA.

"Beiju yingxiong de beiju: Hu Yaobang shishi xianxiang pinglun zhi yi" 悲剧英雄的悲剧：胡耀邦逝世现象评论之一 [Tragedy of tragic heroes: A comment on phenomena surrounding Hu Yaobang's passing]. *Jiefang* 解放, May 1989. Quoted in *Liu Xiaobo qiren qishi* 刘晓波其人其事 [Who is Liu Xiaobo?], edited by Zheng Wang 郑旺 and Ji Kuai 季蒯, 116–21. Beijing: China Youth, 1989.

"Changda bange shiji de shiyi—Xu *Cai Chu shixuan*" 长达半个世纪的诗意——序《蔡楚诗选》 [Poetic feeling across half a century—Foreword to *Selected Poems of Cai Chu*]. *Minzhu Zhongguo* 民主中国, October 10, 2008. http://minzhuzhongguo.org/ArtShow. aspx?AID=6421.

"Cong wawa zhuaqi de canren—Wei Wenge sanshiwu zhounian er zuo" 从娃娃抓起的残忍——为文革三十五周年而作 [Cruelty from the cradle—For the thirty-fifth anniversary of the Cultural Revolution]. *Minzhu Zhongguo* 民主中国, April 2001. Quoted in http:// epochtimes.com/gb/1/3/31/n71014.htm.

Daguo chenlun 大国沉沦 [Fall of a nation]. Taipei: Asian Culture Press, 2009.

"Kuangwang bizao tianze: Lun Zhongguo wenhua de daode zhishang de zhiming miuwu" 狂妄必遭天责：论中国文化的道德至上的致命谬误 [No pride goes unpunished: On the fatal flaw of moral absolutism in Chinese culture]. *Ming Pao Monthly*, August 1989.

"Laisi you lai le, jingcha you shanggang" 赖斯又来了，警察又上岗 [Rice returns, police on duty again]. *Guancha* 观察, March 21, 2005. Quoted in http:// epochtimes.com/gb/5/3/21/ n859124.htm.

Liu Xiaobo 刘晓波 to Hu Ping 胡平, May 12, 2000. *Beijing Spring*, December 2010. http:// beijingspring.com/bj2/2010/240/20101130143040.htm.

[As editor.] *Liu Xiaobo Liu Xia shiji* 刘晓波刘霞诗集 [Selected poems of Liu Xiaobo and Liu Xia]. Hong Kong: So Far, 2000.

"'Liuer jueshi' yanjiang" "六二绝食"演讲 [June 2 hunger strike declaration]. In *Liu Xiaobo qiren qishi* 刘晓波其人其事 [Who is Liu Xiaobo?], edited by Zheng Wang 郑旺 and Ji Kuai 季蒯, 138–39. Beijing: China Youth, 1989.

"'Liusi' lingchen de heian" "六四"凌晨的黑暗 [Darkness at dawn on June 4]. *Epoch Times*, June 6, 2004.

"Meiyou jiyi, meiyou lishi, meiyou weilai: Wei Beijing 'Wenxue yu jiyi' yantaohui er zuo" 没有记忆，没有历史，没有未来：为北京"文学与记忆"研讨会而作 [No memory, no history, no future: For Beijing's "Literature and memory" conference]. *Minzhu Zhongguo* 民主中国, January 28, 2006. Quoted in http://blog.boxun.com/hero/liuxb/503_1.shtml.

"Minjian wangzhan shouwangzhe Ye Du" 民间网站守望者野渡 [Ye Du, guardian of popular websites]. *Minzhu Zhongguo* 民主中国, January 14, 2006. Quoted in http://beijingspring.com/c7/xw/ywzs/20060115003325.htm.

Mori xingcunzhe de dubai 末日幸存者的独白 [A survivor's monologue]. Taipei: China Times, 1993.

Niannian Liusi: Liu Xiaobo shiji 念念六四：刘晓波诗集 [June 4 elegies: Collected poems of Liu Xiaobo]. Hong Kong: Self-published, 2009.

"Qingting Tiananmen Muqin de shengyin" 倾听天安门母亲的声音 [Listening to Tiananmen Mothers' voice]. In *Xunfang Liusi shounanzhe* 寻访六四受难者 [Interviews with June 4 victims], edited by Ding Zilin 丁子霖, 3–27. Hong Kong: Open, 2005.

"Renquan gaoji guanyuan lai le, jingcha you shanggang le" 人权高级官员来了，警察又上岗了 [Human rights high officials are here, police on duty again]. *Guancha* 观察, August 29, 2005. Quoted in http://epochtimes.com/gb/5/8/30/n1035067.htm.

"Renquan yishi de juexing yu zhengzhi gaige: Zailun weilai de ziyou Zhongguo zai minjian" 人权意识的觉醒与政治改革：再论未来的自由中国在民间 [Awakening of human rights consciousness and political transformation: More on a free China's future in the people]. *Boxun* 博讯, January 4, 2003. http://blog.boxun.com/hero/liuxb/49_1.shtml.

Shenmei yu ren de ziyou 审美与人的自由 [Beauty and freedom]. Beijing: Beijing Normal University Publishing, 1988.

Sixiang zhi mi yu renlei zhi meng 思想之谜与人类之梦 [Mysteries of thought, dreams of man]. Vol. 1. Taipei: Storm and Stress, 1990.

"'Tiananmen Muqin' liying dedao de rongyu" "天安门母亲"理应得到的荣誉 [An honor Tiananmen Mothers deserve]. *Beijing Spring*, March 2002. http://beijingspring.com/bj2/2002/100/200372001835.htm.

"Tiechuang zhong de gandong: Yu zhong du *Lun Jidutu*" 铁窗中的感动：狱中读《论基督徒》 [Touched behind steel bars: Reading *On Being a Christian* in prison]. *Boxun* 博讯, September 8, 2008. http://blog.boxun.com/hero/200809/liuxb/2_1.shtml.

"Tiyen siwang: 'Liusi' yi zhounian ji" 体验死亡："六四"一周年祭 [Experiencing death: Elegy for the first anniversary of June 4]. In *Niannian Liusi: Liu Xiaobo shiji* 念念六四：刘晓波诗集 [June 4 elegies: Collected poems of Liu Xiaobo], 15. Hong Kong: Self-published, 2009.

"Wang Yi jingdong le wo: *Wang Yi wenji* xu" 王怡惊动了我：《王怡文集》序 [Wang Yi shocked me: Foreword to *Collected writings of Wang Yi*]. *Minzhu Zhongguo* 民主中国, November 6, 2004. Quoted in http://blog.boxun.com/hero/liuxb/218_1.shtml.

"Wei 'Shiji Zhongguo wangzhan' songxing" 为"世纪中国网站"送行 [Seeing off the Century China website]. *Guancha* 观察, July 26, 2006. Quoted in http://blog.boxun.com/hero/2006/liuxb/43_1.shtml.

"Wo cong shiyisue kaishi chouyan—Wei 'Wenge' sanshinian er zuo" 我从十一岁开始吸烟——为"文革"三十年而作 [I started smoking at eleven—For the thirtieth anniversary of the Cultural Revolution]. *Cheng Ming Magazine*, May 1996. Quoted in https://docs.google.com/document/d/1RzO00D1IG3zfBeTXROFZfogqDj5KEttZhtCQlZlI0io/preview.

"Wo de renshen ziyou zai shiji fenzhong nei bei boduo: Gei 'Sulian de gulage he Zhongguo de laogai' guoji yantaohui" 我的人身自由在十几分钟内被剥夺：给"苏联的古拉格和中国的劳改"国际研讨会 [My person freedom was taken from me in ten minutes: For the "Soviet Gulag and Chinese labor reeducation" international conference]. *Guancha* 观察, May 1, 2006. Quoted in http://epochtimes.com/gb/6/5/1/n1304190.htm.

"Wo renshi de Yang Zili he Lu Kun" 我认识的杨子立和路坤 [The Yang Zili and Lu Kun I know]. *Epoch Times*, April 24, 2001. http://epochtimes.com/b5/1/4/26/n81002.htm.

"Wo yu hulianwang" 我与互联网 [The internet and I]. *Minzhu Zhongguo* 民主中国, February 14, 2006. Quoted in http://blog.boxun.com/hero/liuxb/513_1.shtml.

Xuanze de pipan: Yu Li Zehou dui hua 选择的批判：与李泽厚对话 [Critique of choice: Conversations with Li Zehou]. Beijing: Beijing Normal University Publishing, 1988.

"Yifeng xin jiu gou le" 一封信就够了 [One letter is enough]. In *Liu Xiaobo Liu Xia shiji* 刘晓波刘霞诗集 [Selected poems of Liu Xiaobo and Liu Xia], edited by Liu Xiaobo, 275. Hong Kong: So Far, 2000.

"Yong zhenhua dianfu huangyan zhidu: Jieshou 'Jiechu Minzhu Renshi Jiang' de daxieci" 用真话颠覆谎言制度：接受"杰出民主人士奖"的答谢词 [Subverting a regime of lies with truth: Outstanding Contribution Prize for Democracy of China acceptance speech]. *Cheng Ming Magazine*, May 2003. Quoted in *Liu Xiaobo Wenji* 刘晓波文集 [Collected writings of Liu Xiaobo], edited by Liu Xia 刘霞, Hu Ping 胡平, and Tienchi Martin-Liao 廖天琪, 237–41. Hong Kong: New Century, 2010.

"Yu zhong suibi" 狱中随笔 [Prison notes]. *Independent Chinese PEN Center.* July 24, 2012. http://chinesepen.org/Article/wxdgy/201207/Article_20120724183749.shtml.

"Zai diyu de rukouchu: Dui Makesizhuyi de zai jiantao" 在地狱的入口處：对马克思主义的再检讨 [At the gates of hell: Further reflections on Marxism]. In *Liu Xiaobo qiren qishi* 刘晓波其人其事 [Who is Liu Xiaobo?], edited by Zheng Wang 郑旺 and Ji Kuai 季蒯, 101–5. Beijing: China Youth, 1989.

"Zhan zai shijian de zuzhou zhong: 'Liusi' shi zhounian ji" 站在时间的诅咒中："六四"十周年祭 [Standing in the curse of time: Elegy for the tenth anniversary of June 4]. In *Niannian Liusi: Liu Xiaobo shiji* 念念六四：刘晓波诗集 [June 4 elegies: Collected poems of Liu Xiaobo], 62. Hong Kong: Self-published, 2009.

Zhongguo dangdai zhengzhi yu Zhongguo zhishi fenzi 中国当代政治与中国知识分子 [Contemporary politics and intellectuals in China]. Taipei: Tonsan, 1990.

"Zixu: Laizi fenmu de zhenhan" 自序：来自坟墓的震撼 [Preface: A shock from the grave]. In *Niannian Liusi: Liu Xiaobo shiji* 念念六四：刘晓波诗集 [June 4 elegies: Collected poems of Liu Xiaobo]. Hong Kong: Self-published, 2009.

"Ziyouren miandui tiechuang de weixiao: Wei Qin Geng *Zhongguo diyi zui: Wo zai jianyu de kuaile shenghuo jishi* zuo xu" 自由人面对铁窗的微笑：为秦耕《中国第一罪——我在监狱的快乐生活纪实》作序 [Foreword to Qin Geng's *China's first sin: A chronicle of the happy times I spent in prison*]. *Guancha* 观察, October 12, 2006. Quoted in https://docs.google.com/document/d/1jJNFUY0WsvXhcQiakXKdKjcUQxLX2othIcybGJXB6co.

OTHER CHINESE-LANGUAGE WORKS

Cai Shufang 蔡淑芳. *Guangchang huobei: Yige Xianggang nüjizhe yanzhong de Liusi xieguang* 广场活碑：一个香港女记者眼中的六四血光 [Living monument at the Square: Bloodshed on June 4 in the eyes of a female Hong Kong reporter]. Hong Kong: Sibixiang, 2009.

Chai Ling 柴玲. *Chai Ling huiyi: Yixin yiyi xiang ziyou* 柴玲回忆：一心一意向自由 [Chai Ling remembers: A heart set on freedom]. Hong Kong: Greenfield, 2011.

Chen Jiaying 陈嘉映. "Women zhe yidai" 我们这一代 [Our generation]. *Beijing Spring*, June 2011. http://beijingspring.com/bj2/2010/240/2011620171819.htm.

Chen Kuide 陈奎德. "Dang xianzheng zhongsheng xiangqi: Xinnian xianci" 当宪政钟声响起：新年献词 [When the bell tolls for constitutionalism: Messages for the new year]. In *Lingba Xianzhang yu Zhongguo biange* 零八宪章与中国变革 [Charter 08 and China's transformation], edited by Zhongguo Zixun Zhongxin中国信息中心, np. Washington, DC: Laogai, 2009.

Chen Xiaoping 陈小平. "Laowantong Liu Xiaobo: Wo youxin chengren, jianlao nai wo he" 老顽童刘晓波：我有心成仁，监牢奈我何 [Grumpy old Liu Xiaobo: I am willing to die for a cause, so what am I afraid of about prisons?]. *Independent Chinese PEN Center.* June 25, 2009. http://chinesepen.org/Article/sxsy/200906/Article_20090625102827.shtml.

Cui Weiping 崔卫平. "Liu Xiaobo huoxing zhishi fenzi de kanfa" 刘晓波获刑知识分子的看法 [Intellectuals on Liu Xiaobo's sentencing]. *China in Perspective*, October 20, 2010. http://chinainperspective.com/ArtShow.aspx?AID=8606.

Ding Zilin 丁子霖 and Jiang Peikun 蒋培坤. "Women yu Xiaobo de xiangzhi, xiangshi he xiangjiao" 我们与晓波的相知、相识和相交 [How we met and got to know Xiaobo]. In *Ziyou jingguan* 自由荆冠 [Thorned crown of freedom], edited by Chen Kuide 陈奎德 and Xia Ming 夏明, 39–57. Hong Kong: Morning Bell, 2010.

Feng Congde 封从德. *Liusi riji* 六四日记 [June 4 diaries]. Hong Kong: Morning Bell, 2009.

Gao Yu 高渝. "Gongmin Liu Xiaobo" 公民刘晓波 [Liu Xiaobo, citizen]. *Dongxiang* 动向, February 2009. Quoted in http://chinesepen.org/Article/hyxz/200902/Article_2009021901 4241.shtml.

Hao Jian 郝建. "'Heima,' 'Heishou' he wenzhang haoshou Liu Xiaobo" "黑马"、"黑手"和文章好手刘晓波 [Dark horse, black hand, and virtuosic writer Liu Xiaobo]. In *Ziyou jingguan* 自由荆冠 [Thorned crown of freedom], edited by Chen Kuide 陈奎德 and Xia Ming 夏明, 219–22. Hong Kong: Morning Bell, 2010.

Hu Ping 胡平. "Liu Xiaobo yu Nuobeier Heping Jiang" 刘晓波与诺贝尔和平奖 [Liu Xiaobo and the Nobel Peace Prize]. In *Ziyou jingguan* 自由荆冠 [Thorned crown of freedom], edited by Chen Kuide 陈奎德 and Xia Ming 夏明, 11–15. Hong Kong: Morning Bell, 2010.

———. "Wo he Xiaobo de jiaowang" 我和晓波的交往 [My relationship with Xiaobo]. *Beijing Spring*, November 2010. http://beijingspring.com/bj2/2010/120/2010111204151.htm.

Huang Shuxin 黄舒心. "Chen Jun: Liao Xiaobo zouguo de qilu he neixin de zhengzha" 陈军：刘晓波走过的歧路和内心的挣扎 [Chen Jun: Liu Xiaobo's forked paths and inner struggles]. *Mingjing Magazine*, October 2010. Quoted in *Ziyou jingguan* 自由荆冠 [Thorned crown of freedom], edited by Chen Kuide 陈奎德 and Xia Ming 夏明, 225–30. Hong Kong: Morning Bell, 2010.

———. "Wang Juntao: Liu Xiaobo de jianchi, shuaixing yu wanshi bugong" 王军涛：刘晓波的坚持、率性与玩世不恭 [Wang Juntao: Liu Xiaobo's conviction, headstrongness, and irreverence]. *Mingjing Magazine*, October 2010. http://chinesepen.org/Article/sxsy/201010/Article_20101019235329.shtml.

Jiang Qisheng 江棋生 et al. (fifteen signers). "Liusi ye women kangyi jingfang dui Liu Xiaobo xiansheng shibao" 六四夜我们抗议警方对刘晓波先生施暴 [On the night of June 4 we protest police brutality against Mr. Liu Xiaobo]. *Guancha* 观察, June 5, 2008. Quoted in http://chinesepen.org/Article/sxsy/200806/Article_20080605023311.shtml.

———. "Shuo liangjian wo yu Lingba Xianzhang de shi" 说两件我与零八宪章的事 [A thing or two about Charter 08 and me]. In *Lingba Xianzhang*零八宪章 [Charter 08], edited by Li Xiaorong 李晓蓉 and Zhang Zuhua 张祖桦, np. Hong Kong: Open, 2009.

Jiang Weiping 姜维平. "Wo suo zhidao de Liu Xiaobo" 我所知道的刘晓波 [The Liu Xiaobo I know]. *Open Magazine*, August 2009. Quoted in http://chinesepen.org/Article/hyxz/200908/Article_20090804040446.shtml.

Jin Zhong 金钟. "Wentan 'heima' Liu Xiaobo" 文坛"黑马"刘晓波 [Literary dark horse Liu Xiaobo]. In *Liu Xiaobo qiren qishi* 刘晓波其人其事 [Who is Liu Xiaobo?], edited by Zheng Wang 郑旺 and Ji Kuai 季蒯, 141–54. Beijing: China Youth, 1989.

Jing Wa 井娃. "Zhongguo yuzhong zuojia wenxuan, xianci" 中国狱中作家文选·献辞 [Selected writings and messages from imprisoned Chinese writers]. In *Zhongguo yuzhong zuojia wenxuan* 中国狱中作家文选 [Selected writings from imprisoned Chinese writers], edited by Huang Heqing 黄河清 and Wang Yiliang 王一梁, np. Hong Kong: Morning Bell, 2009.

Li Guiren 李贵仁. "Xiamei, ni zai nali?" 霞妹，你在哪里？ [Sister Xia, where are you?]. *Independent Chinese PEN Center*. January 6, 2011. http://chinesepen.org/Article/wk/201101/Article_20110106235320.shtml.

Liang Wendao 梁文道. "Guangming, cibei yu heping" 光明、慈悲与和平 [Bright, compassionate, and peaceful]. In *Jiedu Liu Xiaobo* 解读刘晓波 [Reading Liu Xiaobo], edited by Xinxi Ziyou Guanchashi 信息自由观察室, 28–35. Hong Kong: Suyuan, 2011.

Liao Yiwu 廖亦武. "Shi xu: Wei Liu Xiaobo Liu Xia shiji er zuo" 诗序：为刘晓波刘霞 诗集而作 [Foreword to the selected poems of Liu Xiaobo and Liu Xia]. In *Liu Xiaobo Liu Xia shiji* 刘晓波刘霞诗集 [Selected poems of Liu Xiaobo and Liu Xia], edited by Liu Xiaobo 刘晓波, 22–32. Hong Kong: So Far, 2000.

Link, Perry. "Chenmo de liliang—Wei Liu Xia sheying zhan suozuo xuwen" 沉默的力量——为刘霞摄影展所作序文 [Silent strength—Introduction to Liu Xia's photography exhibit]. *China in Perspective*, February 11, 2012. http://chinainperspective.com/ArtShow.aspx? AID=14113.

Liu Dawen 刘达文. "Liu Xiaobo, shenjiao sanshi nian" 刘晓波，神交三十年 [Spiritual connection to Liu Xiaobo over three decades]. *Frontline*, November 2010. Quoted in http://chinainperspective.com/ArtShow.aspx?AID=8996.

Liu Xia 刘霞. "Dong mian" 冬眠 [Hibernation]. In *Liu Xiaobo Liu Xia shiji* 刘晓波刘霞诗集 [Selected poems of Liu Xiaobo and Liu Xia], edited by Liu Xiaobo, 313. Hong Kong: So Far, 2000.

———. "Gei Luoer Wa Sitaiyin" 给洛尔·瓦·斯泰因 [For Lol V Stein]. In *Liu Xiaobo Liu Xia shiji* 刘晓波刘霞诗集 [Selected poems of Liu Xiaobo and Liu Xia], edited by Liu Xiaobo, 340. Hong Kong: So Far, 2000.

———. "Meiguo Bihui banfa Ziyou Xiexuo Jiang gei Liu Xiaobo: Wo de daxieci" 美国笔会颁发自由写作奖给刘晓波：我的答谢辞 [PEN American Center giving Freedom to Write Award to Liu Xiaobo: My acceptance speech]. In *Lingba Xianzhang yu Zhongguo biange* 零八宪章与中国变革 [Charter 08 and China's transformation], edited by Zhongguo Zixun Zhongxin 中国信息中心, np. Washington, DC: Laogai, 2009.

———. "Yijiubajiu nian liu yue er ri: Gei Liu Xiaobo" 一九八九年六月二日：给晓波 [June 2, 1989: To Liu Xiaobo]. In *Liu Xiaobo Liu Xia shiji* 刘晓波刘霞诗集 [Selected poems of Liu Xiaobo and Liu Xia], edited by Liu Xiaobo, 374–75. Hong Kong: So Far, 2000.

Liu Xianbin 刘贤斌. *Ruowei ziyou gu* 若为自由故 [If for freedom]. Washington, DC: Laogai, 2011.

Liu Xiaofeng 刘晓峰 and Bing Dao 冰岛. "'Kuangren' Liu Xiaobo" "狂人"刘晓波 [Madman Liu Xiaobo]. In *Liu Xiaobo qiren qishi* 刘晓波其人其事 [Who is Liu Xiaobo?], edited by Zheng Wang 郑旺 and Ji Kuai 季蒯, 71–81. Beijing: China Youth, 1989.

Martin-Liao, Tienchi 廖天琪. "Moran huishou, Xiaobo zheng zai denghuo lanshan chu" 蓦然回首，晓波正在灯火阑珊处 [Suddenly you turn, and Xiaobo is there by the dim light]. *Guancha* 观察, January 1, 2010. Quoted in http://blog.boxun.com/hero/201001/liaotq/1_1. shtml.

Meng Taoer 孟涛儿. "Yige Zhongguoren de chengzhang" 一个中国人的成长 [A Chinese's growth]. *Ziyou xiezuo* 自由写作, January 1, 2011. http://chinesepen.org/Article/wk/201101/Article_20110101011453.shtml.

Niu Han 牛汉 and Chen Huaji 陈华积. "*Zhongguo* zazhi, Ding Ling yu bashi niandai wenxue" 《中国》杂志、丁玲与八十年代文学 [China magazine, Ding Ling, and literature in the eighties]. *Shanghai wenhua* 上海文化 3 (2010). Quoted in http://21ccom.net/articles/read/article_2010081816056.html.

Niu Han et al. "Zhongguo beiwanglu" 《中国》备忘录 [A memorandum for *China*]. *Zhongguo* 中国 12 (1986). Quoted in Wang Zengru 王增如, *Ding Ling ban Zhongguo* 丁玲办《中国》 [Ding Ling and *China*], 252. Beijing: People's Literature, 2011.

Rui Di 瑞迪. "Nuowei Nuoweihui weisheme jiang Heping Jiang shouyu Liu Xiaobo?" 挪威诺委会为什么将和平奖授予刘晓波？ [Why did the Norwegian Nobel Committee award the Peace Prize to Liu Xiaobo?]. *Radio France International Chinese*, December 10, 2010. http://chinese.rfi.fr/%E4%B8%AD%E5%9B%BD/20101210-挪威诺委会为什么将和平奖授予刘晓波？

Su Xiaokang 苏晓康. "Ba jijin jian'ao cheng wenhe" 把激进煎熬成温和 [Forging moderate from radical]. *Open Magazine*, November 2010. http://open.com.hk/old_version/1011p39. html.

———. "Wenming juexing" 文明觉醒 [Civilization awakes]. In *Xunfang Liusi shounanzhe* 寻访六四受难者 [Interviews with June 4 victims], edited by Ding Zilin 丁子霖, 1–27. Hong Kong: Open, 2005.

Tong Qingbing 童庆炳. Foreword to *Shenmei yu ren de ziyou* 审美与人的自由 [Beauty and freedom], by Liu Xiaobo 刘晓波. Beijing: Beijing Normal University Publishing, 1988.

Tu, James. "Liu Xiaobo yu quanwei zhuyi de tongluren" 刘晓波与权威主义的同路人 [Liu Xiaobo and authoritarians]. *Apple Daily*, December 31, 2008.

———. "Manhuai yingxiong zhuyi" 满怀英雄主义 [Full of heroism]. *Apple Daily*, October 9, 2010.

Wan Runnan 萬潤南. "Guanyu Xiaobo de diandi jiyi" 关于晓波的点滴记忆 [Some memories of Xiaobo]. In *Jiedu Liu Xiaobo* 解读刘晓波 [Reading Liu Xiaobo], edited by Xinxi Ziyou Guanchashi 信息自由观察室, 339–44. Hong Kong: Suyuan, 2011.

Wang Xiaoshan 王小山. "Liu Xiaobo shi wode laoshi" 刘晓波是我的老师 [Liu Xiaobo is my teacher]. *Ming Pao*, January 13, 2010.

Wang Zengru 王增如. *Ding Ling ban* Zhongguo 丁玲办《中国》 [Ding Ling and *China*]. Beijing: People's Literature, 2011.

Wei Jingsheng 魏京生. "Rujin de Nuobeier Heping Jiang gei renmen tigong le sheme?" 如今的诺贝尔和平奖给人们提供了什么？ [What does the Nobel Peace Prize offer people today?]. In *Jiedu Liu Xiaobo* 解读刘晓波 [Reading Liu Xiaobo], edited by Xinxi Ziyou Guanchashi 信息自由观察室, 180–81. Hong Kong: Suyuan, 2011.

Wen Yujie 温玉杰. "Shiren de quwen yishi: Jin fei xi bi de Liu tongxue" 诗人的趣闻轶事：今非昔比的刘同学 [Anecdotes about a poet: My classmate Liu then and now]. *Jilin Daxue Zhongwen Xi qiqiji boke* 吉林大学中文系七七级博客 (blog), nd. No url.

Woeser, Tsering 唯色. "'Yi tian dou guo zhong, bie shuo shiyi nian le!': Ji Liu Xia" 一天都过重，别说十一年了！" ：记刘霞 ["One day is too long, let alone eleven years!": On Liu Xia]. *Invisible Tibet—Woeser's Blog*, December 26, 2009. http://woeser.middle-way.net/2009/12/blog-post_26.html.

Wu, Harry. *Qincheng Jianyu: Zhongguo de zhengzhi jianyu* 秦城监狱：中国的政治监狱 [Qincheng Prison: China's political prison]. Washington, DC: Laogai, 2012.

Xinxi Ziyou Guanchashi 信息自由观察室, ed. *Liu Xiaobo dangan* 刘晓波档案 [Liu Xiaobo file]. Hong Kong: Suyuan, 2011.

Xu Youyu 徐友渔. "Yi Liu Xiaobo jian Kuai Dafu" 忆刘晓波见蒯大富 [Remembering Liu Xiaobo's meeting with Kuai Dafu]. *Open Magazine*, November 2010. http://open.com.hk/old_version/1011p20.html.

Ya Yi 亚衣. *Liuwangzhe fangtan lu* 流亡者访谈录 [Interviews with exiles]. Hong Kong: So Far, 2005.

Ye Fu 野夫. *Jiangshang de muqin* 江上的母亲 [A mother by the river]. Taipei: Homeward, 2009.

Yi Ping 一平. "Fei diyi, fei chouhen, fei baoli yu Zhongguo zhi weixian: Yougan Liu Xiaobo 'Wo meiyou diren: Wo de zuihou chenshu'" 非敌意、非仇恨、非暴力与中国之危险：有感刘晓波《我没有敌人：我的最后陈述》 [No enemies, no hatred, no violence, and China's danger: Thoughts on Liu Xiaobo's "I have no enemies: My final statement"]. *Minzhu Zhongguo* 民主中国, March 15, 2010. Quoted in http://blog.boxun.com/hero/201003/yiping/1_1.shtml.

Yin Hongbiao 印红标. *Shizongzhe de zuji: Wenhua Dageming qijian de qingnian sichao* 失踪者的足迹：文化大革命期间的青年思潮 [Footsteps of the missing: Trends of thought among Chinese youths during the Cultural Revolution]. Hong Kong: Chinese University Press, 2009.

Yu Shicun 余世存. "Erlinglingsi dierjie Ziyou Xiezuo Jiang banjiang ceji" 二零零四年第二届自由写作奖颁奖侧记 [Notes to the 2004 second annual Freedom to Write Award ceremony]. *Minzhu Zhongguo* 民主中国, December 30, 2004. Quoted in http://blog.boxun.com/hero/yushicun/47_1.shtml.

Zha Jianying 查建英. *Bashi niandai fangtan lu* 八十年代访谈录 [The 1980s: Interviews]. Hong Kong: Oxford University Press, 2006.

Zhang Boli 张伯笠. *Taoli Zhongguo* 逃离中国 [Escape from China]. Hong Kong: Morning Bell, 2013.

Zhang Min 张敏. "Liu Xiaobo fangtan lu" 刘晓波访谈录 [Interview with Liu Xiaobo]. *Beijing Spring*, October 2010. http://beijingspring.com/bj2/2010/120/2010103101356.htm.

Zhongguo Zixun Zhongxin 中国信息中心. "Bie zai saorao Liu Xiaobo" 别再骚扰刘晓波 [Stop harassing Liu Xiaobo]. *Guancha* 观察, June 4, 2008. Quoted in http://beijingspring.com/c7/xw/rqmy/20080604201056.htm.

———. "Liu Xiaobo de beiju de wenxue jiangzuo zao jingfang pohuai" 刘晓波的悲剧的文学讲座遭警方破坏 [Liu Xiaobo's tragedy in literature lecture sabotaged by police]. *Guancha* 观察, November 30, 2008. Quoted in http://weiquanwang.org/?p=12096.

Zhou Duo 周舵. "Xiexing de liming" 血腥的黎明 [Bloody dawn]. *Independent Chinese PEN Center.* March 9, 2009. http://blog.boxun.com/hero/200903/zhouduo/1_1.shtml.

———. "'Xiexing de liming' xupian: Taowang, beibu, huoshi, chuguo he guiguo" 《血腥的黎明》续篇：逃亡、被捕、获释、出国和归国 [Bloody dawn, part two: Escape, arrest, release, going abroad, and coming home]. *Independent Chinese PEN Center.* May 30, 2009. http://blog.boxun.com/hero/200905/zhouduo/6_1.shtml.

Zhou Yicheng 周义澄. "Liu Xiaobo yu gongchandang" 刘晓波与共产党 [Liu Xiaobo and the Communist Party]. In *Jiedu Liu Xiaobo* 解读刘晓波 [Reading Liu Xiaobo], edited by Xinxi Ziyou Guanchashi 信息自由观察室, 385–401. Hong Kong: Suyuan, 2011.

NON-CHINESE-LANGUAGE WORKS

Barmé, Geremie. "Confession, Redemption, and Death: Liu Xiaobo and the Protest Movement of 1989." In *The Broken Mirror: China after Tiananmen,* edited by George Hicks, 52–99. London: Longmans, 1990.

Colquhoun, Robert. *Raymond Aron.* Vol. 1, *The Philosopher in History, 1905–1955.* Beverly Hills: Sage, 1986.

Five, Kaci Kullmann. "Banquet Speech." *Nobel Peace Prize.* December 10, 2010. http://nobelpeaceprize.org/en_GB/laureates/laureates-2010/banquet-speech/.

Havel, Václav. "China's Human-Rights Activists Need Support." *Wall Street Journal,* December 19, 2008.

———. *Disturbing the Peace: A Conversation with Karel Hvíždala.* New York: Vintage, 1991.

Laignel-Lavastine, Alexandra. *Esprits d'Europe: Autour de Czeslaw Milosz, Jan Patočka, István Bibó* [Spirits of Europe: A study of Czeslaw Milosz, Jan Patočka, and István Bibó]. Paris: Calmann-Lévy, 2005.

Link, Perry. "Love and Dissidence: The Remarkable Saga of Liu Xia and Liu Xiaobo." *New Republic,* January 25, 2012. http://newrepublic.com/article/politics/magazine/100036/liu-xia-xiabao-china-dissident-photography-nobel-peace.

Mandela, Nelson. *Conversations with Myself.* New York: Farrar, 2010.

Müller, Herta. "Wenn der zweite Schuh herunterfällt" [When the second shoe falls]. *Frankfurter Allgemeine Zeitung,* March 26, 2010.

Zha, Jianying. "Servant of the State." *New Yorker,* November 8, 2010. http://newyorker.com/magazine/2010/11/08/servant-of-the-state.

INDEX

ABOUT THE AUTHOR AND
THE TRANSLATOR

Yu Jie (author), born in the western Chinese city of Chengdu in 1973, is an award-winning writer whose work addresses pressing and often controversial political and social issues in contemporary China. Yu's career has included publications in mainland China which, prior to the ban on his work, earned him a reputation as a talented and brave young intellectual. He has also published widely in the considerably more open publishing market in Hong Kong and Taiwan, where his critical and unflinching essays have made him "one of China's most prominent essayists and critics," as described by the *New York Review of Books* in 2012. Also a leading democracy activist and coauthor of Charter 08, he was arrested and tortured in 2010 for his close ties and work with Nobel Peace Prize laureate Liu Xiaobo. After a year of inhumane treatment, he immigrated to the United States in early 2012 to continue to write works "that will not betray the expectations of my friends." Most notable among these publications is *The Life of Liu Xiaobo*, which has been published in Hong Kong and Taiwan. In late 2012, Yu Jie was awarded the Civil Courage Prize of the Train Foundation for his efforts to promote freedom and peaceful change in China.

HC Hsu (translator) is the author of *Love Is Sweeter* (2013) and *Middle of the Night* (2015). An award-winning essayist and short-story writer, his works have appeared in both English and Chinese. His translations of Hu Lancheng, Chu Tien-wen, Chen Kehua, Yuan Ch'iung-ch'iung, and others have also been widely published. He received his PhD from the Europäische Universität für Interdisziplinäre Studien.